DOS PASSOS' PATH TO *U.S.A.*

DOS PASSOS' PATH TO *U.S.A.*

MELVIN LANDSBERG

A POLITICAL
BIOGRAPHY
1912–1936

THE COLORADO
ASSOCIATED
UNIVERSITY PRESS
BOULDER • 1972

THE COLORADO ASSOCIATED UNIVERSITY PRESS
BOULDER, COLORADO
COPYRIGHT 1972 BY COLORADO ASSOCIATED UNIVERSITY PRESS
ISBN: 87081 - 018 - 9

LIBRARY OF CONGRESS CATALOG NUMBER: 72-75880
PRINTED IN THE UNITED STATES OF AMERICA
DESIGNED BY DAVE COMSTOCK

Portions of Chapter I appeared in the *American Quarterly*, XVI (Fall 1964), pp. 373–85. Copyright, 1964, Trustees of the University of Pennsylvania.

Quotations from Dos Passos' letters to Frederica Pisek Field and William Henry Bond and reproduction of designated photographs are by permission of the Harvard College Library. I am grateful to John Dos Passos and Elizabeth Dos Passos (Mrs. John Dos Passos) for permission to quote from John Dos Passos' writings and to use photographs of him and his family.

IN MEMORY OF MY FATHER

FRANK LANDSBERG

CONTENTS

PREFACE AND ACKNOWLEDGMENTS

I BEGAN THIS BIOGRAPHY MANY YEARS AGO BECAUSE I GREATLY enjoyed Dos Passos' *U.S.A.* and could find few facts about it and its author. My primary purpose being to describe the genesis of Dos Passos' political and social views in the trilogy, I have devoted this book mainly to the years 1912–1936. I believe *U.S.A.* to be Dos Passos' major literary work and an outstanding and enduring literary achievement. Yet it is biographically significant for reasons beyond its literary merit. It was the culmination of Dos Passos' youthful involvement in public affairs and of two decades of his life spent trying to influence them. Desiring public good with most uncommon fervor, Dos Passos has all his life accepted political commitment in an uncertain world, but also the need to re-examine and alter commitment. During the years surveyed here, he espoused, cherished, and then virtually abandoned a desire for political revolution in the United States.

This story of Dos Passos' political development through 1936 has analogues in the lives of other American writers and intellectuals between the two world wars, and will probably be of interest to the political as well as to the literary historian. My own admiration of the novelist's moral perspicuity and dedication, his honesty, courage, and acumen grew steadily as I learned more and more about him; however, in describing his development I have been concerned far less with urging a thesis than with presenting a detailed narrative account. Readers who lived through the 1920s and 1930s or have read widely about them will, I think, wish to interpret much of the account according to their own knowledge and experience.

For help in telling the story, I wish above all to thank John Dos Passos, who answered scores of questions, some of which were heavily demanding of his time and energy. As his letters to me usually took the form of replies to lists of questions, I have presented the materials wherever in the story they are appropriate, rather than quoting full letters as such. Whenever possible, I have checked information furnished to me by Dos Passos against earlier material and information from other sources.

For information through interviews or correspondence, I am grateful to Roger Baldwin, Van Wyck Brooks, Elliot Cohen, E. E. Cummings, Mrs. Margaret DeSilver, Cyril F. dos Passos, Elizabeth Dos Passos (Mrs. John Dos Passos), Max Eastman, Waldo Frank, Joseph Freeman, Lewis Galantière, Lewis Gannett, Coburn Gilman, Mrs. Paxton Hibben, Robert Hillyer, Gardner Jackson, Eugene Lyons, John McDonald, Kenneth Murdock, Dudley Poore, Professor Chandler Post, Mrs. Dawn Powell, Mark Saxton, Gilbert Seldes, Herbert Solow, Mrs. Charles R. (Adelaide) Walker, Morris R. Werner, and Edmund Wilson.

For criticism and suggestions I am indebted to Professors Richard V. Chase and William Leuchtenburg, who helped me prepare an early version of this work when I was a student at Columbia University. I will always be grateful for Professor Chase's concern, tact, and good humor, as well as for his criticism. Professor Joseph Dorfman of Columbia University later read the material dealing with Thorstein Veblen and offered additional valuable criticism. For encouragement to publish the book, I wish to thank Lovell Thompson, Mark Saxton, Professor James L. Colwell, Professor John Wrenn, and Helen Clapesattle. Mr. Saxton, Professor Wrenn, and Miss Clapesattle read the entire manuscript and made many helpful suggestions. Professors William Phillips, Mark Schorer, and Daniel Aaron aided me with information regarding Dos Passos' correspondence. Philip Babcock Gove helped resolve a difficulty with Bolshevik terminology, and Malcolm Cowley settled a problem in literary terminology. Professor Harvey Fried, Lillian A. Hamrick of the U.S. Department of Labor Library, S. Branson Marley, Jr., of the Library of Congress, and Ron Walrath of the Minnesota Historical Society helped me with bibliographical difficulties, and Mrs. Sylvia Sheldon and Mrs. Marion Kreith helped with some translations. Professors Oswald P. Backus, Giuseppe G.A. Bolognese, Vernon Chamberlin, J. Theodore Johnson, Jr., and Francis Lide of the University of Kansas provided valuable advice. In all instances the final decision, and responsibility for error, has been my own.

For help in consulting letters and manuscripts, I wish to thank

Miss Felicia Geffen, Mrs. Matthew Josephson, Miss Margaret Mills, and Joanne Le Goff of the American Academy of Arts and Letters, Mrs. Helen H. Bretnor of the library of the University of California at Berkeley, W. B. McDaniel, 2d, of the library of the College of Physicians at Philadelphia, Mrs. Ann Colley of the University of Chicago library, Kenneth A. Lohf of the Columbia University library, William H. Bond, Kimball C. Elkins, Suzanne Flandreau, William E. Jackson, Carolyn E. Jakeman, Joseph McCarthy, Mary Meehan, and Mrs. Kathy Zutes of the Harvard University library, Mrs. Amy Nyholm of the Newberry Library, John D. Gordan and Robert W. Hill of the New York Public Library, David Posner of the library of the State University of New York at Buffalo, Myra Champion of the Pack Memorial Public Library, Mrs. Neda M. Westlake of the University of Pennsylvania library, Alexander P. Clark of the Princeton University library, Ruth Kohlstadt of the Rutgers University library, John S. Mayfield of the Syracuse University library, Mrs. Mary M. Hirth of the University of Texas library, Mrs. Connie G. Griffith of the Tulane University library, John Cook Wyllie, Miss Anne Freudenberg, Harold Eads, and William Ray of the University of Virginia library, and Donald Gallup and David R. Watkins of the Yale University library.

For much day-to-day aid, I am grateful to the staffs of the New York Public Library and the Columbia University, University of Colorado, and University of Kansas libraries. At the University of Kansas library, I have received help from Thomas R. Buckman, George Caldwell, Mrs. Marilyn Clark, William Stuart Forth, John L. Glinka, L. E. James Helyar, Marjorie Karlson, Mrs. Martha Kehde, Alexandra Mason, John M. Nugent, Eleanor L. Symons, and Mrs. Susan Unger.

Several generous grants from the University of Kansas aided me in preparing this book.

Melvin Landsberg

Lawrence, Kansas
August 1970

PUBLISHER'S NOTE. John Dos Passos died on September 28, 1970, while this book was in production.

I.

FATHER AND SON

U.S.A. IS AN IMPOSING TRILOGY DEALING AT ONCE WITH many individuals and with American society during well over a third of a century. The first volume, *The 42nd Parallel* (1930), is devoted primarily to several decades preceding World War I. The second volume, *Nineteen Nineteen* (1932), deals with the war years. The third volume, *The Big Money* (1936), carries the story through the 1920s and into the 1930s. The assembled trilogy, published in January 1938, marks the first appearance of an introductory sketch also named "U.S.A."[1]

The main body of *U.S.A.* consists of fifty-two sections of narrative fiction, each of which is devoted to some one of twelve chief characters; two or more sections are given to each of the twelve. The sections are intermingled, and many of the chief characters meet. Minor characters appear, but only in sections devoted to the major ones. Supplementing the narrative fiction are three auxiliary devices: "Newsreel," "The Camera Eye," and the biographies. More than 140 installments of these three are interspersed among the narrative sections. While the auxiliary devices differ markedly from one another in form, all three may be described loosely as historical.

John Dos Passos wrote the trilogy over about a decade, during which time his political views continued to develop. The work was the culmination of an even longer period of participating in and pondering on current American history. Because of the author's political interests, convictions, and expectations, as well as the scope of its subject matter, *U.S.A.* can with some justice be considered an American epic. Like national epics, it is partly political in theme and has myth as one of its subjects — though it indicates that the important myths in the contemporary world are created by newspapers and public relations men. National epics customarily join legend with prophecy. *U.S.A.* contains a legend of an earlier, more democratic America, and if the prophesying sibyl sits mute, her presence is unmistakable.

This book relates some of Dos Passos' steps on the path to *U.S.A.* In particular, it tells of his attempts from his college years on to understand, cope with, and describe American society. When he started his many years of work on *U.S.A.*, at about thirty-two, his country was already heavily industrialized. Radios and motion pictures had mass audiences. Automobiles had altered the economy. The progressives, who sought legislation to control giant corporations, had fallen from national power after 1920. Democracy seemed to founder before industrial growth.

World War I, which began while Dos Passos was at college, had shattered nineteenth-century beliefs in inevitable social progress. Advanced nations had not only gone to war, but had also used their science to multiply hatred and destruction. Financial and industrial leaders, Dos Passos believed, bore much responsibility for the war.

This recent history he tried to describe when he wrote *U.S.A.* He wrote of a changing society, with its inventors, profiteers, reformers, revolutionists, trimmers, and victims. He wrote in the belief that political and social insight has never been more vital than in the twentieth century.

Not surprisingly, the path we are to trace began in the peculiar circumstances of John Dos Passos' childhood, and in his complex relationships with his parents. His ailing, dependent mother and his aggressively successful father both deeply influenced his emotional development, while just listening to his father talk gave him a provocative introduction to social, economic, and political doctrines.[2]

John Randolph Dos Passos (1844–1917) was the son of a poor immigrant from Madeira and of Lucy Catell, said to be of Quaker origin. He came to New York in 1867, after work as office boy and as apprentice in a Philadelphia law office, service in the Pennsylvania state militia, and attendance at law lectures at the University of Pennsylvania. "The same dream of big things that leads so many ambitious young men all over the United States to come to New York led his footsteps hither," a colleague said of him in a eulogy a few days after his death. "Many of those young men are disappointed, but he was not — he made good."[3]

He not only made good; he displayed unusual versatility and originality in the way he did it. First he became a well-known criminal lawyer. Perhaps his greatest triumph in this phase of his career was getting the murder verdict against Edward S. Stokes set aside after Stokes had been found guilty of killing the Civil War financier "Jim" Fisk in a quarrel over a mistress.[4] Afterward Dos Passos, Sr., opened an office in the Mills Building, opposite the New York Stock Exchange,[5] and soon was enjoying a lucrative practice among the brokers and operators. When he found that there was no good book available on his specialty, the law of commercial exchange, he wrote what became the standard work on the subject.[6]

There is real irony in the fact that the elder John Dos Passos did much to make possible the consolidation of American business, which was to further the growth of industry (one of his son's earliest *bêtes noires*) and strengthen the influence of corporations upon government. Many Wall Street firms employed him as a confidential adviser, for he was both a master of corporation law and a most skillful reconciler of conflicting business interests. After the original "Sugar Trust," formed in 1887, was declared illegal by the New York Court of Appeals, H. O. Havemeyer called upon him to organize the new American Sugar Refining Company. Dos Passos, Sr., did more than merely draw up papers; he actually planned the formation of the corporation. And for this he received the largest fee on record for such work up to that time. According to his obituary in the *New York Times*, he was credited with much of the advice that long enabled the trust to keep out of reach of the law. He also helped to form the American Thread Company and Cramp's Ship Works, and to reorganize the Texas and Pacific, the Reading, and the Erie railroads.[7]

Sometime in the course of this busy professional life, probably during the 1880s, John Randolph Dos Passos, already a married man, met Mrs. Lucy Madison, an attractive young widow. A long love affair followed, and on January 14, 1896, in a Chicago lakeshore hotel, she bore him, out of wedlock, a son, whom they named John after his father.

The mother was a Southern gentlewoman, born Lucy Addison Sprigg in Cumberland, Maryland, before the Civil War. Her family

Courtesy of Elizabeth Dos Passos (Mrs. John Dos Passos)

Self-confident and assertive, Dos Passos' father, John Randolph Dos Passos, who designed corporations and wrote on public affairs.

A Southern gentlewoman, Dos Passos' mother, Lucy Madison, probably in 1894, two years before his birth.

moved to Petersburg, Virginia, when she was very young and there lived out the ordeal of the war. Her father, an engineer, assisted the Confederate Army. Lucy and her two younger sisters, writes Dos Passos, were famous beauties among the needy Southern gentlemen of postwar Virginia. At eighteen Lucy married R. R. Madison and bore him a son, who now became young John's half brother. For a time after her husband's death, Mrs. Madison worked in government offices to support herself and her child.[8]

Since Dos Passos' parents could travel openly together in Europe — and his father preferred English to American education anyway — Dos Passos spent a good part of his boyhood abroad. He provides this chronology of his childhood years:

> A couple of winters in Brussels
> 1902–?3 Went to Friends' School in Washington
> 1904–8? Peterborough Lodge in the Hampstead region of London
> 1908–10 or 11 Choate School in Wallingford Conn

In the early summer of 1911, Dos Passos, Sr., having become a widower, married Mrs. Madison, and the boy, known at Choate as John Roderigo Madison, became at college John R. Dos Passos, Jr.[9]

Asked how close, in sympathy and understanding, he had been to his parents, Dos Passos replied: "From the time I was about ten mother was more or less of an invalid and most of her care devolved on me, so we were very close indeed."* Her illness, he added, was described as Bright's disease. "Towards the end she suffered a series of small strokes that left her with considerable aphasure [aphasia]. It was one of these strokes that killed her."

"My relations with my father whom I came to admire greatly before he died," Dos Passos wrote, "were much too complicated to go into here. For a *fictional* approximation see Chosen Country: the Pignatelli family."[10]

The autobiographical "Camera Eye" of *U.S.A.*, even more than the novel *Chosen Country* (1951), describes the early years. In "The Camera Eye" installments of *The 42nd Parallel*, the father

---

*For much of the time Dos Passos was away at school, but his mother had some hired help. In the later years the family's difficulties were eased by Mrs. Harris, a congenial woman who served as trained nurse and housekeeper. Dos Passos, *The Best Times*, p. 19.

Dos Passos as a little boy in Brussels. The Belgian capital was his "earliest known city."

is a self-confident, assertive man. He wears silk initialed hankerchiefs smelling of bay rum, carries liquor in a flask, and enjoys yachting. He sings lustily, recites *Othello* in his lawyer's voice, and tells his son of his diving prowess "when I was your age." The mother, who is exceptionally tender toward her son, is of polite society and seems to accept fully the traditional social distances between Virginia gentry and colored people and laborers. The young son becomes highly conscious that his status is not acceptable socially or ecclesiastically. His illegitimacy sometimes sets him apart, while the occasional cruelty and discomfiture of the people around him warp the fashionable world's veneer before his eyes.[11]

"What a horrible childhood," "a hotel childhood," eighteen-year-old Jay Pignatelli, Dos Passos' semi-autobiographical figure, thinks in *Chosen Country*. "He'd hated all those schools, all his life he'd hated everything but Petite Mère."[12] When she became ill and the father was detained on business, ten-year-old Jay had been her only comfort. He had done his best to run the house, order meals, keep track of happenings about the garden and farm, and, in his childish way, to amuse her continually as his father did.

The portrait of the father is very much like that in "The Camera Eye," though in *Chosen Country* the father is half Italian. "Kate," he tells Jay's mother, "you must think it odd that I class myself as an Anglo-Saxon when I'm only half a one, but I do it unconsciously." He says to his tongue-tied, constrained, inattentive, but nevertheless listening young son: "New ideas give people pain. . . ."[13]

Jay's view of the elder Pignatelli's demeanor is arresting when we remember Dos Passos' own avoidance of self-dramatization both in his actions and his writings; the boy (dubbed Don Modesto by the girl he will marry) squirms when his father boasts of his achievements. Not only does the father possess great self-assurance, but he also demands it of his son. When Jay is little, his father, attempting to teach him to swim, grows angry at the boy's fright. "He's such a strong swimmer Jay," his mother says, "and he wants you to be a strong swimmer too. . . . You've got to learn to keep up with him."[14]

At eighteen Jay, with many of his author's traits and difficulties, asks himself: "Was it the bar sinister or the nearsighted eyes that made him always fumble the ball — what a terrible tennisplayer,

Courtesy of Elizabeth Dos Passos

A childhood spent on two continents. Here the boy is with his mother on board ship.

no good at football or even at soccer — or the foreign speech or the lack of a home that made him so awkward, tonguetied, never saying the right word.''[15]

As a student in law school Jay fidgets under his father's advice and talk about himself. Seeing his father an old man anxious over business and overworking himself, he is troubled and wishes to help; but his father, with a show of spirited impatience, sends him away. On the train Jay thinks of all that he should have said. Back in Cambridge he receives a letter reiterating his father's expectations, and urging him to overcome his hesitancy of speech.

Dos Passos may, as those at least partly autobiographical writings suggest, have found much in his father to disapprove of or dislike, and he may often have been an unwilling, inattentive listener to his father's talk, but he could hardly have helped being stimulated by his father's forceful ideas. The elder Dos Passos lived through his son's years at Harvard and remained an active public figure during the entire period.

John Randolph Dos Passos was an intellectually aggressive man who aspired to be more than a creature of the new age. He was unusually well read, possessing considerable knowledge of classical and modern history and literature, as well as of jurisprudence. He enjoyed being able to refer his actions and opinions to ultimate principles and despised the new crop of lawyers who were nurtured on casebooks rather than on Blackstone. His economic thought, as revealed in his books and pamphlets, shows real development.[16] He always remained fundamentally conservative, but toward the end of his career his conservatism had become the adaptable type that is likely to be almost as unpopular as radicalism in conservative circles.

He was a friend of William McKinley and stumped Pennsylvania and Virginia for him in 1896.[17] At that time he was enthusiastic about the prospect of an American empire and, simultaneously, keen for personal liberty. Sometime about 1896, in a pamphlet entitled *Argument of John R. Dos Passos, Esq. of New York in Favor of Recognition of Cuba by the United States*, he wrote that this country was justified in encouraging the Cuban revolutionists because Cuba was nearby; because politically and morally she ought to be a republic; and because the United States' commercial interests there were so great that the best writers on international law, citing the doctrine of self-preservation, sanctioned

Courtesy of Elizabeth Dos Passos

No wish to be an Englishman. Attending school in a suburb of London, he pleaded to return to America.

the nation's intervening to protect the property and rights and advance the interests and commerce of its citizens.[18] He granted that these arguments alone might not warrant intervention, but one other factor, he thought, did. The King of Spain had proclaimed Cuba under perpetual martial law. Any state which deprives its citizens of the three absolute rights of an individual — the rights of personal security, personal liberty, and private property — is a despotism, and its people are justified in rebelling to rescue themselves. Any outside civilized nation has a duty to acknowledge their belligerency and to succor and support them.

Much less liberal was a pamphlet which Dos Passos, Sr., published in 1900 defending McKinley's policies in the Philippines.[19] In this work, which took issue with the criticisms of Carl Schurz and the anti-imperialists, he displayed legalistic hardness. He insisted that the United States had not promised or acknowledged Philippine independence and was not bound to do so under international law. If the Philippines should ever ask for independence with near unanimity, then the issue would become a real one.

Also belonging to the period of the elder Dos Passos' exuberance over empire was *The Anglo-Saxon Century* (1903), a book far removed both from his professional interests and from the political issues of the moment.[20] It was a plea for a union between the people of the United States and of Great Britain (including the inhabitants of their colonies) — for common citizenship, freedom of commercial intercourse between the two nations, and uniform currency and standards of weights and measures.

Behind the plan was the author's desire to justify the American empire in the same way as the British did theirs, as well as to link the destiny of the new empire with that of the older one. The American Revolution was actually, he wrote, an expansion and propagation of the Anglo-Saxon race and its principles of liberty, law, and government. The growth of Anglo-American power and influence was not determined by conscious will but by underlying forces shaping the progress of the human race. To the Anglo-Saxon peoples these forces had entrusted the civilization and Christianization of the world. Since fate had made the United States a world power, the nation ought to be ready to support the growing business interests of its citizens. It ought to remember the abstract rules of right and not embark on wars for mere aggrandizement; however, for its own sake and for humanity's sake, once it acquired a colony it ought never to let it go.

The elder Dos Passos was not a Republican, but a Gold Democrat. His career as a campaigner for Republican presidential candidates received a sharp, though temporary, check with McKinley's death.[21] In 1904 he published a fulminating campaign pamphlet seventy-nine pages long called *The Trend of the Republican Party* and bearing the legend: "Thou are weighed in the balances of the Constitution and found wanting." The immediate stimulus seems to have been a strong antipathy toward Theodore Roosevelt. Though acknowledging that the party had once preserved the Union and abolished slavery, John Randolph Dos Passos now saw little good in it. It was living on past achievements. McKinley had sought to revive it, but his death had extinguished all hope. It had begun to "do things" to the Constitution long before Roosevelt's accession, the elder Dos Passos charged. Besides victimizing the defeated South, it had tampered with the Presidency, packed the Supreme Court, and muzzled free speech in Congress.

Republican orators claimed credit for the material wealth of the nation, but the elder Dos Passos doubted the justice or even the pertinence of this claim. The incentive to wealth was honorable and useful, he added, and the nation ought to encourage it. But money had become a substitute for character; it was being used to buy social and political position. Of what use was the new material prosperity, he asked, if the nation was not more elevated and refined than before?

The elder Dos Passos once stated in his son's hearing that with his ideas he could not be elected even a notary public or a dog-catcher in any county of the state, not if he had all the money in the world.[22] His idea of a common Anglo-American citizenship would certainly have been used against him, and at least two of his other ideas would have harmed him. First, there was his desire to deny citizenship — or at least the vote — to the foreign-born in the United States. In *The Anglo-Saxon Century*, Dos Passos, Sr., maintained that foreigners assimilated themselves almost immediately to the laws, manners, and conditions of the United States; they became the most fervent advocates of democracy. But four years later, in an address to the Virginia State Bar Association, he reversed that opinion. Liberal naturalization laws were, he now said, a menace. They had destroyed the prestige and honor that had once been attached to American citizenship and had dampened the patriotism of native-born citizens. To make America a union of citizens who understood and valued the rights of life, liberty, and property, he called for the denial of suffrage to the "rabble and refuse of foreign countries."[23]

He issued other calls for restricting democracy. There being no way of curtailing the suffrage, he stated in 1909 in an argument against proposals for direct primaries, the true friend of the people was the one who provided means of protecting them against their own imperfections.[24] The indirect nomination of officials was in sympathy with the form and theory of the United States government, while the increasing number and complexity of public questions made the professional politician necessary.

He expressed his suspicion of democracy again two years later in a pamphlet arguing against a proposition to have United States senators elected directly by the people.[25] The pamphlet as a whole dealt with the rights of property, the nature of the original Union, and the fact that the Senate was an advisory and a judicial as well as a legislative body. The United States Senate, like the British House of Lords, he declared, protected property against attacks by excited masses. Unless the Senate's identity were maintained, he warned, America might be faced with a situation reminiscent of the French Revolution.

Law reform was one of the elder Dos Passos' continuing interests. Seeking to improve criminal court procedures, he attacked the doctrine that a defendant need not testify against himself. He complained also that the law was far harder on a poor defendant than on a rich one. The solution he advocated included a less reverent attitude toward mere legal technicalities and an office of Public Defender to protect the rights of the accused.[26]

To Dos Passos, Sr., law reform included reforming the lawyer, or purifying and ennobling the profession, as he put it.[27] In one of his most memorable books, *The American Lawyer* (1907), he noted that until the Civil War, lawyers had been the social and intellectual aristocrats of the country, but then law had begun to change from a profession to a business. The modern lawyer, Dos Passos, Sr., charged, was dishonest. He did not concern himself with how his conduct affected the administration of justice or the welfare of the state. He knowingly put forth false pleas and defenses; while claiming to be the representative of his client in court, he was actually the principal actor.[28]

In two major books Dos Passos, Sr., dealt with a subject that has never ceased to occupy his son's attention, the concentration of corporate wealth in the United States — probably the most vexing economic problem of the day. His first book on the subject, *Commercial Trusts*, was published in 1901, his second, *Commercial Mortmain*, in 1916. They are significant works because they reveal the development of his outlook on the growth of huge corporations.[29]

In *Commercial Trusts*, Dos Passos, Sr., stressed the fact that modern commerce could not thrive without aggregated capital. Since trusts were simply one form of such capital, there was no sense in attacking them alone, he wrote; a realistic attack would have to include partnerships and corporations and would imperil a system under which the country had developed and become prosperous. Restrictions such as the Sherman Anti-Trust Acts remained unenforced because the natural laws of trade defy human legislation.

By 1916 Dos Passos, Sr., had altered many of his opinions and was warning against the dangers of aggregated capital. The desire to concentrate had become a craze, he said in *Commercial Mortmain*. In a few years every business would be merged into a corporation and great aggregations of capital would run all industrial enterprises and would allow people with brains and talent to be no more than corporate clerks and servants. The commercial and industrial oligarchies might seek control of newspapers; their leaders might one day even be able to dictate the country's financial policy. Already, he noted, some individuals had become so rich that they could force any industry into one corporation and arbitrarily assign to themselves enormous compensation. Was it not possible that the magnates would eventually gain control of all three branches of the federal government, if not by outright bribery, then by indirect methods? One could no longer rely on restraint based on moral sense; money had no conscience.

The belief that the fundamental aim of an individual or a nation was to make money had, he added, become widespread. It had led to an aristocracy of wealth, which claimed social superiority only because it possessed money. This class threatened to become a fourth branch of the government, one that would gradually wipe out the checks and balances of the republican system.

But the answer did not lie with antitrust acts, the elder Dos Passos insisted once again. The country could not treat the normal processes of business as a crime. It should look to certain "natural remedies" to aid it in controlling trusts and other forms of aggregated capital. These remedies included new inventions, the concentration of labor (which he insisted was as obnoxious as that of capital), extravagance, and mismanagement. But he held that the country should give the federal government full power regarding questions of aggregated capital and wealth, though this power should be applicable only to real evils. The nearest approach to a remedy for the problem of unlimited wealth and of trusts, he said, was through taxation, much of which could be imposed under the new income tax amendment. The government might license monopolies for a fee, or it might heavily tax corporations that had attained monopolistic powers, the taxes being a charge for the privilege of enjoying the powers. Under all circumstances, the government should always retain the power of dissolving monopolies.

The effect of all these positive, aggressively argued opinions upon the younger Dos Passos' political development has been complex. It is easy to say that the son, early in life, rebelled against his father's ideas and attitudes. The elder Dos Passos' sympathies were usually with the man on top. Although the son of a Portuguese immigrant, he identified himself with a triumphant Anglo-Saxon race and would have denied suffrage to immigrants. He advocated imperialism on the ground that it would benefit American business. In one of his pamphlets he spoke of man's beast nature and added that "the veil of civilization which keeps men and women within decorous bounds is not very thick";[30] insofar as he called for reform, he seems to have done so, not from an urge to help particular human beings, but from a desire to perfect institutions.

The son, on the other hand, began his adult life with immeasurably more optimistic hopes for human nature, seeing it primarily as something to be liberated rather than controlled. Class and moneyed background, of which his entire rearing made him conscious, seemed to be separating him from the mainstream of human experience. When still a young man, he found himself in sympathy with Boston Italians, exploited immigrant laborers, and Mexican peons. His illegitimacy doubtless contributed toward this sympathy. Deep feelings of deprivation he certainly knew (indicative, perhaps, of their depth is the fact that among his fictional characters sharing his own background, absent fathers are common). The father's self-assurance and eminence may have constituted a challenge to the son to establish his own individuality, and thus further have helped induce his efforts in behalf of outcasts. Psychology is intricate, however; illegitimacy might have led another man to seek to be ultrarespectable.

With all the motives one can offer for John Dos Passos' alien-

Courtesy of Elizabeth Dos Passos

On vacation from Choate, with his parents on Squirrel Island, Maine, July 1909.

ation from his father, the extent to which they shared interests, ideas, and attitudes is significant. The father was and the son became vitally interested in politics and economics. Both men declared that an increasing concentration of wealth might destroy democratic government. The elder Dos Passos believed in reform, and he asserted his views with courage and independence, just as his son was to do; moreover, the elder Dos Passos, like his son after him, had the strength to change his mind publicly about political and economic issues. The father's thinking had an ethical basis, even his advocacy of colonialism having, besides its economic purpose, a genuinely felt ethical one. Members of the family remember the elder Dos Passos as a libertarian and an antimilitarist. ("He was a great individualist," his nephew and law partner recalls, "and believed that no restriction should be placed upon anyone's action, so long as he did not commit a breach of the peace." Dos Passos, to illustrate "how normal for an American an anti-militarist attitude was before 1917," adds: "My father bitterly opposed the Spanish-American War."[31]) Some of the ideas of the elder Dos Passos, such as that of an Anglo-American union, were as unorthodox as any that his son was to express. Both father and son complained of the tendency in America to overvalue material goods, and both contrasted material surfeit with intellectual and artistic distinction.

It is instructive to compare two quotations. The first is from the elder Dos Passos' pamphlet condemning the Republican party, in which he raised the problem of how important material prosperity is.

But the nation is deeply concerned with the question as to the influence which this prosperity has had upon the manhood and character of our people. Are we better for it? Have we made real ethical progress? Do we know ourselves better? Are we more elevated, refined and enlightened? How is our literature? How is histrionic art? Do we better understand the duties of citizenship? In the treatment of our neighbors — of our inferiors — are we just and fair? The picture of prosperity has two sides. The Republican party has only shown the nation the material, sensuous one.[32]

The other quotation is from the son's important essay "A Humble Protest," which appeared twelve years later in the *Harvard Monthly*, an undergraduate literary magazine. The essay is a condemnation of the industrial era.

Except for the single triumph of liberalism over superstition in all its forms, religious, political, moral, which was the French Revolution, can we honestly say that life is intenser, that art is greater, that thought is more profound in our age than in the reign of Elizabeth? . . . You cannot honestly affirm that opportunity for producing great art, — and art is certainly one of the touchstones, if not *the* touchstone of a civilization, — or even the opportunity for a general interest in the forms of beauty, is greater than it was three centuries and a half ago. Most thoughtful people will say it is less. . . .[33]

Like his father, who was not in the habit of calling his protests humble, Dos Passos attacked materialism; but he showed in his essay a concern for the economically depressed classes of society which was absent in the father's writings.[34] Dos Passos also placed a much higher value on the French Revolution than did Dos Passos, Sr., who seems to have steeped himself in the philosophy and values of eighteenth-century American Federalism.

We ought not to forget that eighteenth-century Federalism did not disown revolutions. Nor ought we to forget the elder Dos Passos' pamphlet on Cuba, for part of his reasoning there is based on Locke's defense of the English Revolution of 1688 and on the philosophical justification of the American Revolution. It is important that Dos Passos was exposed to a philosophy that held rebellion to be a possibility and a right. He probably heard it proclaimed with vigor by a conservative parent who admired Burke,[35] abhorred radicalism, and never dreamed of his son's applying revolutionary doctrine to the United States. What might happen, though, if the son should become convinced that personal liberty and personal security were being abolished by an oligarchy (the father used that word over and over again) in the United States and should become despondent about the possibility of democratic redress?

II.

HARVARD

AT HARVARD COLLEGE, WHICH HE ENTERED IN SEPTEMBER 1912, Dos Passos seemed to his friends to have enjoyed a far richer childhood than they. So E. E. Cummings recollected, and young Dos Passos' cosmopolitanism might well have impressed companions. While in Belgium with his mother, he had acquired French virtually as a native language. He had known life in an English preparatory school. (''My father,'' he says, '' . . . would have educated me entirely in England if I hadnt protested vigorously.'') And after his graduation from Choate at fifteen, his father had sent him on a grand tour which included visits to Egypt and Greece.[1]

Dos Passos' appearance attested to both his Portuguese strain and his sojourns abroad. Cummings described him as being at college ''about the least American-looking person I can imagine.'' Stewart Mitchell, another friend, recalled that his ''swarthy appearance, foreign accent, and continental mannerisms'' set him off from his fellow students. But he had spent perhaps the more satisfying part of his youth in Washington, D.C., and on his father's farm in Virginia.[2] Both the European and the Southern backgrounds had important effects on his outlook in later years. *Chosen Country* seems to indicate that his early separation from the United States helped impel him to explore and grasp his native land, and his early revulsion from industrialism may have been due partly to an agrarian temper to which other Southern writers have given regional expression.

Chandler Post, Dos Passos' faculty adviser and instructor in Greek literature and in fine arts, remembered him as a pleasant Latin-looking young man very much interested in cultural matters. There was nothing bohemian about him. He dressed normally and well, and he was neither too shy nor too forward. A friend, Kenneth

Murdock, recalls that Dos Passos was very much "the young intellectual" at Harvard, with interests that were primarily literary and aesthetic. As far as any of his friends could tell, he had no politics. He was generally at the office of the *Harvard Monthly*, but cared nothing about "college life" as such.[3]

Dos Passos' own reminiscences of the college years have varied in content at different periods of his life. In 1956 he wrote: "At Harvard we were much too superior to be interested in politics." "Found socialists boring we were aesthetes those days."[4] But in "The Camera Eye (25)" section of *The 42nd Parallel*, which he wrote when he was an impassioned revolutionary, he implied that he had suffered vague but nettling dissatisfaction with the political, social, and cultural atmosphere prevalent in Cambridge:

> haven't got the nerve to break out of the bellglass
> four years under the ethercone breathe deep gently
> now that's the way be a good boy one two three four
> five six get A's in some courses but don't be a grind be
> interested in literature but remain a gentleman don't be
> seen with Jews or socialists
> and all the pleasant contacts will be useful in Later
> Life say hello pleasantly to everybody crossing the yard
> sit looking out into the twilight of the pleasantest
> four years of your life
> grow cold with culture like a cup of tea forgotten
> between an incenseburner and a volume of Oscar Wilde
> cold and not strong like a claret lemonade drunk at a
> Pop Concert in Symphony Hall
> four years I didn't know you could do what you
> Michaelangelo wanted say
>   Marx
>   to all
> the professors with a small Swift break all the Greenoughs
> in the shooting gallery
> but tossed with eyes smarting all the spring night
> reading *The Tragical History of Doctor Faustus* and
> went mad listening to the streetcarwheels screech grind-
> ing in a rattle of loose trucks round Harvard Square
> and the trains crying across the saltmarshes and the rum-
> bling siren of a steamboat leaving dock and the blue peter
> flying and millworkers marching with a red brass band
> through the streets of Lawrence Massachusetts
> it was like the Magdeburg spheres the pressure out-
> side sustained the vacuum within

and I hadn't the nerve
    to jump up and walk out of doors and tell
them all to go take a flying
                Rimbaud
                at the moon[5]

In examining the development of Dos Passos' political and social thought at Harvard, we are faced with a dual task: noting what seemed significant to him at the time and what seemed significant in retrospect, after he had turned to politics and society as themes for fiction.

When he entered Harvard, Dos Passos had enough Latin, Greek, and French to enable him to take advanced work in these subjects in his freshman year. During his stay, he took one year each of French, German, Latin, and Spanish, and two years of Greek. (*Year* here means one full-year course or two half-year courses.) He took the equivalent of five full-year courses of English literature and comparative literature. Although he was probably not planning to earn a living by writing — the idea, his father kept insisting, was impractical[6] — he was registered for English composition every semester.

A system of "concentration and distribution" had superseded President Eliot's system of free electives. Now course offerings were divided into four groups: (1) Language, Literature, Fine Arts, Music; (2) Natural Sciences [including a course in the history of science]; (3) History, Political and Social Sciences [including anthropology]; (4) Philosophy and Mathematics.

Dos Passos elected no more than the minimum number of courses, an equivalent of six full-year ones, required outside the group in which his major subject, English, fell. In apportioning these, he took approximately the minimum number, one-and-one-half each, in the natural science and philosophy and mathematics groups, and he took the remaining three in the history, political and social science group. All his courses in the philosophy and mathematics group were in ancient philosophy, the emphasis falling on Greek thought, and they seem clearly related to his work in classical literature. His courses in the history, political and social science group were elementary ones in constitutional government, European history, and anthropology.[7] Certainly, Dos Passos did not receive a strong academic background and discipline in history and the political and social sciences.

Courtesy of Elizabeth Dos Passos

At Harvard. "Four years under the ethercone," he later complained.

The curriculum is a clue to the sense in which Dos Passos applied the term "aesthete" to himself: he was preoccupied with literature and art. But there was more involved here than personal predilection. Aestheticism at Harvard took some traditional forms that still prevailed in Dos Passos' time. Van Wyck Brooks writes that during his own years at Harvard, 1904–1907, literary men tended to reject their country and century. Cults and enthusiasms far removed from contemporary America flourished; almost everyone read Pater; and future poets and novelists filled their minds with images from Italian art.[8]

Upon Dos Passos, who in his college stories was depicting much of contemporary America as insipid, this traditional aestheticism had its influence, his choice of courses and his interests after college suggesting that work in past cultures had real satisfactions. However, he grew to be more repelled than attracted by the fashionable enthusiasms, finding them debilitating. Some of his college stories, concerned with vitality and passion and set in exotic lands he had glimpsed, testify to an early — a temperamental — need for experience in a wide, stimulating, contemporary world.

While many of his friends and acquaintances, he says in his most recent memoirs, *The Best Times* (1966), chose to live in the 1890s, he was already breaking off from such aesthetes by his senior year. A major influence was a fellow student, Edward Nagel, stepson of the sculptor Gaston Lachaise and a friend of Cummings. Nagel, who had been brought up mostly in Paris and later became a nonobjective painter, introduced Dos Passos to the world of the modern and got him to reading the Russian novelists in French editions. Though poetry remained for Dos Passos a supreme value, Dostoevski's works, combined with Lawrence's *Sons and Lovers*, set him panting for real life.[9]

While at college Dos Passos contributed approximately thirty short stories, essays, articles, poems, and reviews to the undergraduate literary magazine, the *Harvard Monthly*. In April 1915 the magazine announced his election to its board of editors, which during his time included E. E. Cummings and Robert S. Hillyer, two of his friends with bright futures in literature. Dos Passos was listed as a member through the July 1916 issue.

The first two short stories he published in the *Harvard Monthly* have as their locales areas that he had visited during his trip abroad in 1911–12. The stories reflect the disillusionment that many young

On the *Harvard Monthly* Board in 1916. Dos Passos is in the fourth seat from the left, and in the fifth is Robert Hillyer.

men feel when they discover the chasm between ideal woman and women. Not any socioeconomic problem, but the problem of young men's coping with the existence of women, became a recurrent theme in Dos Passos' college fiction; here we can only offer some examples.

His first contribution, which appeared at the end of his freshman year, was "The Almeh," a short story narrating an incident in the visit of an American youth and an English youth to Cairo. The latter, a painter with a slight English accent (certainly resembling the author and reflecting childhood years in England), becomes enamored of the face of an Arab girl, whose veil falls off in a momentary mishap. Subsequently the two youths discover that she is a dancer at the bazaar and that she has been purchased as a wife for their donkey boy. Their final view is of her preparing a meal in the doorway of a mud hut, screaming in a harsh voice at some grimy, naked nephews, while flies swarm about her.[10]

Although Dos Passos probably did not intend the events to be symbolic, we are tempted to regard as such the two views of the Arab girl, and marvel at the extent to which the story foreshadows some of Dos Passos' travel writings; in the years after his graduation, he continually alternated between fascination with the color and rhythms of some of the traditional life he encountered and realization of the inadequacy of that life.

During his sophomore year, he published "The Honor of a Klepht," another exotic short story describing a man's disillusionment with women. Here, a leader of a klepht band in the days before the Greeks won their independence descends from the foothills of Mount Parnassus to warn a village of a Turkish raid and to bring to safety the girl he loves. Before the girl can gather her mother's goats and come to the appointed meeting place, the Turks enter the village and massacre the inhabitants. The next day the klepht band attacks the Turks. When the klepht chief finds his girl the expensively accoutred mistress of the Turkish governor, he declares her dead and goes to his own death fighting.[11]

The writings of Dos Passos' junior year included book reviews, short stories, and an essay on *Lord Jim*. Of his review of *Insurgent Mexico* by John Reed we shall speak later. He characterized the form that his own travel books were to take when in a review of a travel book by a Harvard graduate, William M. E. Whitelock, he asserted: "The short, informal, personal type seems to have completely superseded the ponderous, heavily-gilt volume of travels of the past generation.'' A third review, of a translation of a novel by the Dutch author Louis Couperus, provides additional testimony to the catholicity of Dos Passos' literary interests at this time. The essay on *Lord Jim* was a report of the conventional classroom type, praising Conrad's books for qualities Dos Passos has tried to give his own — mental stimulation, color, humanity.[12]

The stories Dos Passos published during his junior year were more closely related to his own time and his own experiences than ''The Almeh'' and ''The Honor of a Klepht'' had been. Predominantly satirical, these new stories may leave a reader feeling that the author was unbearably smug. In his defense, we remember that he was reacting to a provincial America actively antagonistic to many of his values. Knowledge of the later Dos Passos suggests, moreover, that even at this time he probably sought more virtues in the people around him than he found. Imaginatively wandering in places startlingly unlike Cambridge, Dos Passos was, in any event, still clearly interested in the habits of his countrymen. Although the stories are not artistically significant, they may mark Dos Passos' debut as an observer and satirist of American life.

''An Interrupted Romance'' combines the boy-wants-girl theme of the earlier stories with satire of commonplace American tourists, whom he must often have encountered in Europe. An American who is supposed to be studying in Paris spends most of his time sitting about lazily at a particular spot on the Champs Elysées. When one day he sees a young and very pretty woman join an old man who habitually sits nearby, the American ponders ways of meeting the woman. She subsequently forgets her lace handkerchief, and he pounces upon it. The next day, as he is approaching the girl to return her handkerchief, he is interrupted by ''his stout aunt from the west, and her two giggly daughters.'' The American departs to show his Baedeker-bearing relatives the way to the Arc de Triomphe. He never sees the old man or the young woman again, although he returns morning after morning.[13]

''The Poet of Cordale,'' a satirical story containing early examples of Dos Passos' skill with dialogue, has rural or small-town America as its locale. When a salesman with a liking for verse is asked to recite something at the July 4 ''speaking'' of his community, he decides upon ''Barbara Frietchie,'' although he is somewhat ashamed of the selection. His recitation brings enthusiastic applause and demands for an encore. The salesman's critical sense then leads him to deliver some of Omar Khayyám's poetry to the

crowd, and he disgraces himself before the Temperance Union
and the minister, as his prosaic wife warned him he would.[14]

"An Aesthete's Nightmare" indicates Dos Passos' amusement
at Harvard devotees of exotic taste, even as "The Poet of Cordale"
reveals his disgust at the lack of taste among the general public
in America. An aesthete returns home with a small marble copy
of the Venus de Milo, which he purchased in Boston and has
just displayed to all his friends. He arranges the Venus so that
the amber light of his lamp will fall on the torso, lights a cone
of incense before a Buddha that dominates his mantelpiece, and
lies back among the pillows of his cot, which he calls a divan.
Falling asleep, he dreams that he is a fifth-century Vandal who
enters Aphrodite's temple, smashes her statue, and scatters her
votaries. When he awakes, he finds his own statuette broken. Remembering the joy of destruction, he soon smashes all the objects
of art in his room and hurls the Buddha through the window.[15]

Since "An Aesthete's Nightmare" probably rebels against a
marble, unattainable ideal of womanhood, and since it sets living
vandalism above dead culture, the story might have aroused an
exceptionally alert critic. From a reviewer for the *Harvard Crimson*,
however, it evoked only a mild defense of folkways at the college.
" 'An Aesthete's Nightmare' proves how rare the extreme aesthete
type is in our midst —" he commented. "Mr. Dos Passos would
never have to resort to such obvious and wholesome objects of
art as the Venus de Milo, a Buddha, and Parrish's 'Pirate Ship'
if he had ever seen the animal in the wild state in his native lair — in
Oxford, for instance."[16]

Probably the European war, as well as his restlessness amid
cultural monuments, suggested the specter of the vandal to Dos
Passos.[17] One story, "Malbrouck," published during his junior
year dealt with actual destruction and with a more somber Paris
than the one described in "An Interrupted Romance." A Parisian
woman in a garret sings, at her little son's insistence, a song about
a warrior who has been slain and will never return. At the conclusion
of the song she breaks into tears, for her husband is at the front.[18]

Dos Passos' writings during his senior year were more numerous than those of the preceding three years combined, and they
were considerably different in character. They included additional
stories, verse for the first time, and, most important for us here,
arresting comments on politics, economics, and the war.

Most of the stories have the same themes as his earlier ones, and suffer from many of the same weaknesses. Some of the stories are divorced from the author's experiences, while others indicate that he had not yet acquired insight into the complexity of the experiences with which he dealt. From the problem of not having lived long enough, Dos Passos usually took refuge in satire, irony, and humor.

But one story, "Romantic Education," satirizes American culture with a far defter touch than its author had shown before. Like "The Poet of Cordale," it confronts the prosaic American world with a passionate, exotic one. In this story a once-beautiful Spanish woman tells an American engineer she has met aboard ship that Americans do not live. She confides her history to him so as to make him realize that there is more to the world than machines — there are love, beauty, art. The American, who has spent most of his days in a power plant, has visited a few middle-class homes, and has been "sweet" on a few girls, now resolves that he will see the world. His resolution brings him ultimately to the Café Vibert, "one of those places where Americans who desire to be naughty are taken by their couriers."[19] Clearly, Dos Passos, in the midst of his cosmopolitan amusement, was aware of states worse than innocence.

Two of the prose pieces published in Dos Passos' senior year were on a new theme, a boy's deep love for his mother, and involved his feelings far more intensely than did the stories we have discussed. Both have autobiographical roots and, like "Malbrouck," show the father in some way absent. In one, a story titled "The Shepherd," a fifteen-year-old boy, just beginning to yearn for adventure and knowledge of the world, loses his way in the mountains and must spend the night by the shed of a shepherd, whose tales of passion and bodily sufferings intensify his desire for experience. But when the boy sees his mother the next day, his visions of freedom grow dim. "As he kissed her slightly wrinkled cheeks, and saw the tears on them, he felt infinitely tender, felt that he must protect his mother against all the world."[20]

The second of the two pieces, "Les Lauriers Sont Coupés," is elegiac in tone and mingles recollections of Brussels, which Dos Passos calls his earliest-known city, with memories of his mother, with whom he lived there. It describes with sensitivity the excitement of railroad stations; the horror of flaming factory chimneys seen from a train window (a significant memory when we consider Dos Passos' lifelong revulsion from industrialism); the odors of cakeshops; the "tiresome fairyland of milliners and dressmakers, and lace shops"; restaurants; Terveuren, the park where the palace of "poor Carlotta," widow of the emperor Maximilian of Mexico, had stood; and a frightening tale (which the boy's *bonne* had told him) of the murder of a king of the gypsies, and of the king's funeral, attended by all the riffraff of Europe. There is one allusion to the war: "So much has intervened — both for me and for Brussels — since then. . . ." The allusion extends the subject of the elegy, which appears at first to be only a portion of the author's childhood. But the conclusion of the sketch reveals that it was the death of Dos Passos' mother the previous year that had inspired the elegy.

> "Nous n'irons plus aux bois, les lauriers sont coupés
> Les amours des bassins . . . "
> ["We'll go to the woods no more, the laurel trees are cut
> The loves of the ponds . . . "]

My mother would sing that in a little crooning voice, sitting beside me in her silk evening gown that was so soft to stroke, — the bonne with her horrid stories had gone by that time, — and I would sink off to sleep amid dim solemn gardens and the pale sadness of autumn woods.

> "Voici l'herbe qu'on fauche et les lauriers qu'on coupe.
> Nous n'irons plus aux bois, les lauriers sont coupés."
> [Behold the grass they mow and the laurel trees they cut.
> We'll go to the woods no more, the laurel trees are cut."][21]

"Les Lauriers Sont Coupés" is Dos Passos' first outstanding piece of prose, one that stands comparison with any of similar length that he has written since. Dos Passos published the piece anonymously, doubtless wishing to keep his grief private.

Some of Dos Passos' verse in the *Harvard Monthly* seems better than most of his prose there, although none of the verse is as noteworthy as "Les Lauriers Sont Coupés." One poem shows the strong influence of the imagistic school. Another may illustrate Van Wyck Brooks' assertion of the influence of Italian art on the literary work of Harvard men. Although the reference to the Virgin is ultratraditional, the author is characteristically looking at the face of a contemporary:

> In a shop window, spangled in long lines
> By rain-drops all a-glow,

An Italian woman's face
Flames into my soul as I go
Hastily by in the turbulent darkness; —
An oval olive face,
With the sweetly sullen grace
Of the Virgin. . . .[22]

Some of the inspiration for the verse must have come from the Harvard Poetry Society, which Cummings, Hillyer, S. Foster Damon, Dos Passos, and others founded in 1915 with the encouragement of Dean Briggs. "The members met irregularly to read their own poems and take the rap of vigorous criticism, or to listen to readings by poets such as Robert Frost, John Gould Fletcher, and Amy Lowell."[23] Dos Passos subsequently collected manuscripts and negotiated publication of *Eight Harvard Poets*, a volume of verse by Damon, Hillyer, Stewart Mitchell, William A. Norris, Dudley Poore, Cuthbert Wright, Cummings, and himself. Cummings said years later that this undertaking indicated Dos Passos' interests at the time. He was very much surprised when Dos Passos developed a political theme.[24]

Pausing from his own poetic work, Dos Passos in 1916 reviewed two anthologies of verse, the *Catholic Anthology* and *Georgian Poetry, 1913–1915*. His review of the latter demonstrates the extent to which the war, if not domestic politics, had affected his thinking and made the traditional aestheticism appear irrelevant. He declared the selections in the anthology to be representative of contemporary English verse, and he praised the "aliveness and closeness to the soil of much of the work." But he found the absence of war poetry arresting: "Everything is from that period — so far away now — when the nineteenth century was still living on into the twentieth." The war had split the centuries apart, he said. He was to remain of this opinion.

He considered the *Catholic Anthology*, which he called representative of Washington Square, less praiseworthy than the English anthology, and believed that both would be less influential than *Des Imagistes*, which contained work "of people of approximately the same artistic creed" and was "really an attempt to add something, to impose a new trend of thought on current literature."[25]

The four years Dos Passos spent at Harvard were marked by concern in the college community over labor problems and over the Mexican crises. Both culminated in spectacular incidents, but neither proved as fateful for the students as the gradual heightening of tension over the issue of preparedness and then of war with Germany.

The start of Dos Passos' freshman year coincided with the opening at Salem of the murder trial of three I.W.W. men, Arturo Giovannitti, Joseph J. Ettor, and Joseph Caruso — an outgrowth of a two-month-long textile strike that the I.W.W. had waged in Lawrence, Massachusetts, between January and March 1912. During that strike most inhabitants of the eastern United States first heard of the I.W.W.

A day before the murder trial opened, mill workers in Lawrence participated in a scheduled parade and in an unscheduled battle with police. These were a prelude to a twenty-four-hour general strike the next day in protest against the three men's imprisonment. About two months later a jury acquitted Ettor, Giovannitti, and Caruso of the charge of murder. Workers carrying red lights and cheering continuously accompanied the three to I.W.W. headquarters in Lowell, where Ettor addressed a crowd of 10,000 people.[26]

Dos Passos mentions the demonstrations in "The Camera Eye (25)" section of *The 42nd Parallel*, and he devotes "The Camera Eye (20)" section to an accident in Lawrence that took the life of a student strikebreaker from Matthews Hall, where Dos Passos lived during his freshman year. Although the strike did not affect Dos Passos' political views, it may have served as his vivid introduction to the I.W.W. What is equally important, the defense of Ettor and Giovannitti anticipated that of Sacco and Vanzetti, or seemed to, in some respects. The strike was thus an event that assumed importance in retrospect.

By the time Dos Passos was ready to graduate from Harvard, the great social and economic problem facing the world appeared to him to be industrialism. His glimpses of it had so astonished and horrified him that he was bothered far less by conventional economic questions than by the threat it seemed to pose to the quality of human life. Veblen, whom Dos Passos read at length during his sophomore or junior year, looked with some favor on industrialism.* By working with machines, he said, significant

*Dos Passos speaks of reading Veblen with great enthusiasm at college. "I think I read him all," he writes, "at least as much as had already been published. I forget whether that was in my sophomore or junior year. I started with 'The Theory of the Leisure Class' which amused me stylistically. . . ." Letters from Dos Passos to M.L., June 26, 1956, July 12, 1966.

numbers of men might learn to think according to the methods of modern material science.[27] This hope was one piece of Veblenism which Dos Passos never shared.

"A Humble Protest," Dos Passos' youthful indictment of industrialism, appeared in the June 1916 issue of the *Harvard Monthly*. The date gives this work, his longest and most ambitious essay published at college, something of a valedictory character. It is noteworthy for two reasons: Dos Passos' early travel writings and *Manhattan Transfer* repeatedly decry industrialism, stressing its aesthetic, sensory, and social horrors; and the essay suggests that Dos Passos' outlook on economics was by that June unorthodox enough to make him potentially receptive to the humanitarian arguments of socialists.

A number of influences and tendencies, including an emphasis on simplicity and spiritual attainment reminiscent of Thoreau's, appear in the essay. The course in the history of science which Dos Passos was taking during his final year might have influenced the essay, and some of the passages indicate that his course in ancient philosophy, in which the students must have encountered Heraclitus, may have had its effect. Dos Passos declared that man has a tendency to believe that "what is, is right and must endure forever"; even an enlightened person finds difficulty in realizing that "no state of society is inevitable or ultimate, and that, so far as the limitations of our perceptions go, its flux is eternal."[28]

Dos Passos had been reading *Les Villes tentaculaires* (The tentacular cities) by the Belgian poet Emile Verhaeren, as well as works by other literary critics of industrialism, when he wrote the essay. Verhaeren resembled Walt Whitman, already a favorite of Dos Passos, in accepting industrialism and huge cities as historical phenomena to be celebrated. But while Verhaeren, after a struggle, succumbed to hope and saw beauty in the conventional ugliness and the inhumanity of the modern metropolis,[29] the horrors, not the hope, affected Dos Passos when he read the poem. It might be possible to consider life's aims, Dos Passos wrote, as two: the desire to create and the desire to know. They had not fared well under the rule of science, with its concomitants, industrialism and mechanical civilization. Except for the triumph of liberalism over every form of superstition — religious, political, and moral — that had characterized the French Revolution, life was not more intense, nor art more great, nor thought more profound than during the Elizabethan renaissance in England. Part of the reason might be that science had influenced man to slight the role he plays in the universe, for science had led him to see the universe through instruments and columns of tabulated facts rather than as it appears to him at first hand.

The French Revolution, which Dos Passos considered more significant than even the "limited Italian Renaissance," had affirmed the humanism, the belief in the fullness of man, that had been inherited from the Greeks and, in another form, from Jesus. The greatest tragedy in modern history, said Dos Passos, was that this liberating humanism had been conquered by "that bastard of science, the Industrial Revolution." Under industrialism, three fourths of mankind slaved so that the other fourth might "in turn be enslaved by the tentacular inessentials of civilization." Half the occupations of mankind utterly demoralized both body and soul; the material luxuries they produced destroyed man's capacity for art and knowledge.

Dos Passos did not close the essay until he had linked industrialism with the World War to show in still another way the fallacy of equating industrialism with progress. In the light of flaming Belgian towns, he wrote, men were looking aghast at each other. Was this machine civilization? Germany, the nation which had pushed industrialism to its height and developed the great art of music, had succumbed to barbarism.[30]

Strong as this denunciation of industrialism is, we must remember that it is stated in measured academic prose addressed to the intellect. "A Humble Protest" masked emotions far more intense than most of its readers suspected.

Dos Passos has said that his views of society and politics during his later Harvard years were influenced by the *New Republic* — a periodical which became for a while a "major rallying ground" for young cultural nationalists — and he undoubtedly responded to some of its arguments, but his writings in no sense mirrored them and at times took decisive issue with them.

The *New Republic*, founded by Herbert Croly with the collaboration of Walter Weyl and Walter Lippmann, first appeared in November 1914. Charles Forcey, a historian of the periodical, has written of Croly: "National cohesion, the creation of a setting where creative art and life might flourish, was his essential goal." The magazine preached a radical progressivism, and during its initial two years contended for a long list of domestic reforms, including industrial democracy (one of its major ends, requiring, it maintained, a strong labor union movement); protection of labor's right to strike; minimum wage legislation; restrictions on child labor; free speech; academic freedom; law reform; and prison reform. Dos Passos was interested in these reforms, though he must have been particularly attentive to the *New Republic's* discussions of the European war.[31]

The *New Republic* sounded a keynote in foreign affairs when in its first issue it proclaimed that independence in the sense of isolation had proved to be a delusion. At the beginning of the war, Americans, the periodical said, had considered themselves free from "inherited national antipathies" and "distracting international entanglements" and had "constituted themselves into a supreme court . . . to sit in judgment on the sins of Europe." But the progress of the war had shown Americans that they were involved economically and sentimentally in European affairs. No matter which side won, the United States would be affected by the treaty of peace. Despite the periodical's fondness for Theodore Roosevelt, it took a position midway between Bryan, who was against increasing armaments at all, and General Wood, who, according to the *New Republic*, wanted to increase them too much. A victory by the Central Powers, the periodical said, would be dangerous to the security of the United States.[32]

Dos Passos would certainly have pondered such arguments because from his freshman year, agitation for "preparedness" had been evoking major controversy at Harvard. At first the agitation was in large part jingoism and politics. Major General Wood, the Army Chief of Staff, speaking at Harvard in November 1912, suggested a plan for compulsory military service to help form a 600,000 man reserve. Universities would cooperate in the program, he said, and their graduates would devote a year to becoming officers. America's growing power and possessions required a large army, he continued, not only to protect the country but also to prevent war.[33]

Some time after General Wood's speech, the *Harvard Crimson* published a dissenting letter. "This year," the correspondent wrote, "there has been a perhaps unparalleled attempt to impress upon Harvard men the necessity for allying themselves with the United States Army or Navy." Instead of fostering a martial spirit, should not Harvard direct the interest of its students to the movements for disarmament and arbitration? The newspaper noted that the letter expressed the views of many Harvard men but replied that in the present state of civilization peace was a remote possibility.[34]

"Preparedness" at Harvard. The university regiment on its first practice march, April 30, 1916.

That same year the War Department established two summer camps to train college men to be reserve officers. President Lowell favored the idea of the camps.[35] The War Department considered its first experience with them successful and in the next academic year announced plans for five in 1914.

Attempting to explore the problems of international arbitration and the maintenance of peace, Harvard students during Dos Passos' sophomore year founded the International Polity Association. A large number of university organizations, following examples set in Europe, combined in establishing this organization to sponsor authoritative lectures on the facts of international relations. Norman Angell, best known as the author of *The Great Illusion*, early became a favorite political analyst for the association. Speaking before it in April 1914, he said that nations were arming because they feared aggression. An international organization would quell such fears, but a proper world opinion had to come first. Europe was looking for America to lead."[36]

After the outbreak of World War I the dispute between proponents and opponents of preparedness became more intense. The *Harvard Crimson* on November 18, 1914, announced that the War Department had authorized formation of a machine gun company from among students of Harvard and the Massachusetts Institute of Technology. The issue containing the announcement carried two letters of protest from students.

Outside Harvard, pressures for preparedness were meanwhile increasing. When early in 1915 Wilson ignored demands for increased arms, preparedness spokesmen redoubled their propaganda, and after the Germans sank the *Lusitania* in May, these spokesmen inundated the public with words. Motion picture producers released films depicting invasions of the United States by goose-stepping soldiers. "Not in many years," a biographer of Wilson writes, "had the American people been subjected to such pressure by an organized minority."[37]

Despite this situation, antipreparedness editors gained control of the *Harvard Crimson* in 1915, much to the annoyance of alumnus Theodore Roosevelt. The paper published a series of editorials denouncing summer military camps as a menace; it reported that General Wood had said the camps would emphasize the spreading of "sound" information on the United States' military needs, and it was on this very ground that the newspaper opposed the camps.[38]

On March 7, 1915, John Reed ('10) appeared at the Harvard

Union to lecture on "Life in the Trenches." In response to a question, he said that, because he felt that no foreign nation could effectually subdue the United States, he favored complete disarmament. Reed was already a legendary figure at Harvard and in Greenwich Village. An uninhibited and outspoken Westerner, he had won recognition as a writer and orator at Harvard despite his background and behavior, which were considered not altogether "good form." After his graduation he continued writing and in 1913 went to work on the staff of *Masses*. During the I.W.W.-led strike of New Jersey textile workers that year, he was thrown into jail with Carlo Tresca and William Haywood. When the *Metropolitan Magazine* sent him to Mexico, he frequented Pancho Villa's headquarters and accompanied him into battle. Reed's reports, subsequently republished in *Insurgent Mexico* (1914), gave him a national reputation as a war correspondent. When the World War broke out, the *Metropolitan Magazine* sent him to Europe.[39]

Not Reed's politics, but his prose, attracted Dos Passos.[40] Reviewing *Insurgent Mexico* for the *Harvard Monthly* in November 1914, Dos Passos thanked Reed for not offering pet theories to explain Mexico's unrest, pet criticisms of United States foreign policy, and panaceas. What he liked about the book was the author's objectivity, his quality of adventurous youth, his descriptive ability, and his understanding of the Mexican people. Dos Passos' review almost two years later of Reed's *The War in Eastern Europe* again confined itself to the artistry of the author.[41]

Within a few years an already upset world would be topsy-turvy, and Dos Passos would be interested in Reed's politics. But for the nineteen-year-old listening to Reed at the Union in 1915, what was important was that Reed was traveling and seeing the war — in fact, doing everything that the restless college student wished he were doing. A decade and a half after hearing the talk, Dos Passos gave a report of his encounter with Reed to *Monde*, where it appeared in translation on January 18, 1930. The newspaper account being clumsy, I shall paraphrase it somewhat.

Harvard, Dos Passos wrote, had an institution called the Union, with a library, a restaurant, reading rooms, and lecture halls. The Union had been established in a burst of democratic enthusiasm as a meeting place for students of all colors, beliefs, and conditions. Frequenting that place in my day was most unfashionable — one saw only Jews, a Negro, and people who were at the university to study — and being seen there gave a student quite a reputation.

The only time that I saw John Reed, he continued, was at the Union, in one of the small lecture rooms on the top floor, when he came during a break in his work as a foreign correspondent. Our conversation mingles in my memory with his articles, which I was then reading. I remember having arrived late. A strong, lively fellow, with bearing and speech suggesting a football captain's, was standing and speaking emphatically. It was Reed. When he had finished, the student world in which I lived appeared to me frightfully paltry. Whereas for millions of men the solid rock of everyday life had been shattered by wars and upheavals, we students were living under a bell glass, nourished by the disheartening concoction of ancient cultures. John Reed had escaped from the bell glass. He spoke as if he had never lived under it. Since he had been able to come out from under, others could too.[42]

The campaign for preparedness that General Wood had initiated had by Dos Passos' senior year become one of preparing to fight in the European war. The historian Samuel Eliot Morison, returning from a western university, found Harvard students as well as faculty committed to the side of the Allies even earlier, near the beginning of 1915. In Dos Passos' senior year, 1915–16, fifteen students and graduates complained to the *Harvard Crimson*, which had now (like Wilson) espoused preparedness: "The militarist fever seems to be sweeping over professors and students alike . . . to an unprecedented degree."[43]

That academic year the student council initiated and the university created a Harvard regiment, and military training became a course counting toward a degree. At the inauguration meeting of the regiment, on December 20, President Lowell said that the training was preparation for the summer camps. In March, Harvard men had a University Flying Corps to train military aviators. The Navy Department announced a summer training cruise for civilians. Harvard had Preparedness Week two months later. The Harvard Regiment contributed its numbers to the 80,000 who marched in one of the gargantuan parades in support of Wilson's preparedness program. At a mass meeting at the Union, a campaign was launched to increase enrollments for the Plattsburg Camps and for the naval cruise. Theodore Roosevelt published an article in June urging Harvard men, both graduates and undergraduates, to enroll for the military training camps to be held during the coming summer. These camps were, he wrote, "the entering wedge for a system of universal and obligatory military training" for wartime service.[44]

Meanwhile, the voices of Norman Angell and another notable English author, G. Lowes Dickinson, were influential among such Harvard men as did not consider preparedness a solution to every problem. Dickinson, speaking at the Union in February, maintained that the crucial question confronting the world was not how to settle the present war but how to prevent future ones. He supported the measures proposed by the League to Enforce Peace. Competitive arms races led directly to war, he said. Hope for preventing war lay in establishing an international court and in limiting the sovereignty of nations. At the end of the war, the time would be appropriate for the presentation of a plan for international reconstruction, but the belligerents would not have one. Dickinson therefore believed that individuals should maintain their passion for peace.

Norman Angell asserted that the United States was courting danger by arming without making up its mind what it wished to fight for. The country had to enter into treaties of reassurance with other nations, lest its power be regarded as a menace after the war. The United States also had to undertake to help enforce a rule of civilization among nations. Although Angell's ideas were not altogether pacifistic, the International Polity Association seems to have been regarded as a center of pacifism at the university.[45]

Dos Passos was neither a doctrinaire pacifist nor a disciple of Dickinson or Angell; however, he and the other Harvard Poets were as a group pacifistic, opposed to imperialism and to the militaristic propaganda of General Wood and Theodore Roosevelt. Insofar as Dos Passos favored preparedness, it was Woodrow Wilson's brand rather than Theodore Roosevelt's.[46] His articles in the *Harvard Monthly* show that his attitude was similar to that of the *New Republic* in regard to the possibility of American isolation; that he was aroused by stories of German ruthlessness and vandalism, and once went beyond the *New Republic* in calling for belligerency; and that he then drew back while the periodical became progressively more bellicose. He grew increasingly restless over a diet of conflicting reports and opinions. "My notions were shifting around in so many directions at once at that time it's hard to track them down," he explains. "None of these notions got very hard outlines until they were exposed to the reality of war."[47]

Somewhat surprisingly, Dos Passos' earliest identifiable political editorial defended the summer military camps. In the July 1915 issue of the *Harvard Monthly* there appeared two unsigned editorials under the title "Summer Military Camps: Two Views." One was by Dos Passos. Writing as a democrat who deplored extreme pronouncements by both militarists and pacifists, he denied that the camps were the first step toward compulsory military training "or something equally barbaric." He asserted that students attending them might come back "with a little snobbery knocked out of them, with a larger sympathy with their contemporaries from other colleges — and perhaps, too, with a smattering of slang to spice their conversation."[48]

Four months later the *Harvard Monthly* published Dos Passos' first signed comment on the war, an editorial titled "The Evangelist and the Volcano." This editorial anticipated Dos Passos' statement in his review of *Georgian Poetry, 1913–1915* that the war had split the centuries apart. Rather than attribute blame, Dos Passos voiced profound shock — a feeling which, as he doubtless knew, he shared with many an intellectual throughout the world. He began by describing common American pronouncements on the war: "It's all them Kings and Queens gettin' land for their princelings," and "If King George was made to fight, and the rest of them Kings——." What Americans had to realize, Dos Passos said (his democratic instincts never leading him to countenance provincial naivetés), was that the catastrophe was too large to be blamed on either King George or the Kaiser. The ideals of civilization were tottering, and it was not because of the virtue of the inhabitants that America was not, in the words of Bryan, "wallowing in the slime of war." The destiny of America as well as of the European powers was being decided on the French and Turkish battlefields. Taking the United States to task for pouring forth humanitarian cant in the face of forces that everybody was at a loss to understand, he likened the country to an evangelist preaching to a volcano — at a safe distance.[49]

Apparently Dos Passos could not find any of his answers satisfactory for long. By March 1916, though not blaming the war on the Kaiser, he was condemning Germany as a threat to European civilization. In the *Harvard Monthly* of that date appeared Arthur K. McComb's denunciatory review of Robert Herrick's *The World Decision*, and an editorial by Dos Passos sharply attacking the review.[50]

The American novelist Herrick saw the war as fundamentally one between Latin and Teuton. From Rome the Latin tradition of civilization had inherited law, justice, beauty, and mercy. This tradition respected individual rights and liberties, beauty of conduct, and beauty of art. It did not believe that people should be alike politically and economically; instead, it held that each individual ought to work out his own salvation. To this view of life the Teutonic tradition opposed one of deadening militarism, materialism, efficiency, and lack of imagination and individuality. The German state was not merely barbaric; it was consciously Darwinian, for it believed that the country that seizes the most will survive.

Herrick charged that the pacifists cynically refused to see the true issue of the war. Since there was no room in the world for both the Latin and the Teutonic ideals of civilization, the war had to be fought to a finish and one of them had to die. If Germany won, the danger would be less from new aggressions on her part than from the attractiveness her triumph would lend to her creed.

McComb attacked the book largely from the viewpoint of pacific cosmopolitanism. Dos Passos, responding with fervid humanism to Herrick's argument, called the book brilliant. He said the pacifist just then was like the man who, when told that his home is burning, sits down to plan a new fireproof edifice instead of salvaging his furniture. Dos Passos agreed that there was a fundamental conflict between two types of civilization: "the Latin ideal, the ideal of art and literature and the life of the spirit; and the Teutonic ideal, efficiency, material prosperity." To be neutral, except as a technicality, was impossible. Rather than chatter about world peace, Dos Passos wrote, one should choose his ideal of European civilization and, if necessary, fight for it.

Nevertheless, Dos Passos' views were more pacific than those of the *New Republic* in June 1916, after Germany's *Sussex* pledge. At that time he commented editorially about a conference on foreign relations that the Federation of International Polity Clubs was sponsoring at Western Reserve University. Although he did not mention Norman Angell, he supported a thesis which Angell was continually stressing. People were beginning to realize, Dos Passos wrote, that if the United States wished to prove its idealism and engage the powers of darkness, it would have to stop temporizing and undertake a policy of constructive pacifism. Once again he condemned Midwestern isolationism, and now he condemned too the extremes of a movement in which he had some interest, socialist pacifism.[51] Dos Passos hoped that the conference would avoid the "Scylla of 'grape-juice' moralizing and the Charybdis of long-haired ultra-socialism.'' If it did, the students would emerge to spread the message in torpid sections of the country that nationality involved responsibility, that isolation was impossible, and that the United States had, intelligently and unselfishly, to use its power for good in world politics.[52]

The writings in the *Harvard Monthly* suggest that Dos Passos became interested in politics late. His interest was mainly in the war. Although he favored Wilson's progressive reforms, he was not sufficiently concerned to write about them. In his comments on the war, Dos Passos betrayed an uncertainty and an inconsistency that were not characteristic of his discussions of literature. But early, fluttering attempts though they are, his writings on the war foreshadow a pattern in his future career as a political commentator. Though he might be far less than certain, he would seek or accept commitment when he thought issues crucial. In articles and other such public statements, he would speak with considerable decision. The role of disengaged logician would never be permitted Dos Passos; he would always be too much the combatant in behalf of fundamental decencies to play that dispassionate role. And yet, although his commitments were of the heart as well as of the mind, an unusual honesty and lack of egotism, coexisting with his moral fervor, would lead him time after time to change views in response to new events and evidence.

III.

THE WORLD WAR

WHEN DOS PASSOS LEFT HARVARD IN JUNE 1916, HE WAS so eager to see the war that he wished to enroll in ambulance service at once. No longer did he have to consider the needs of an ill mother. But his father, whose wishes had persuaded the restless student to finish college, now checked him. Fearing for his son's life and hoping the conflict would end soon, Dos Passos, Sr., wanted young John to postpone going to France. He suggested as a compromise that Dos Passos go to Spain to study the language and prepare for a course in architecture which he hoped to take. So in the summer and early fall Dos Passos remained on his father's farm in Virginia, where he read a great deal, wrote letters and articles, attempted a novel, "The Walls of Jericho," and followed closely the heightening debate about the war.[1]

One of the articles, his first after college, appeared in the *New Republic* in October under the title "Against American Literature." It revealed the author's continuing anxiety about industrialism and dislike of materialism, and showed his agreement with such critics of American society and literature as Van Wyck Brooks, although it did not refer to any of them by name. The article indicated, too, that Dos Passos had already been strongly influenced by Walt Whitman's vision of America. "It was the 'genteel tradition' of the early nineteen hundreds I was complaining about," he writes. "I dont imagine I had read Norris or Dreiser at that time. I think I had read Stephen Crane and already loved Mark Twain and Whitman."[2]

The New York lawyer Eliot Norton wrote Dos Passos, Sr., that his son's article hadn't gone deep enough. Exuberantly the elder Dos Passos replied that it was not as deep as a well nor as wide as a churchdoor — ''but he gave the world liberty to call him a grave man. . . .''[3] With Norton, one wishes the article had gone into greater detail in its analysis, wishes above all that Dos Passos had said more about Whitman. Since he did not point to or interpret specific ideas in that poet's work, we cannot say to what extent he later adhered to those of Whitman's ideas that were impressing him in 1916. In his requirements of, and his disappointments in, American character and in his devotion to contemporary and socially relevant themes, he would in the next two decades be very close to the Whitman of *Democratic Vistas*.

Gentle satire was the predominant mood in American literature, Dos Passos complained in the article. Washington Irving was ''typical of its least significant manifestation,'' while Edgar Lee Masters, Edith Wharton, and Katharine Fullerton Gerould exemplified ''its modern — and bitter — form.'' Although this satire changed ''chameleon-like'' with variations in European thought, it had up to now ''pretty faithfully represented that genial, ineffectual, blindly energetic affair, the American soul.'' ''Much of our writing, particularly in the upper realm of the novel, the region of Edith Wharton and Robert Herrick, is sincere, careful, and full of shrewd observation of contemporary life,'' Dos Passos said; ''yet I defy anyone to confine himself for long to purely American books without feeling starved, without pining for the color and passion and profound thought of other literatures.'' The reason, he said, was that American literature was genteel, abstract, and rootless. Having been transplanted from England to New England and then to the Middle West, it lacked a basis in folklore and tradition. For this characteristic Whitman, ''our only poet,'' had substituted dependence on the future, but because of the desire of American readers for genteel expression and conventional ideas, he had failed to reach the audience he had sought. Industrialism had now broken the bridges to the past, Dos Passos added, and made retreat impossible. America had to accept Whitman's challenge or become ''the Sicily of the modern world,'' culturally impoverished though materially rich.[4]

Given this way of thinking, it is not surprising that Dos Passos became interested in *Seven Arts*, a new periodical of similar views founded by James Oppenheim as editor and Waldo Frank as associate editor. (Later Van Wyck Brooks became another associate editor.) The two founders believed the country was at last arriving at a self-consciousness that was the beginning of greatness. In such an epoch, art ceased to be a private matter; it became not only an expression of the life of the nation but also a means for its enhancement. The founders hoped their periodical would enable artists, particularly those as yet unknown, to reach an emotionally starved community.[5]

In this prewar era Dos Passos was reading with admiration both Waldo Frank and Randolph Bourne, an early and frequent contributor to the *New Republic*.[6] Both men may have fostered his hopes for a forward-looking literature. Frank was praising Dreiser for describing the crass life of an America that was passing, and Sherwood Anderson for depicting in *Windy McPherson's Son* a new America seeking the truth. He was condemning life in New York and other "cancerous cities." Bourne was writing on a great variety of topics, including feminism, city planning, and progressive education. He was castigating "puritanism"; combating efforts by Anglo-Saxons in America to eradicate the cultures of alien groups; and declaring that culture is not a knowledge of classics, but sensitive taste manifesting itself in contemporary endeavor. Frank and Bourne were writing as alert members of a new generation which was, they thought, morally, economically, and artistically to redeem America; if young writers after the war believed themselves to be a betrayed generation, it was in part because some of them had come to maturity with greater expectations than their predecessors had known or their successors were to entertain.[7]

The presidential campaign of 1916 did much to heighten the political expectations of progressives. Democratic success in the election depended on the party's gaining the votes of former supporters of the Progressive party, and a Democratic Congress under Wilson's leadership enacted that year the most extensive and important progressive legislation in United States history up to that time.

At the Democratic Convention, which met in St. Louis in mid-June, peace became another cause. Ironically this cause, which Dos Passos later stigmatized Wilson for betraying, emerged out of the blue (the billowing red, white, and blue, in fact). Annoyed by Republicans' claims that their party alone embodied patriotism, Wilson arranged that Americanism should be the theme of the convention and that there should be numerous demonstrations of Democrats' loyalty to the flag. The platform which Wilson approved was not pacifistic; it merely promised a neutral foreign policy, advocated reasonable preparedness, and supported America's entrance into a postwar league of nations. But during the keynote address, by former governor Martin H. Glynn of New York, a development occurred which determined the tone of the convention and of the campaign.

Glynn evoked no more than dutiful responses when he spoke of Wilson, preparedness, and 100 per cent Americanism, but when he moved on to historical precedents for refusing to go to war under provocation, the immense crowd rose to their feet, demanding that he not scant his recital. Sensing their mood, Glynn cited precedent after precedent while his listeners chanted responsively and engaged in a series of frenzied demonstrations.

Leaders of organized labor, independent progressives, and many socialists endorsed Wilson, although progressives and socialists were generally not happy about his championship of preparedness. Walter Lippmann, Herbert Croly, Lincoln Steffens, John Dewey, John Reed, and Jane Addams were among Wilson's supporters. Wilson at the end of September charged that the Republicans were a war party and that election of Hughes would mean intervention in Mexico and Europe. "It was as if he had finally found the one great issue," Arthur S. Link writes, "and time and again he expounded this theme, in the Midwest and in the East, until it became the staccato note of his addresses. Moreover, by implication he promised to keep the United States out of war if the people sustained him." The millions of pamphlets and thousands of newspaper advertisements which the Democrats published throughout the nation stressed peace.[8]

Dos Passos did not approve of Wilson either early or without reservations. Stewart Mitchell recalled that in early July 1916, when Dos Passos visited him, Dos Passos was "cool, if not hostile" toward Wilson. He approved of the President's economic and social reforms but was unhappy with his talk of war.[9] He seems nevertheless to have come to share with many of his friends the enthusiasm for Wilson during the summer of 1916. "The first campaign in which I was heavily involved emotionally," he has written, "was Wilson's against Hughes. . . . We were mad for Wilson the peacemaker. 'He kept us out of war' was the slogan of the Wilson soapboxers."[10]

Dos Passos' thoughts, opinions, and feelings at this period are most vividly expressed in a series of letters which he wrote to his college friend Arthur K. McComb. These letters reveal, on the one hand, an abundant energy demanding outlet and direction and, on the other, a remarkable enthusiasm for and sensitivity to public virtue. Dos Passos' private voice, absent or carefully subordinated in most of his published work, sounds clearly here.

A letter of August 7, 1916, reflects a brief running controversy over pacifism and industrialism in which the two friends had engaged in the *Harvard Monthly*. When after his rejoinder to McComb's review of *The World Decision*, Dos Passos published "A Humble Protest," his friend retorted that wealth, and hence industry, are in some ways the condition of art. Property rights and trade are, he added, deterrents to war.[11] From his father's farm in Virginia, Dos Passos wrote insisting that pacifists were relying too much on catchwords and were too devoted to commerce to be effective. "Can you," he now asked, amid the boom inspired by the European war, "give up prosperity that you may win peace?"

"I am trying, among other cakes baking," he added, "to get out an article on 'Shelley and the Modern Age' deploring the strange sanity of American young men, their lack of idealism, and their 'redbloodedness'. . . ."[12]

About three weeks later he wrote a letter expressing his desire to use his energy, to roam the world, to agitate, to work for a new enlightenment. The letter provides remarkable insight into his motivations for more than a decade:

Apropos of the war, I have again relapsed into chaos — I have no ideas Except a vague and very teasing desire to hack and hew, to agitate against the bogies which are being battened by warfumes and are gradually obscuring the fair sky of democracy (the last phrase I shall recommend to Mr. Wilson) The New Republic is losing verve. Heavens the need to agitate! for sanely enthusiastic [*sic*] to put shoulders to the wheel —

I am dying to get to Belgium to exhaust surplus energy by "going to and fro in the earth and walking up and down in it"

Really Arthur I am darned serious — "the forces of reason" must get together, must make a fuss — We want a new Enlightenment — new Byrons new Shelleys new Voltaires before whom 19th century stoginess on the one hand and 20th century reaction on the other shall vanish and be utterly routed "like souls from an enchanter fleeing."

G. B. S. has already formed a nucleus — where are his successors?[13]

Dos Passos wrote McComb that since he was too young for Belgian Relief, he would take the *Espagne* to Bordeaux and thence go on to Madrid. In the spring he planned to go to Paris and attempt by hook or by crook to get to the front, hopefully the Rhine.[14]

In another letter, containing a Madrid address for further correspondence, Dos Passos, in his phrase, "enraged over" a report: "A certain journalist writes an article criticizing unfavorably Mr. Wilson's policies. Said journalist asks for a passport to visit England. Said journalist is calmly refused one by the State Department."[15] He was already angry about the treatment Bertrand Russell had received in England.[16] Did the item about the passport make him apprehensive of even more flagrant repressions that war could bring in redblooded and provincial America?

There might be a germ of some of his later characterizations of American soldiers in his facetious comment that November 16 on "Against American Literature":

I am writing another [article] to the effect that America doesn't need art and that art is the antidote for the disease of romantic discontent — and we not needing it — are in the position of a small boy being forced by his grandmother to take castor oil for fear the green apples he ate last week'll make him ill. You see, Americans don't eat green apples intellectually — I take as a text Flaubert's "chaque notaire porte en soi les ruines d'un poète" — Americans . . . carry within them the ruins of baseball players. . . .

Although — absolutely seriously — I believe that most of the hope of the Western World lies in us — still I fear it'll take many a generation of pummelling to bring anything out of our unyeasted dough.[17]

Feeling politically powerless, Dos Passos was repeatedly uneasy and jocular about his intense seriousness. In January 1917, having had a glimpse of wartime France, he wrote McComb a poignant letter culminating in a private declaration of war against warmakers. The graceful things, the mellow things in life were being covered with "a pompous noise of drums and trumpets," he cried. The worst fact of all about the war was people's resignation.

. . . I cant get the grotesque sight of the one-legged men in Bordeaux out of my head — and the hospitals — everywhere hospitals.

And then the grotesque, sublime silliness of officialdoms — the censorships, the patriotic porridge. . . .

I honestly see no reason on earth why a society for the assassination of statesmen shouldnt be formed that would promptly and neatly do to death all concerned in any declaration of war, "just" or "unjust."

If Anarchists can murder people so successfully, I don't see why Pacifists can't.[18]

The dates of Dos Passos' departure from and return to the United States help to explain his shock at the President's taking the country into the war. He left for Spain on October 14, 1916, when oratory for Wilson and peace was near its height. When his father died of pneumonia on January 21, while he was studying at the Centro de Estúdios Históricos, he terminated his stay in Spain and sailed for home about February 20, after the United States had broken diplomatic relations with Germany over that nation's repudiation of the *Sussex* pledge and its initiation of all-out submarine warfare.[19]

"The crazy spring of 1917," Dos Passos later called the months that followed.[20] On February 26 Wilson asked Congress for authority to wage an undeclared naval war. About a dozen senators, including La Follette and Norris, successfully filibustered against the administration's bill, but Wilson announced on March 9 that he was, nevertheless, going to place gun crews on merchant ships. German submarines sank three American merchantmen on March 18. All along, the spring of 1917 rang with appeals and counterappeals from interventionists and pacifists and with vituperative attacks by most newspapers upon La Follette and his sympathizers.

The revolutionary socialist *Masses*, edited by Max Eastman, opposed intervention because it viewed the war as a capitalist debacle, pointing out how industrialists with munitions to sell and financiers with overseas investments dominated the preparedness organizations.[21] The *New Republic*, on the other hand, supported America's entrance into the war. It contended that peace "would have to be based on public law, that until nations were ready to fight for the maintenance of that law, the strongest aggressor would have his way." While acknowledging the truth of the pacifists' cry that Wall Street wanted war, the editors declared that the government was intervening because it feared Germany's aggressive imperialism.[22]

Dos Passos, who was reading both these periodicals and viewing the European war with consternation, supported *Masses'* position. He says he greatly feared at the time that intervention would prolong the conflict and foster autocracy and totalitarianism at home. But it is unlikely, he adds, that *Masses* influenced his attitude; rather, he probably read the magazine because he agreed with it.[23] His sharp differences with the *New Republic* appear to have been due to sentiments which he shared with a great many other Americans. Most progressives feared militarism and were as likely as Max Eastman to identify intervention with Wall Street.[24]

Nevertheless, some time before and in the course of America's entering the war, Dos Passos had moved leftward on a road which now brought him to socialism. Many events in his previous history must have played their parts. The process, which he does not remember well, he ascribes to his receptivity at the time rather than to any contact with "reds" or reading of "red" literature. "In fact," he says, "I think I lived mostly in books and read mostly classics." At Harvard he had not been greatly impressed with *Masses* when, probably in 1915, he had first seen it in Edward Nagel's room, but he had after a time found himself sharing its "enthusiasm for and sympathy with the common man."[25] Many years later he recalled that *Masses* was impelled by "a feeling that if you could throw off conventions, clothes, institutions, class rule and give the natural good in man a chance, the world would be a better place for man to live in and that man himself would grow more worthy of his inherent possibilities." Since finding himself in sympathy with *Masses*, Dos Passos added, "I've tended to feel more as the common man feels (with the underdog against the topdog) than as any of the castes and oligarchies feel."[26]

There was sympathy with socialist pacifism, at least, in Dos Passos' letter to McComb from Spain in January 1917; describing a finicky pension guest, he commented that the man's one redeeming feature was his socialism. And he remembers being much impressed by an antiwar speech he heard Max Eastman make sometime in 1917.[27]

As America entered the war and mobilized, Dos Passos was in New York, staying with his aunt and preparing to go overseas with the Norton-Harjes Ambulance Service. With more than a grain of seriousness, he wrote McComb a mock philippic, interrupted, he noted facetiously, by a call to dinner: "My only hope is in revolution — in wholesale assassination of all statesmen, capitalists, war-mongers, jingoists, inventors, scientists — in the destruction of all the machinery of the industrial world. . . . My only refuge from the deepest depression is in dreams of vengeful guillotines."[28]

Besides his eagerness to see what the war was like, he had another motive for leaving, one which was probably a mingling of psychological and political impulses: "I had a horror of serving in the army. . . . Later, after I'd seen the front lines a little, I felt quite differently. In fact I went to a great deal of trouble to get into the army . . . and I've always been glad that I did. It was the most valuable part of my education during these years."[29]

Before he embarked for France, he seems to have gone to a meeting of Emma Goldman's No-Conscription League, only to find that the police had banned the meeting. If he went, he says, he probably did so largely to see the show.[30] With his turbulent emotions he could not have been an entirely passive spectator. A letter to McComb reveals his self-dissatisfaction and guilt:

> I've been spending my time of late going to Pacifist meetings and being dispersed by the police. I am getting quite experienced in the cossack tactics of the New York police force. . . . Every day I become more red — My one ambition is to be able to sing the *internationale* —
>
> What about Roger Sessions? Did he get arrested or anything? [There was talk that the composer — whom Dos Passos had liked at Harvard, though they were not close friends — would be a conscientious objector; he was, in fact, too young for the draft in 1917.]
>
> I think we are all of us a pretty milky lot, — dont you? — with our tea-table convictions and our radicalism that keeps so consistently within the bounds of decorum. Damn it, why couldn't one of us have refused to register and gone to jail and made a general ass of himself? I should have had more hope for Harvard.
>
> All the thrust and advance and courage in the country now lies in the East Side Jews and in a few of the isolated "foreigners" whose opinions so shock the New York Times. The're so much more real and alive than we are anyway — I'd like to annihilate these stupid colleges of ours, and all the nice young men in them — instillers of stodginess in every form, bastard culture, middle class snobism —
>
> And what are we fit for when they turn us out of Harvard? We're too intelligent to be successful business men and we haven't the sand or the energy to be anything else — [31]

We might remember the letter for what light it sheds on such characters in Dos Passos' novels as John Andrews, Jimmy Herf, and Richard Ellsworth Savage. And the letter is clearly anticipatory of another aspect of Dos Passos' fiction: his identification of being alive with being politically and socially, as well as privately, tolerant and humane.

Dos Passos sailed for France about June 20, 1917.[32] He left an America that was markedly less tolerant and humane than it had been the year before. Freedoms that he and his friends had enjoyed all their lives were fading. Soldiers and sailors were roaming New York and interfering with meetings against war and conscription. "Suddenly you couldn't speak as you wished," E. E. Cummings declared later, "and you were subject to a draft." He too enlisted in the Norton-Harjes Ambulance Service. Robert Hillyer, another of the Eight Harvard Poets who enlisted in the ambulance service, published in the April *Masses* the poem "To Congress Concerning the Bill for Universal Military Service." It castigated advocates of the bill as tyrants "mad with the fury that foretells your end."[33]

After entering the war the United States gave way to "an hysteria of fear," write Professors Samuel Eliot Morison and Henry Steele Commager, who hold Woodrow Wilson and his subordinates in large part responsible. "The Espionage Act of 15 June 1917 and the Sedition Act of 16 May 1918 were as extreme as any legislation of the kind anywhere in the world." George Creel, Wilson's chairman of the Committee on Public Information, mobilized the mind of America as deliberately and as unequivocally as Baruch mobilized the industry and Baker the manpower.[34] As the conflict progressed, Wilson used the Sedition Act to strike hard against left-wing opposition to the war effort. Everyone of some slight standing in the I.W.W. was arrested; when successors were elected, they too were arrested. The Socialist party in the spring and summer of 1917 voted "continuous, active, and public opposition to the war," and subsequently almost every major party official was indicted. The government restricted or denied mail service to anarchist and Socialist periodicals. *Masses* ceased publication at the end of 1917, after the government curtailed its mailing privileges and indicted Eastman, Reed, and others of its staff.[35]

Dos Passos saw as a moral crisis the administration's manner of bringing the country into war and its unprecedented severity against dissenters. His wartime experiences would seem to increase the immensity of that crisis — and would kindle emotional and artistic fires. Forty years later he wrote: "It was the defeat of what seemed to me the normal antimilitarism of the US through what I considered Wilson's betrayal that opened the way to my considering revolution the only way out—the only way back to primitive American self government — It is an attitude towards which — when I throw myself back into the conditions of those days — I still have considerable sympathy."[36]

Manned by "gentlemen volunteers." Vehicles of the Norton-Harjes Ambulance Service in France.

Dos Passos went to France with Section 60 of the Norton-Harjes Ambulance Service. Richard Norton (Eliot Norton's brother), commander of the service, was an archaeologist who had been director of the American School of Classical Studies at Rome from 1899 to 1907, and had conducted investigations in Central Asia and the Cyrenaica. Arriving in France shortly before the first battle of the Marne, Norton decided that many lives could be saved if enough ambulances were provided to transport wounded men to hospitals without delay. He was successful in getting support from America, and by the end of its career the Norton-Harjes Ambulance Service had over eight hundred men and about as many ambulances.[37]

Dos Passos' letters to McComb reveal much about his state of mind while in the ambulance service. In a letter of June 20, 1917, from the S.S. *Chicago*, hours before sailing for Bordeaux, he exhorted his friends: "But at least you must write — all of you — long letters to the New Republic — long articles in the Masses — " At college Edward Nagel had infected Dos Passos and Cummings with the fascinations of the school of Paris; in the arts all was abolished and had to be invented anew! Now Nagel's name became a code word for dawn in politics: "I expect dark days. My only hope is that something'll happen in France and Austria. But it's a slim one — Oh God how long? But anyway write — read my letters carefully as I may try to transmit censurable news. Nagel — the name — will stand for dances of revolution and all the psychological fringe thereof."[38]

Another letter, written when Dos Passos was Europe-bound, mentioned that he had overheard Archie Roosevelt and Major Theodore Roosevelt, Jr., two fellow passengers, exult over America's military pre-eminence after the war. "And this from Princes of the Blood," Dos Passos commented.[39]

As he proceeded toward Europe, his thoughts were still with Harvard: "By the way — if the Monthly starts up next year at college — it can count on a hundred dollars from me — that is if I'm not dead broke by that time — But by God you must make it whiz. You ought to be able to print one red hot issue before getting suppressed anyway — I almost wish I were back in college — If I only had something to blow off steam in — I'd love to lambaste conscription and the daily press and the intellectual classes and Harvard's attitude — "[40]

Writing in July from Sandricourt Training Camp (in the Department of the Oise, north of Paris), he was filled with concern about the effect of the draft among his friends. Again he asked about Sessions. Had he been jailed? "But, God, I'm glad to be out of the vast American wilderness — I don't feel now as if I could ever go back, though I know I shall — "

> Politically I've given up hope entirely—the capitalists have the world so in their clutches . . . that I don't see how it can ever escape. There are too many who go singing to the sacrifice — who throw themselves gladly, abjectly beneath the Juggernaut. It's rather a comfort to have given up hope entirely — you can take refuge in a pleasantly cynical sullenness, and shake the pack off your back and give three leaps and stride away from the whole human tribe. Of course I have twinges, and shall probably ere long take up again my self-inflicted burden — Till then, let all go hang. . . . Of the Great Revolution I hear no more — I believe in nothing.[41]

However he might detest the war, he found himself curiously stimulated by it. "France in agony of misery is far more liveable," he wrote from a small village in Champagne, "than America in orgy of patriotic bunk. . . . I've not been so happy for months. There's a rollickingness about it all that suits me. Dumas — glorious Dumas — rises in a chant of wine and women and death amid the dull stupidity. Poor humans — how damned adaptable we are."[42]

The French being about to launch an offensive in the Verdun sector, the ambulances were moved up. From a small village behind the lines, Dos Passos wrote on August 10: "I've built myself a snailshell of hysterical laughter." Of Nagel in France, he confided, there were increasing signs. He added: "I've come to firmly believe that the only thing that can save America is Nagelism there. . . . Bobs [Robert Hillyer] & Van [Frederik Francis van den Arend, another college friend] and I talk most excitedly of going home to Junius letters and that sort of thing. . . ."[43]

Dos Passos and Van were sitting in a pitiful, forsaken garden and Van was just opening a letter from McComb when a shell shrieked overhead and exploded. "Oh Arthur can't we do something, we who still have eyes in our heads and thoughts in our minds? Can't we stop this wailing over the dead? — Our life is a wake over the corpse of an elaborately garbed Liberty that I suspect was purely mythical anyway. . . . I'm tired of wailing. I want to assassinate. . . . I shall have to come home — to heave 'arf a brick into the temple of Moloch if nothing else — at least to disturb with laughter the religious halo of the holocaust."[44]

While in the Verdun sector, Dos Passos and Hillyer spent some of their time writing alternate chapters of the novel that Dos Passos had begun as ''The Walls of Jericho.'' Not inappropriately, theirs was a novel championing rebellious youth.[45]

The United States government, acting with the American Red Cross, took over the ambulance service in September 1917. Announcing the news, Dos Passos lamented to McComb: ''The government has taken over the Red Cross with the usual noisome results. . . . What to do to escape the net of slavery drawn tighter and tighter about us, I don't know. I can't believe the war will end until people end it, by force, or by annihilation. Why we who don't believe in it should be made miserable by the cowardice of our fellows — I can't see. I am beginning to desire to m'enficher of the whole affair and escape to Siam — but it's at war — God! everywhere is at war.''[46]

Dos Passos' loss of gentleman volunteer status is described in ''The Camera Eye (32)'' section of *U.S.A.*, which reveals his admiration for Richard Norton and his distaste for inexperienced Red Cross majors. Join the army, Dos Passos was told, or retire. After some detached service, he went off to Paris, where he continued work on the novel and wandered in delight through the city's autumnal streets and gardens. Suddenly there was a rush call for ambulances, and he was able to enlist in the American Red Cross as a civilian.[47]

Between November 1917 and June 1918, Dos Passos was in Italy. He encountered a little action on Monte Grappa, in Bassano, and whenever he could, he raced about Italy to see the paintings and architecture. Two letters of December 1917 voiced more worries about friends. A rumor, again false, had Cuthbert Wright in prison. The noose was ''tightening about everyone's neck.'' ''God! I feel like a dirty hound for being here in Italy instead of trying to do something at home — But it is so hard — without money or influence, or even with it — still it would be worth doing just to show the damn tyrants that we aren't all cowards.'' He had no news, he wrote, of E. E. Cummings and Slater Brown. He had written to all sorts of people about them. ''I hate the negative attitude of utter detestation I get into. It is stupid and monastic. But bitter hate is the only protection one has against the cozening influences of a world rampant with colossal asininity.''[48]

A letter of May 1918 renounced direct action but approved of criticism and agitation: ''No I believe no more in the gospel of energy — One thing the last year has taught me has been to drop my old sentamentalizing over action; action when it is anything at all is a foolish running about, a sheep-like scurrying from the wolves, or a wolfish snarling stalking of the sheep; let us have none of it. A voice of one crying in the wilderness, rather . . . I still believe in that. To turn ones nose to the moon and bay — To blow trumpets and have the walls of Jericho crumble."[49]

But criticism was scarcely more welcome than sabotage in 1918. Professor Chandler Post recalled being somewhat embarrassed when he encountered Dos Passos in Italy. Post was now a captain in Army intelligence, and Dos Passos was under suspicion.[50] In a matter-of-fact tone barely concealing the excitement of thirty-eight years before, Dos Passos has recounted the origin and conclusion of the difficulty:

When I was in Italy with Red Cross Section 1 the Italian Intelligence Service interested itself in my mail. I had a good friend in Spain who was very pro-ally. I intermingled my exortations to him to keep his country neutral with a somewhat too explicit description of the Italian army on the Brenta. . . . officers selling the men's rations; all that sort of thing . . . Now I know that these things date back to the Sumerians but they shocked me at the time. There resulted a great row. Red Cross said go home young man.[51]

His virtually dishonorable discharge from the Red Cross distressed and bewildered Dos Passos. On July 12 he wrote from Paris: "The extreme lack of decency, of small obvious humanness, in people comes out every day. They are preposterous. I refuse to take them seriously." From aboard the S.S. *Espagne* he informed McComb: "I was notified that if I attempted to go to Spain or Switzerland, I should be arrested. . . ." Nine days later he reported, still from the ship: "I spend my time reading the Confessions of Rousseau and finishing up my novel and avoiding my fellow passengers."[52]

Out of the fiction Dos Passos wrote en route to and later in New York came *One Man's Initiation — 1917*. When he was in France after the war, he met "Trilby" Ewer, who was about to become foreign editor of the *Daily Herald*, an independent labor paper in England. Through him Dos Passos got the manuscript of the novel to George Allen and Unwin and when the publisher showed interest, Dos Passos managed to get to London and to raise a guarantee of several hundred dollars. England, he felt in sending the manuscript there, had much more freedom of expression about the war than did Woodrow Wilson's America. Still, England had Mrs. Grundy, and Dos Passos had to allow some bowdlerization before the novel appeared, on October 20, 1920.[53] It is to *One Man's Initiation — 1917* that we must go for suggestions of many of the day-by-day experiences that determined Dos Passos' verdict on the European war.

In its broad outlines the book is autobiographical. Martin Howe is an American ambulance driver in France. He intends to go to Spain after the war.[54] He is literary-minded; from time to time he finds himself repeating snatches of poetry. His moral and aesthetic sensibilities are keen. At the beginning of the book we encounter him on a boat bound for France. He is as bewildered about the nature of the conflict as Dos Passos must have been in 1917. "Perhaps it's only curiosity," he says to the young American woman who tells him how splendid it is of him to come all this way to help France. When she begins to sputter about the atrocities of the Germans, he wonders whether the reports are all true.

One of the chief themes of the book, a theme adumbrated in Dos Passos' college writings, is that the war is an unnatural horror. Martin Howe has not been in Paris long when he sees a young man who wears for a nose a triangular black patch that ends in a mechanical device with little black metal rods that take the place of the jaw. A short while later he trembles in his bunk as he hears a siren, for it resembles the cry of a woman in a nightmare. A man is brought in wounded by machine-gun bullets; where the curved belly and the genitals should be there is only a depression filled with blood. A physician indicates the lunacy involved in the war when he tells Martin that the soldiers in the trenches are much nearer in their states of mind to their antagonists than they are to civilians in their own countries. On leave in Paris, Martin and his friend Tom Randolph agree that someday soldiers and generals alike will have to "jump to their feet and burst out laughing at the solemn inanity, at the stupid, vicious pomposity" of what they are doing.[55]

A chain of events leads to a climax in which Martin reaffirms his own humanity and sanity. In Paris he and Tom encounter an Englishman who is trying to drink away the memory of a particularly lurid piece of cruelty: just before leaving the front he had seen a man tuck a hand grenade under a German prisoner's pillow.

The prisoner said "Thank you." Then the grenade exploded. Martin cannot forget the story. Later, at a crossroads near the front, he sees an old wooden crucifix that someone has propped up; it is tilted, and the scarred cracked figure of Christ holds "despairing arms" against the sky. As Martin waits for a column of troops to pass by, he sees one of the soldiers kick away the prop. Still later, Martin and two French soldiers drink wine together in the doorway of a deserted house. One soldier tells of how he killed a German with a bayonet and cries that he is ashamed to be a man. The other boasts that he bayoneted three and received the *Croix de Guerre*; he adds that all the *Boches* should be put to the bayonet.

The climax comes when a German prisoner who has been put to work aiding the stretcher-bearers is felled by exploding artillery shells. Martin goes out to help him:

Sweat dripped from Martin's face, on the man's face, and he felt the arm-muscles and the ribs pressed against his body as he clutched the wounded man tightly to him in the effort of carrying him towards the dugout. The effort gave Martin a strange contentment. It was as if his body were taking part in the agony of this man's body. At last they were washed out, all the hatreds, all the lies, in blood and sweat. Nothing was left but the quiet friendliness of beings alike in every part, eternally alike.[56]

A strong undercurrent of description of the landscape continually re-enforces the idea that the war is unnatural. Dos Passos shows how the weapons are violating inanimate nature itself.

Martin Howe's initiation is not, however, only to war. The one specific reference to an initiation occurs in a conversation between him and a French soldier, Merrier. Martin says that he is not resigned to the political situation. He wishes to do something someday, but first he wants to see. He wants to be initiated in all the circles of hell. "I'd play the part of Virgil pretty well," Merrier comments, "but I suppose Virgil was a staff officer."[57]

Merrier leads Martin and Randolph into a farmhouse where he, they, and three other men discuss the war. There Martin is introduced to carefully formulated ideologies of rebellion. Not only is the situation autobiographical, but it also provides an important clue to the development of Dos Passos' revolutionary ideas. In "A Preface Twenty-Five Years Later" to the book, Dos Passos wrote:

In reporting a conversation we had with a congenial bunch of Frenchmen one night in a little town where the division was *en repos*, I tried to get some of this down on paper. As an American unaccustomed to the carefully articulated systems of thought which in those days were still part of the heritage of the European mind, I remember being amazed and delighted to meet men who could formulate their moral attitudes, Catholic, Anarchist, Communist, so elegantly. Reading it over I find the chapter scrappy and unsatisfactory, but I am letting it stand because it still expresses, in the language of the time, some of the enthusiasms and some of the hopes of young men already marked for slaughter in that year of enthusiasms and hopes beyond other years, the year of the October Revolution.[58]

Responding to questions about his countrymen, Howe says he doubts whether Americans think. They do not know what the war is. Never having had any experience in international affairs, they believe everything they are told. He and Randolph hold that in entering the war the United States denied its excuse for existing, freedom from "that gangrened ghost of the past" with its bitter hates. The two friends believe that America has turned its back on its heritage. It is now a military nation — an organized pirate nation like the others. As for American idealism, Howe says, it is camouflage. Is none of it sincere? "The best camouflage is always sincere." What terrifies him, Martin adds, is "their" power to enslave minds:

"I shall never forget the flags, the menacing exultant flags along all the streets before we went to war, the gradual unbaring of teeth, gradual lulling to sleep of people's humanity and sense by the phrases, the phrases. . . . America, as you know, is ruled by the press. And the press is ruled by whom? Who shall ever know what dark forces bought and bought until we should be ready to go blinded and gagged to war? . . . People seem to so love to be fooled. Intellect used to mean freedom, a light struggling against darkness. Now the darkness is using the light for its own purposes. . . ."[59]

One by one the men in the farmhouse offer their own solutions. The blond Norman wants government by the Church, not through physical force but through spiritual force. Merrier calls for socialism — a socialism that will spring from the natural need of the members of the lower classes to help one another. It must not come from the governors, who wish to use it only to tighten their control. The rich, he adds, must be "extinguished." The anarchist Lully thinks that property should be abolished; then government, which should be purely utilitarian, will no longer be worshiped.

André Dubois calls for a revolution after the war. They all drink: "To Revolution, to Anarchy, to the Socialist state." It is the working people, Dubois says, who have the power and nerve. Since men are easily duped, it is for the intellectuals to fight the lies that are choking everybody alike.

As they walk home together, Martin turns to Tom Randolph and says: "With people like that we needn't despair of civilisation." The hope is repeated in the last scene of the book, when Martin stoops over the dying Norman and learns that Merrier, Lully, and Dubois have all been slain. The last words we hear the Norman say are, "It's not for long. To-morrow, the next day . . ."[60]

One Man's Initiation — 1917 suggests how Dos Passos under the impact of actual experience shed many opinions about the war that he had held at Harvard. Gone was any lingering notion that the war was a defense of culture by the Latin nations. One event in the book not only belittles that view but also suggests the impossibility of remaining aloof from one's world, of avoiding commitment. Examining a fine Gothic abbey leads Martin to yearn for monastic solitude and detachment, but when the Germans shell the abbey, he and his companion observe that the French are using its cellar as an ammunition dump and its lantern as an observation post.[61] As Dos Passos drove his ambulance through the European abattoirs in 1917 the insanity of the war continually made revolution seem sane by contrast.

But however revealing firsthand observation may have been, Dos Passos did not form his opinions by that means alone. Even before his ambulance service, he was alert to Europe's literary and intellectual ferment. Sailing home from Europe after his father's death, he had been "moved to frenzy" by Henri Barbusse's *Le Feu* (1916), a novel (soon translated into English as *Under Fire*) portraying the war as seen by a regiment of French infantrymen. *Le Feu* is not reticent about the soldiers' agony, and it does not depict the men as enduring it with patriotic fervor; the verdict of many of them is: "Two armies fighting each other — that's like one great army committing suicide!"[62] At the conclusion of the novel, soldiers declare they must endure injustice and win the war, but afterward they must establish equality and overcome militarism, even if doing so means fighting Frenchmen.

Romain Rolland was a second European who influenced Dos Passos. During the years before the war, when Rolland was writing *Jean Christophe*, he looked to rapprochement between France and Germany, to European federalism, and to a fraternity of independent thinkers throughout the world. He happened to be in Switzerland when the war broke out, and from there he attempted to maintain communications between European intellectuals, combat the hatred that the press was inspiring in every belligerent nation, and bring to the public news of movements toward international understanding.

Reading *Jean Christophe* in July 1916, Dos Passos had developed an overpowering "youth against the world" zeal, which was probably reflected in his August 7 letter complaining to McComb about a lack of idealism in American young men. Though he voiced irritation at Rolland's view of art in that novel, finding it sentimental, Rolland's remonstrances against hatred during the war and his insistence that intellectuals guard their integrity impressed Dos Passos — "mostly," he says, "before I went to France." His recollections of *Jean Christophe* continued to excite him there.[63]

Although not a contemporary, Arthur Rimbaud was a third important European influence upon Dos Passos' political and social views during the war. One week in the summer of 1917 Dos Passos never went anywhere without a book of Rimbaud's verse in his pocket. Rimbaud's poems describe early visions of his power as a poet, express contempt for European bourgeois civilization and deliver apocalyptic prophecies of its doom, and portray the author's compulsion to travel and seek a destiny in remote lands. Before his twentieth birthday, Rimbaud not only abandoned literature but fled from Europe. Subsequently he became a trader in Africa.

Dos Passos was probably impressed by the career as well as the poetry of this arch-romantic and anarchist. At college he had felt a compulsion to travel similar to that which Rimbaud expressed, and like Rimbaud he had been drawn to lands innocent of industrialism. Now, as bourgeois-industrial civilization appeared to have crumbled, Rimbaud may have loomed before Dos Passos as a poet-prophet.[64]

An apocalyptic era seemed to be at hand. The powerful Petrograd Soviet in the spring of 1917 demanded that the Russian government adopt a policy of seeking peace without annexations or indemnities and agitated for an international socialist meeting to effect peace. After the October Revolution Trotsky invited all the belligerent nations to conclude an immediate armistice, and on December 5 Russia signed a truce with Germany. The progress of the Russian revolution in 1917 incandesced the expectations of leftwing intellectual pacifists throughout Europe and America, although the expectations were dimmed by a fear of Germany.[65] During and after the negotiation of the Treaty of Brest Litovsk, Lenin was counting on a general European revolution.

Following his discharge from the Red Cross, Dos Passos was back in America between August and November 1918.[66] During this time he caught disconcerting glimpses of events on the home front, many of which he indignantly recreated in *U.S.A.*. Newspapers were carrying reports of a second trial of the editors of *Masses*. Max Eastman was meanwhile editing the *Liberator*, the successor to *Masses*. In the *Liberator* Dos Passos probably read John Reed's descriptions of the Bolshevik Revolution, his account of Eugene V. Debs' stubborn opposition to the war, and his portrayal of the mass trial of 101 I.W.W. men, including William Haywood, before Judge Landis.

Quite as determined to return to the battle areas as many another pacifist might have been to remain away, Dos Passos attempted to get into various army units. Myopia was one obstacle; one-time friends possessed by patriotic fury and deeming him unworthy to serve were another. In September, with the aid of a sympathetic physician who ignored the fact that he had memorized the eye chart poorly, he finally got into the army ambulance service and joined a unit located at Camp Crane in Allentown, Pennsylvania. From camp he wrote McComb to explain his enlistment: "I'm glad I'm here even if I seem to grumble. I've always wanted to divest myself of class and the monied background — the army seemed the best way — From the bottom — thought I, one can see clear. . . ."[67]

In another letter to McComb, referring to the trouble with the Red Cross, he added: "My scandal was hushed up . . . through the exertions of a heroical aunt. I got into the army voluntarily . . . because I am very anxious to see things through and think them through, in actual experience rather than hearsay."[68]

The ordinary Americans at the camp, a markedly different group from Captain Norton's gentlemen volunteers, provided some of the education for which the novelist was later grateful. To McComb he wrote: "You cant imagine the simple and sublime amiability of the average American soldier — Here is clay for almost any moulding. Who is to be the potter? That is the great question."[69]

For the moment Dos Passos himself was clay. He wrote that he repeated the words "Organization is death" over and over again — in anagrams and in different languages. In his serio-facetious tone, he declared: "God, there is strife to come — there must be much sharpening of pens. . . ." The dark conquers eternally, till the world crumbles into dust, he philosophized more somberly; but "the lamp that flickers and goes out is greater and more beautiful in the moment's intensity of flare than all the eternity of dark that follows."[70]

Of combat in World War I Dos Passos saw no more, the armistice having been concluded by the time he returned to France. He was stationed in Alsace for a while, and between March and July 1919 he was in a detachment of American soliders studying at the Sorbonne.[71]

In Paris that spring after the armistice, distinctions of military rank must have seemed particularly irritating to him. He believes that these distinctions increased the desire of young middle-class radicals to have the underdog rise.[72] Seeing as related evils capitalism, some of the nightmarish aspects of industrialism, the war, and now the peace being prepared at Versailles, he excitedly awaited the general strike which the General Labor Federation had called for May 1, 1919. In a fashion which became characteristic, he sought firsthand knowledge of the unrest. "Loafing around in little old bars full of the teasing fragrances of history, dodging into alleys to keep out of sight of the M.P.s, seeing the dawn from Montmartre, talking bad French with taxidrivers, riverbank loafers, workmen, *petites femmes*, keepers of *bistros*, *poilus* on leave," Dos Passos has written of numbers of American radicals, "we eagerly collected intimations of the urge towards the common good. It seemed so simple to burn out the tentcaterpillars that were ruining the orchard."[73] Riots occurred in Paris when troops and police interfered with May Day demonstrations which the government had forbidden; but, despite the inspiration which Bolshevik successes provided, no second French Revolution occurred.[74]

Discharged at Gièvres in July 1919, Dos Passos went to Spain the next month. From there he wrote in April 1920 to McComb in Bâle: "Write me lots about Erasmus. I am in a moment when I need the fillip of stories of great people who died very long

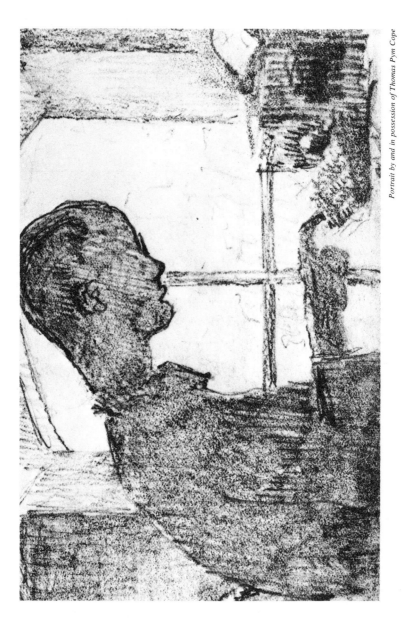

In Paris, 1919, relating some of his experiences. Dos Passos' nearsightedness meant coming close to read books and typewriter keys and straining to recognize faces.

ago.'' He had begun *Three Soldiers* in France during 1919, and he completed it in Spain in 1920.[75]

Late that summer Dos Passos returned to the United States to ''peddle'' his novel. After something like fourteen rejections, he had to undergo the agony of watching the editors at the George H. Doran Company delete what the publisher considered offending obscenities. Burning to convey the incalculably greater obscenities of the war itself, the young author with difficulty held his peace. Only after the success of *Three Soldiers* did Doran, on June 23, 1922, issue an American edition of *One Man's Initiation — 1917*.[76]

Dos Passos' first wartime novel is the hurriedly written effort of an amateur. His second, the story of the disastrous careers of soldiers Andrews, Chrisfield, and Fuselli in the American army, is the work of an accomplished novelist. It is also a type of fiction that became characteristic of Dos Passos. He had been greatly affected, he says, by novels wherein a story is the ''skeleton on which some slice of history is brought back to life.''[77] *Three Soldiers* and most of his subsequent fiction recreate contemporary history in this way.

In *Three Soldiers* Dos Passos displays an increased ability to present material dramatically. It is difficult to forget, for instance, the scene in which a crowd of still-green American soldiers in a French café gape at and comment about a prostitute until she screams with rage. Equally memorable is the scene in which the boy Stockton refuses to get out of bed. When the guards yank him out, he falls dead. The sergeant's ''Well, I'll be goddamned'' is, of course, the apt phrase.

The appearance of the apt phrase is significant. It is usually through the use of dialogue that Dos Passos fixes scenes in a reader's memory, and if the book succeeds dramatically, it is because Dos Passos has caught and used with extraordinary skill the talk of American soldiers in the years 1917 and 1918. The dialogue is there, not only the phonetic variations and the peculiarities of grammar, but, more important, the phrases.

Consider the vivid description of an American military unit's voyage to France on a troop transport. We are told of Fuselli's ''watching the top of the mast move, like a pencil scrawling on paper, back and forth across the mottled clouds.''[78] The image is striking, but it is a solitary one. What holds us is the way the dialogue tells us that a shipload of diverse Americans, the sorts Dos Passos wanted to and did encounter in the army, is in the hold of the ship. Not only the anticipated drama of the situation, but also an underlying clash of traditions is reflected in the speech.

> "They got sentries posted to keep us from goin' up on deck," said someone.
> "God damn them. They treat you like you was a steer being taken over for meat."
> "Well, you're not a damn sight more. Meat for the guns."
> A little man lying in one of the upper bunks had spoken suddenly, contracting his sallow face into a curious spasm, as if the words had burst from him in spite of an effort to keep them in.
> Everybody looked up at him angrily.
> "That goddam kike Eisenstein," muttered someone.[79]

Despite its title, Dos Passos' book is primarily about one soldier, John Andrews; the other two, Chrisfield and Fuselli, are treated less fully and serve in part to place Andrews in high relief. Andrews is an individual for whom art and similar private concerns are more important than public "duties." Besides, he has come to believe that these duties have been dishonestly described and imposed. Since wartime government is oblivious to private desires, his survival depends on prudence, a quality in which he is deficient. Chrisfield asserts a less sophisticated individuality; he does not have well-defined ends of his own, and he has no idea of the way in which the war leaders are imposing their catchwords upon him. Fuselli, in his lack of individuality, differs from both of them. He is the end product of the media that give the masses of America their ideology as well as their entertainment.

Three Soldiers certainly attempts some representation of the American character, which Dos Passos had mulled over in his Harvard stories and letters, and it probably also attempts to represent the kind of rootlessness that Dos Passos had written about in "Against American Literature." But concern with rootlessness would be clearly subordinate to portrayal of the army; at the moment all three men are members of that vast machine, and as such all three suffer, though they belong to widely differing social groups.

Andrews, the only educated person of the three, is a Harvard man, an artist, and a Southerner; divorced from his region, he has been swept into an inhospitable industrial culture. Chrisfield is a farm boy and a nativistic Midwesterner. Fuselli is a second-generation Italian American and the only fully urban man of the three. Though very different from Andrews, he too is deracinated,

American industrial culture having replaced that of his forebears. He seems almost a collection of responses. As the plaything of forces with which Dos Passos has been concerned for a lifetime, he is highly significant, although he is too individual a character to bear on his shoulders the burden of being mass man.

Fuselli aims at material success but does not know that the conventional explanations of how it is achieved are not true, particularly in the army. In civilian life he dreamed of getting rich but actually held a job with no prospects. In the army his aim is to win promotions. The war, he believes, is a lucky thing for him; it gives him a chance to rise in the world. He must smile at the right people, never do anything that will antagonize anybody, and show how clever he is. He does not miss freedom, and has no conception of what freedom means to someone like Andrews. After he has leaned out of a troop train and kissed a girl furiously, amid the cheers of his companions, he remarks: "It's great to be a soldier. Ye kin do anything ye goddam please." His idea of the war is derived from the movies.[80]

Lacking intelligence, experience, and aggressiveness, Fuselli, in spite of his many self-serving stratagems, is an eternal dupe — a victim of his own fears as well as of propaganda; thus, when Wild Dan Cohen says that the Germans dropped a message giving the Allies three days to evacuate a hospital, Fuselli refuses to believe him and concludes that it would be a good idea not to be seen too much with Cohen.

But although Fuselli is a ridiculous figure presented with sad irony, the picture of the war that he has accepted is the common one. Members of his unit indignantly eye a soldier who says that the Germans seem to be advancing and that one cannot believe everything he reads in the newspapers. When Fuselli takes exception to a Frenchman's talk about revolution, Eisenstein, a Polish-Jewish immigrant, comments that Fuselli is a typical American.

> "You talk like a socialist," said Fuselli. "They tell me they shoot guys in America for talkin' like that."
> "You see!" said Eisenstein to the Frenchman.
> "Are they all like that?"
> "Except a very few. It's hopeless. . . ."[81]

It is Eisenstein who says this, not Dos Passos, whose commentary (except for the titles of book sections) is characteristically implicit. But Dos Passos depicts many of Fuselli's countrymen

as a poor lot indeed. Officers, though not all of them, use their
curt voices like whips, change their attitudes obsequiously at a
frown from a superior, and engage in illegal cruelty. Y.M.C.A.
officials tell the men that the war is a great Christian undertaking
and lead them in singing "We're going to get the Kaiser." At
the end of the war some of the enlisted men, cut from the same
cloth as Fuselli, have learned so little that they boast and bet about
which of their companies — infantry or engineering — sustained
more casualties.

Chrisfield, a twenty-year-old from Indiana who left school
at twelve to work on the family farm, resembles a frontiersman
in his combativeness, his fierce demand for independence, and his
deeply rooted folk prejudices. We can go far toward knowing him
by attending to only a few of his comments: "Ah didn't git in
this here army to be ordered around by a goddam wop"; "Ah'd
lahk te cepture a German officer an' make him shine ma boots
an' then shoot him dead. . . ."; "But Ah'd a damn side rather
shoot somebody else Ah know. . . . An' Ah'll do it too, if he
don't let off pickin' on me"; "They like ridin' yer. A doughboy's
less'n a dawg to 'em. Ah'd shoot anyone of 'em lake Ah'd shoot
a nigger."[82]

Chrisfield is surely a far more terrifying provincial than any
Dos Passos had put into his college stories. Yet one wonders to
what extent Dos Passos is inviting a favorable comparison of
Chrisfield with the wheedling Fuselli. A decade after the publication
of the novel, Dos Passos pointed to "faint traces of democratic
government" in the South as a vestigial remnant of pre-industrial
America.[83] It is perhaps Chrisfield's being denied the equality that
a white native Westerner claims as his birthright that leads to his
desperation. A man of uncontrollable rages, he cannot stand the
idea of having to work while Sergeant Anderson, with whom he
fought when the latter was a private, can lounge about. He refuses
to obey Anderson and invites punishment by threatening him. When
he embarks on an attempt to kill Anderson soon after he has been
punished, he says "Make the world safe for Democracy" over
and over again, without thinking of what the words mean.[84]

Andrews says that he is Chrisfield's sort, only "they" have
tamed him, and the two do resemble each other in a fierce, instinctive
rebelliousness (perhaps it is significant that between them they share
some of the name of Romain Rolland's tempestuous Jean Christophe). However, Chrisfield's portrait makes it clear that Dos Passos

was not writing as a nineteenth-century Russian-style populist, finding multitudinous virtues in the peasantry. Possibly Andrews is voicing some kind of populism, in a mood of disgust with himself.

When Chrisfield tells Andrews that he envies his learning, for learning helps a person get along in the world, Andrews replies in terms that recall Dos Passos' criticism of tame Harvard pacifists. What use is there in getting along, he asks, if one does not have a world to get along in? He belongs to a crowd that just fakes learning, Andrews says, a tame generation that doesn't deserve to survive. It is people like Chrisfield who are important.[85]

Despite Andrews' comment, the differences are not in Chrisfield's favor. Chrisfield has accepted the war, and he can rejoice in its cruelty. During the same American attack in which he finally murders Anderson, he kicks a German prisoner repeatedly and laughingly accedes to a sentry's killing him. In Andrews' conversation with Chrisfield just before Andrews goes to Paris, the two men are farther apart than at any other point in the book. Chrisfield has become a corporal, and, with no Anderson to arouse his fury, he seems to be more comfortable than before. But he dreads the trials of individual freedom and independence — trials which, we shall see, had in civilian life proved too much for Andrews. Soon after Andrews tells Chrisfield that he does not want to live like a king or a sergeant — but like John Andrews, Chrisfield remarks: "It's funny, ain't it? You an' me was right smart frinds onct. . . . Guess it's bein' a non-com." When Chrisfield adds: "Reckon a feller wouldn't know what to do with himself if he did get out of the army . . . now, would he, Andy?" Andrews jumps to his feet and bids him farewell in a harsh voice.[86]

To understand Andrews, one must pay attention to the passages in which he comments on his life before he entered the army. His childhood environment certainly did not help make him amenable to group discipline. He was originally from Virginia, where he lived alone with his mother in an isolated old house belonging to her family. His mother, the only person who ever had any importance to him, had led a terribly thwarted life and was very unhappy. She taught him to play the piano and would spend hours making beautiful copies of his compositions. After he left Harvard and before he went into the army, his life, he says, consisted of "slaving in that iron, metallic, brazen New York to write ineptitudes about music in the Sunday paper."[87] In spite of his lack of technical training, his chief desire was to create music, but apparently he was unable to do it. He threw himself into the army because he was sick of revolt, of thought, of being free and getting nowhere. He wanted to lose his individuality, to become one of a mass behaving all alike.

Almost from the start of the novel, Andrews is shown realizing his mistake, valuing his individuality, gasping for freedom. He has not escaped the kinds of exasperations he knew as a civilian in industrial civilization, soldiers even more than metropolitan newspaper writers being cogs in a machine. "Making the Mould," "The Metal Cools," "Machines," "Rust," "The World Outside," "Under the Wheels," read the successive section headings of the book.

To Andrews the war appears ridiculous and hateful. From friends and acquaintances who, like Roger Sessions, were planning to write music, Dos Passos could have got hints for creating Andrews. It is also significant that both Andrews and Romain Rolland's German-born Jean Christophe are composers. As Andrews washes windows in the barracks, the phrase "Arbeit und Rhythmus" recurs in his mind; then it occurs to him that he is being trained to kill anyone who speaks the German language. In the Y.M.C.A. hut among men watching propaganda films, a contribution of the machine age, he feels "blind hatred stirring like something that had a life of its own. . . ."[88] Later he taunts Y.M.C.A. men who repeat the wartime shibboleths.

Andrews is concerned lest he lose the thread of his own life and become an automaton. He lacks the philosopher's ability to weigh future goods against present ones. His need to desert is the result of the same kind of irrational fury that impels Chrisfield to kill Anderson. Though Andrews knows that, since the war is over and the armistice signed, he will soon be free, he cannot argue with himself; his spirit is so contorted with revolt that he wonders whether he has gone mad. When he is mistreated by M.P.s and then marched away like an automaton, "a nightmare voice" shrieks and shrieks. After he has escaped from prison, he refuses to heed his friends' advice that he go back to his unit, where he probably has not been missed and where the records can be altered in any case. "One more order shouted at my head," he cries, "is not worth living to be eighty. . . ."[89]

Although Andrews' desertion is primarily the result of emotional revulsion, he also sees it as a revolutionary gesture. In the hospital he blames himself for having been willing to sacrifice himself as a soldier for a useless cause but unwilling to do the same for everything that defines him as an individual. After his desertion it occurs to him that every man who stands up courageously to resist military service and die loosens the grip of the nightmare that has overtaken the world. He tells Geneviève Rod, the French girl with whom he has fallen in love, that now that by pure accident he has made a gesture toward human freedom, he does not wish to temporize and be properly demobilized.

Andrews' turning to political themes seems especially significant when we consider the incident of the Gothic abbey in *One Man's Initiation — 1917*, and Dos Passos' references to his own aestheticism at college. Before Andrews' desertion, he is preparing a musical composition based on a subject as remote from the war as the Queen of Sheba's visit in Flaubert's *The Temptation of St. Anthony*. When the M.P.s take him away to prison, he leaves a composition called the ''Soul and Body of John Brown'' unfinished on his writing table. The subject of the composition provides a small but important irony. A most unusual subject for a white Virginian to take to his heart, it points to Andrews' complex links with his own background, as well as to his rejection of any role as master.

Andrews' rebellion is, nevertheless, fundamentally against what he conceives to be his own enslavement. He never becomes a doctrinaire revolutionist, though he begins to think in general terms. At the time of his first trip to Paris, he does not seem interested in a discussion, by Henslowe and some of his friends, of the fate of the Russian revolution. Later he thinks of the great figures of the Italian Renaissance and muses that whichever wins, tyranny from above or spontaneous organization from below, there can be no individuals. If he looks with favor on the May 1 general strike in France against the war with Russia and wonders whether it can succeed, his attitude is the result of despair. It scarcely rises above Chrisfield's in sophistication or even a pretension to it. Andrews' final comment on society — one which in the eyes of Geneviève Rod deprives him of even the modicum of respectability of a socialist — is that there will perhaps always be ''organizations growing and stifling individuals, and individuals revolting hopelessly against them, and at last forming new societies to crush the old societies and becoming slaves again in their turn.''[90]

At Harvard, Dos Passos had written that flux is eternal, and at Camp Crane he had repeated over and over again that organization is death. Yet, though he gave Andrews a background similar in part to his own and some similar sentiments, he was a far different man from Andrews. His wartime career was markedly different from the unfortunate composer's and considerably less rash. Politically he was always more knowledgeable, critical, and responsible. He sought facts and accepted political commitment, but never refused to re-examine both facts and commitment. Still, does he not repeat through Andrews' story the cry in his letter to McComb: "The lamp that flickers and goes out is greater and more beautiful in the moment's intensity of flare than all the eternity of dark that follows"?

Three Soldiers established Dos Passos' reputation as a novelist: it was recognized immediately as the first capably written American novel to depart from the inspirational pattern for writing about the war, to treat the conflict realistically, and to criticize it severely. Henry Seidel Canby, writing in the *New York Evening Post*, noted that the book was one of a number — heralded by Barbusse's *Le Feu* — which sought to show the effect of war on a sensitive civilized mind; *Three Soldiers* was the first for America that could be called literature. He feared that, like *Le Feu*, the book would be discussed as an argument for pacifism, and the creative skill displayed in it would be ignored. Andrews should be seen not as a spokesman for his generation, Canby wrote, but as an artist and an individualist who, much more than his companions, values a type of life that war makes impossible and who entered the army with no concern for group patriotism, loyalty, and duty.[91]

Remembering the wartime hysteria, W. C. Blum, in the *Dial*, declared that the publication of *Three Soldiers* proved at least that the war was over and American books about the war need no longer be worse than American books in general. He observed that Dos Passos' attitude toward officers was that of a surprising number of enlisted men — a fact, he added, treated as secret only by the newspapers. The author, Blum wrote, did not have to be ironical. "He sits still, and the unforgettable idiocy of everybody in sight supplies the irony. . . ."[92]

The conflict was still too recent for the public to receive Dos Passos' indictment of wartime thought and morality with indifference. If one of the themes of *Three Soldiers* is the extent to which hysteria dominated the country during the war, the book made its point not only by what it contained but also by the way in which the influential *New York Times* commented on it. That newspaper's review, which occupied all of page one of the Sunday book review and magazine section, bore the headline: "Insulting the Army." The reviewer, Coningsby Dawson, began with the sentence: "This is the kind of book that any one would have been arrested for writing while the war was yet in progress." To him it represented not what soldiers had thought during the war, but what the least worthy of them imagined they had thought, now that they were free to complain. "The men depicted in 'Three Soldiers' got out of the war what they brought to it — low ideals and bitterness. They would have got the same out of life if there had been no war. They were spineless, self-centred weaklings, with a perpetual chip on their shoulders — deserters in spirit from whatever duty beckoned."[93]

Dawson reviewed the book in the light of his own experiences with the Canadian forces. Some two weeks later the paper took note of this fact and announced that the next day it would print "a like condemnation which is not open to that sort of criticism from those who have been praising 'Three Soldiers' as a true picture of war as it was encountered by young Americans."[94]

The "like condemnation" was again a Sunday, page-one article. After recording his surprise that Dos Passos had not been a slacker and that he possessed a really creditable war record, the author, Harold Norman Denny, proceeded to explain the difference between front-line ambulance service and front-line infantry fighting. If the author had been in the combat forces, Denny said, he would have written another type of book; the three neurotic characters were well-drawn, but Dos Passos failed in not presenting a background of American soldiers as they truly were. Dos Passos seemed to believe that Americans were not fighting for just or adequate reasons, Denny remarked, perceiving a crucial point that Dawson had not mentioned. To a man with that point of view, the war might seem intolerable, but even then a true man would not whine. Denny closed his article with the comment: "Perhaps it is malicious to point it out, but the paper cover surrounding 'Three Soldiers' is of an intense, passionate yellow."[95]

Neither Dawson nor Denny, we may assume, had read *One Man's Initiation — 1917*; the nature of their reviews makes it unlikely that they knowingly would have neglected it as a means of discrediting the author.

Before *Three Soldiers* was published, Dos Passos had embarked on a trip through Spain and the Near East, and it was somewhere in the Arab lands that he first saw reviews of his book.[96] When he returned, the *New York Times* pictured him as expressing surprise that it had received so much unfavorable criticism. He had tried to show "the effect of the army on the under dog in the army," he explained. There were in the army "enormous numbers of people who had a better time and were more prosperous than ever before in their lives." The *New York Times* did not choose to notice that this explanation constituted a further criticism of wartime America. "What earned the indignation which the book caused," its spokesman stated, "was its presentation of those whom Mr. Dos Passos calls 'under dogs' as men with real grievances against military system and discipline — as men who had suffered cruel wrongs and were deserving of sympathy."[97] When Congress declared war, woe to that minstrel boy who did not have a soldierly bone in him.

IV.

A REVOLUTIONARY
POSTWAR WORLD

IN MARCH 1921, AFTER A HALF YEAR IN THE UNITED STATES, Dos Passos sailed for Lisbon with E. E. Cummings, the trip, by small freighter via the Azores, taking twenty-three days. After traveling in Spain with his friend, he embarked upon a journey through Turkey, the Soviet Caucasus, Iran, and some of the Arab lands. With him he carried credentials from the *Metropolitan Magazine* and the *New York Tribune*, for both of which he intended to do color articles. He returned to the United States about late February 1922.[1]

What was he seeking in his travels? His extraordinary wanderlust asked no more specific goal than a journey, but among his many urges was one to experience ways of life more vivid and colorful than that of the industrial West. We have found testimonies to this urge in Dos Passos' writings during and immediately after his college years. He had written of veiled Arab women, the verse of Omar Khayyám, a shepherd's rousing a boy's desire for freedom and adventure. And in "Against American Literature" he had complained of a lack therein of folklore, tradition, and passion. In the lands he now visited, the past lived on.

It was dependence on the future, however, that Dos Passos had urged American writers to learn from Whitman. The literary future was not, for Whitman, separable from the social and political one. For Dos Passos, after his experience of the war, the two were never to seem separable. The war fed Dos Passos' desire to enlighten and agitate, to seek revolutions that would liberate man. The Communists were, in many countries, working for revolution. What was to be expected of them? His life in Spain before and after the war and his journeys in 1921–22 left him with a host of impressions, questions, and tentative answers about industrial and nonindustrial society in the twentieth century. These resulted in numerous articles and two travel books, *Rosinante to the Road Again* and *Orient Express.*

From Dos Passos' postwar journalism, and from the periodicals he read and contributed to, we can be certain that he was highly aware of the millenarianism among leftists after the Bolshevik Revolution and of the repression of the left in the United States. His observations immediately after the armistice and now in 1921–22 suggest those of Wordsworth in revolutionary France, although Dos Passos is self-effacing in his writings. His articles are written with a revolutionary fervor comprehensible only when we recall his wartime passion and the expectations of social revolution among socialists and anarchists everywhere. They are written too with an intense resentment of the American government and press because of excesses that both committed after the war, when people feared turmoil and revolution at home.

Revolution had for so long been an apocalyptic term among socialists and anarchists that leftists in America were committed to the October Revolution long before they knew quite what it entailed. Unsuccessful and harshly persecuted at home, the left enthusiastically greeted the Bolshevik enterprise as the triumph of a syndicalism and socialism similar to its own.[2] The General Executive Board of the I.W.W. in 1919 and 1920 referred with favor to Soviet Russia and the Third International, though in 1920 the I.W.W. resisted affiliation with any international trade-union organization dominated by the Comintern or dedicated to a dictatorship of the proletariat. After the Comintern adopted a policy of infiltrating the A.F.L., the I.W.W. refused to cooperate and die. A new General Executive Board soon voiced hostility toward the Comintern.[3]

The Socialists in 1918 proclaimed their enthusiastic support of the October Revolution, and right and left wings of the party alike sought to identify themselves with the Bolsheviks. But the Socialist forces had been transformed. The postrevolutionary left, for whose emergence Russian émigrés were in good part responsible, contained many members of Socialist foreign-language federations. In February 1919 leaders of this left drew up a manifesto calling for a Bolshevik-style organization and prepared to gain control of the Socialist party. The old leaders had no intention of yielding control. After a national referendum in the spring of 1919 gave the left wing twelve of the fifteen seats in the national executive committee, the old leaders charged fraud and expelled much of the left-wing opposition. The Socialist party convention opened in August 1919 with the right wing in control but with two thirds of the party members gone. Although a referendum led the Socialist party to apply for affiliation with the Comintern, its bid was rejected in 1920. Splits, resignations, and defections to Communist groups meanwhile were reducing the number of Socialists. The imprisoned Debs polled 919,799 votes in 1920, but these were largely votes of protest. The war and Communist inroads had virtually annihilated both the Socialist party and the I.W.W.[4]

Along with a diffuse pro-Bolshevism among socialists and anarchists in 1918, there developed in the country at large a widespread and usually uncritical antiradicalism that was far more significant. After the war, revolutionary radicals were few in number and — whatever some of them may have thought — were without prospects of launching a revolution. But some of the participants in the hysteria over radicalism wielded immense political and economic power. They used it to bolster reactionary capitalism and at times to weaken some of the liberties that distinguish democracy from totalitarianism. The restriction of accustomed freedoms during World War I had helped make Dos Passos an opponent of the existing political and economic system in America. The year of peace immediately following the conflict persuaded him that the groups he thought responsible for the war were intent upon extending their economic power and suppressing dissent in fields which had previously been beyond their reach. Since much space in *Manhattan Transfer* and *U.S.A.* is devoted to the antiradical hysteria of 1919, we shall review the events in some detail.[5]

In 1919, when some radicals began to advocate Bolshevism and work for revolution, the country was neither psychologically nor economically in a state of peace. The wartime demand for absolute loyalty persisted, and the public considered Bolsheviks pro-German. Organized labor had abandoned its wartime quiescence and now became more militant than at any time during the next fifteen years. Meanwhile industrialists, who had emerged from the war with more prestige than in the muckraker days, were determined to end collective bargaining and destroy the gains that organized labor had made during the Progressive era.

In 1919 most of the press, many politicians, and some private organizations created unreasonable apprehension over a series of spectacular events bearing traces or evidence of radical activity. Each event kindled fears in the light of which subsequent ones were viewed. The first event, between February 6 and 10, was a general strike by all of Seattle's organized labor in support of a shipyard workers' strike. The public for the first time devoted virtually its entire attention to the issue of domestic Bolshevism, and most newspapers seized upon it as a postwar source of sensational news and exaggerated it unconscionably.

Next came the discovery that someone had sent bombs through the mails in an attempt to murder thirty-six government officials, industrialists, and financiers on or about May Day. May 1 brought riots in the European style as radicals held mass meetings, rallies, and red-flag parades reaffirming their dedication to international socialism. It was soldiers and patriots who precipitated the riots, when they broke up radical parades and meetings and demolished Socialist headquarters in Boston, New York, and Cleveland; nevertheless, newspapers everywhere in the country described the clashes as dress rehearsals for a revolution. A month later came more bombs. Within a single hour on June 2, explosions in eight cities damaged public and private buildings, including the home of Attorney General Palmer, and killed two people.

Formulating the problem of Bolshevism so as to advance their own interests and programs, conservative patriotic societies, such as the National Security League and the American Defense Society, and employer groups, such as the National Metal Trades Association, the National Founders Association, and the National Association of Manufacturers, linked patriotism with the open shop. The American Legion greatly exaggerated the danger of domestic Bolshevism, and Legionnaires continually brawled with Socialists and assaulted radicals. The conservative groups so increased the public's fears that the Overman Judiciary Subcommittee of the United States Senate and the Lusk Committee of the New York State Legislature undertook investigations of Bolshevik influence in America. Following its hearings in February and March, the Overman Committee declared there was immediate danger of revolution, and the Lusk Committee, which first met on June 12, also reached exaggerated conclusions concerning Bolshevik power.

Despite the A.F.L.'s belief in capitalism and its strong denunciations of Bolshevism, its frequent strikes made the public apprehensive. By late summer 1919, when labor was quickening its efforts to gain wage and hour advantages and the right to bargain collectively, it was definitely on the defensive about accusations of Bolshevism. In September, moreover, the newly formed Communist and Communist Labor parties began to participate in strikes not their own so as "to develop the revolutionary implications." The general public was thus prepared to view all strikes as crimes or revolutionary conspiracies when three historic strikes occurred in the fall of 1919: the Boston police strike, which began on September 9; the nationwide steel strike, between September 22 and January 8; and the coal strike in November. The steel strike demands particular notice because it is an event in which Dos Passos involved Mary French in *The Big Money*.

A National Committee for Organizing Iron and Steel Workers, with Samuel Gompers as honorary chairman, John Fitzpatrick as acting chairman, and William Z. Foster as secretary-treasurer, had by the summer of 1919, despite violence and intimidation by the steel companies, established a union in every significant mill town in the nation. When Elbert H. Gary of U.S. Steel refused to bargain collectively, the unions, disregarding Gompers' suggestion that they wait for an industrial conference which Woodrow Wilson was calling, declared a strike.

Although many newspapers criticized Gary for his intransigence, within a short time Bolshevism and re olution became the reputed issue. William Z. Foster denied radicalism, but he had been a syndicalist. The Communist organizations and the I.W.W. identified themselves with the strike. Riots occurred. After General Wood established martial law in Gary, Indiana, Army intelligence discovered revolutionary literature and evidence of a bomb plot there. During the final two months of the strike, conservative A.F.L. officials, who had been unhappy about it from the beginning, affirmed that some of the strike leaders were anarchists and Bolsheviks. It was the public's identification of the strike officials with Bolshevism that doomed the steel unions' struggle. But for the steel companies, if not for the revolutionary strike leaders, the real issue was collective bargaining. The outcome of the strike was a triumph for the companies' public relations men, whose tactics Dos Passos described a decade and a half later in *U.S.A.*

As a result of such events as these — as well as race riots and mob violence, including most notably a deadly battle between aggressive Legionnaires and Wobblies in Centralia, Washington — many government officials became honestly fearful of revolutionary radicalism. The Department of Justice sent all major newspapers and magazines warnings about the menace of Communism, but it delayed vigorous action until a critical United States Senate on October 19 passed a resolution nudging it to effect some deportations. Federal and local authorities then raided headquarters of radical organizations and detained a large number of aliens, most of them members of the Union of Russian Workers. Congressional and newspaper opinion forced a hesitant Labor Department to accede to their deportation. On December 21 the steamship *Buford* (which the press nicknamed the "Soviet Ark") sailed from New York with 43 anarchists (most were theoretical anarchists, but the group included Emma Goldman and Alexander Berkman), 199 members of the Union of Russian Workers, and 250 soldiers and guards. Most of the press was jubilant, but the *New Republic*, the *Nation*, and the *Dial* declared that the deportations marked the end of the United States as a haven for the oppressed of all countries.

The Justice Department next turned upon the Communist and Communist Labor parties. On January 2, 1920, it conducted raids in 33 cities and arrested more than 4,000 suspected Communists. By making many of the arrests without warrants, holding the suspects incommunicado, often under frightful physical conditions, and starving and beating the suspects, the department dimmed some of the distinctions between contemporary American democracy and Bolshevism for a generation of radicals, including Dos Passos.

Beginning in November 1919, the federal and state governments hastened to crush types of political and economic radicalism which had, as a rule, been tolerated before the war. In the spring and fall of 1919 the House of Representatives refused to seat Victor Berger, who was appealing a conviction for violating the Espionage Act by speaking against the war. The House reaffirmed its refusal in January, after Berger's re-election. Upon Attorney General Palmer's urging, both houses of Congress in January prepared and passed peacetime sedition acts, which never, however, became law. In 1919 at least twenty state legislatures passed criminal anarchy and sedition laws, most of them severely punishing opinions, however unrelated to acts; and thirty-five states had such laws by 1921. In New York the State Assembly denied seats to its five Socialist members at the beginning of the January 1920 session. Upon the recommendation of the Lusk Committee, the legislature outlawed the Socialist party, required loyalty oaths of all teachers, and established a system for licensing private schools. Although Governor Alfred E. Smith vetoed this legislation, it became law a year later under his successor.

The public did not examine the meaning of Bolshevism or attempt to distinguish it from such movements as socialism and anarchism. The behavior of the Socialist party and the I.W.W. in 1919 and the initial ignorance among radicals as to the meaning of Bolshevism might have made drawing such distinctions difficult, even if the public had been inclined to try it. But the public did not differentiate between liberals and radicals, reformers and revolutionaries either. "It was automatically assumed," Robert K. Murray writes in *Red Scare*, "that anyone who was not a 'conservative' was a 'radical,' and hence even those who advocated the mildest reforms were dumped into the 'Red' classification."[6]

As speaking freely and acting independently became more dangerous, they grew less frequent. Education became, after labor, the most suspected and most criticized area of American life: schools such as Barnard, Vassar, Wellesley, Radcliffe, Yale, and the University of Chicago were widely described as radical institutions or nests of Bolshevism; professors who browsed left of center were "parlor pinks"; schoolteachers were dismissed, in a few instances for belonging to Communist groups, but usually for far less substantial reasons. Ministers in many places stopped preaching the social gospel, lest they lose their pulpits.

The scare reached its peak in January 1920. By the following fall the public was losing interest, except in a few areas such as New York and California. The Bolshevik threat in Europe had diminished, many dissenters had decided upon a prudent silence, and the public was realizing that the number of Bolsheviks in the United States had been much exaggerated. Most important, Americans were turning to those peacetime diversions which Dos Passos' fiction later juxtaposed with the economic and political events of the decade.

Dos Passos' reaction to this antiradical hysteria in the postwar United States was intensified by the degree of political sophistication he gained from Europe. During two decades when Americans were prone to view Socialists, Communists, and anarchists as a single murderous species, he was aware of distinctions. For a knowledge of them, his experiences in Spain were in large part responsible. Spain was the European nation he knew best and in which he felt most at home — more so even than in the Paris of the twenties, although he had been brought up speaking French.[7] Spanish life, literature, and politics influenced his criticism of American society and possibly his work as a novelist.

"Young Spain," which appeared in *Seven Arts* in August 1917, was Dos Passos' first published study of the country. Waldo Frank recollected that Dos Passos might have come to the *Seven Arts* office with that manuscript in hand. If not, he came with some other "which impressed me so that I asked him to do a piece on Spain."[8]

What struck Dos Passos strongly about the country, he said in his article, was the depth of its roots in the infinite past. No war or revolution had ever succeeded in shaking the intense anarchistic individualism bred in its isolated village communities, a characteristic which made Spain the most democratic country in Europe. This characteristic accounted not only for the pride of the Spaniard but also for the two types that dominated the Iberian mind — that of Don Quixote (or Loyola), the individual who believes in the power of man's soul to dominate all things, and that of Sancho Panza (or Don Juan Tenorio), the individual who sees the whole world as food for his belly. The present atrophy of the country after a century of revolution might well be due, he wrote, to the attempt to force centralized government on a land whose life was centrifugal.

Spain, he said, was ripe for a revolution; only a sort of despairing inaction prevented it. The country's governing politicians were unbelievably corrupt and inefficient, labor was wretchedly underpaid, and the cost of living was rising steadily. Famine was the mother of revolution. Though important obstacles stood in the way, the tension was bound to snap.

Some Spaniards, members of the generation for which the war of 1898 had been a great spiritual crisis, were engaged, he wrote, in a searing criticism of Spain and of the modern world in general. Dos Passos was sufficiently critical of modern business to declare that, although Pío Baroja was a better artist than Vicente Blasco Ibáñez, the latter's socialistic ideas would probably be more fruitful than Baroja's "old-fashioned cosmopolitanism" and his advocacy of "things Anglo-Saxon" and "the efficient Roosevelt virtues."

At the conclusion of the article, Dos Passos quoted a Spanish friend as saying to him that the future belonged to America, where life had become once more a primal fight for bread; from animal brutality came the vigor of life, but Spaniards were still content with simple things — the warmth of the sun and the flavor of bread and wine — and let all the rest of life be a ritual. But Dos Passos contrasted Spain with "the restless industrial world of joyless enforced labor and incessant goading war" and did not seem to agree with his companion.[9] Individualism and historical distinctiveness were for him qualities to cherish. Certainly, any socialism that he contemplated for Spain would have been neither centralized nor monotonously industrial.

Back in Spain after his discharge from the army in 1919, Dos Passos took time for a journalistic dash to neighboring Portugal that led to publication in the *Liberator* of his first report on postwar Europe. The article, "In Portugal," which was concerned with revolutionary progress in the small nation, severely criticized the republican government. It had fulfilled none of its promises, Dos Passos wrote. Illiteracy remained above 75 per cent. Labor was more poorly paid than anywhere else except in the Balkans. Foreign and domestic capital were undisturbed. Portugal took its orders on foreign policy from Great Britain and might be described as "a British colony without the advantages of British administration."

The piece was a clear, if implicit, defiance of the anti-Red feeling in the United States. Behind much of the unrest, Dos Passos noted, was the hope that Communism was bringing to the masses. "But in Portugal, as everywhere in the world," he wrote, "the giant stirs in his sleep." Talks in Lisbon with workmen and with the editor of the syndicalist newspaper left Dos Passos thinking that the days of the politician and of the bourgeois were numbered and might be over already if it were not for British dreadnaughts; but listening to some imprisoned Young Syndicalists singing the "Internationale," he reflected that they could do little but sing until something happened to the ships.[10]

Many of Dos Passos' articles on Spain at this period consisted of material intended for the book *Rosinante to the Road Again*, the bulk of which was written during his sojourns in 1916 and 1919 and most of which appeared originally as ten articles published between October 20, 1920, and February 8, 1922, in the *Freeman*.[11] The articles usually differed little from their counterparts in the book, though an article might be more topical or more pointed.

An article in the *Nation* thus made use of material intended for *Rosinante to the Road Again* to launch bitter criticism of the domestic anti-left campaign and of the foreign activities of the United States, Dos Passos blaming both upon the militarism and imperialism to which he felt America had succumbed when it had entered the war. The article, like the book, describes a discussion among a group of Spaniards during the winter of 1920 as to how good a country the United States is. When he had been in Spain in 1917, Dos Passos said in the article, the Spaniards had been naming children and squares after Wilson, but between the winter of 1919 and the spring of 1920, he had watched this admiration of America crumble, along with America's ostensible ideals.

One cause had been the reception of the Spanish commission to a labor congress in America. All the members of the commission had been chosen by their government and all, except one Socialist, were conservative liberals. "They landed in the middle of the anti-Bolshevik hue and cry," Dos Passos commented bitterly, "when the great docile sewer of canalized hate was being turned away from the Germans against anyone who hoped, however vaguely, that the exploiting system of capital would not be eternal." The president of the commission, a former government minister, had been erroneously attacked in the press as a Bolshevik, and the Socialist in the party had been exposed to official rudeness. As a result, the liberals had returned home convinced that the heart of the octopus they were fighting lay in the United States. For similar reasons, Spanish intellectuals now considered the United States a colossus trampling out the hopes of the Western world.

America had once been, Dos Passos wrote, a refuge from oppression for all the world. Now it was a hated militarist nation. In a sense its reputation was unjustified, for forces of good will existed; they had been given real, if accidental, expression in the Fourteen Points. The trouble was that the jingo press of America led Europeans to think that the country's Hun-haters and lynchers, its Bolshevik-baiters, its Palmers and Burlesons were typical Americans. No voices could be heard above those of the shrieking devotees of military capitalism; the barbarities of the Marines in Haiti were known throughout the world, but the protests against them lay buried in the liberal weeklies.

America had to develop, Dos Passos wrote, a large organized public that would instantly and loudly repudiate every governmental abuse, whether internal or external. Something must surely be left of the proud independence of the pioneers and of the individuality of Yankee sea captains.[12]

In *Rosinante to the Road Again* essays on Spanish literary men are strung on a thread of narrative reflecting Dos Passos' bewitchment with Spanish life. Although the narrative thread is rather tenuous, the reader feels that he has been exposed to much more than a collection of essays. No doubt the reason is that the author and the people he discusses are engaged in the same quest: understanding and explaining Spanish civilization.

The explorers Telemachus and Lyaeus appear in the introductory and final chapters and in interludial chapters among essays Dos Passos writes in the first person. In the *Odyssey* Homer presents Telemachus as a diffident young man lacking his father Odysseus' decisiveness. Unable to control his mother's suitors, who waste his family's substance, the son embarks on a search for his father. Dos Passos' use of Telemachus, then, is probably an allusion to his own psychological problems and cultural concerns. In "The Camera Eye" of *U.S.A.* he later contrasted his father's booming confidence with his own incapabilities and diffidence. As for his cultural concerns, he felt the United States' divorce from its pre-industrial past to be a loss of strength, industrialism signifying to him a dearth of joy and vitality, two qualities he celebrated in Spanish life, partly perhaps because of his awareness of his Iberian origins.

Lyaeus is another name for Bacchus, Lyaeus' spontaneous and carefree behavior being contrasted with his companion's considerable prudence and solemnity. Just as Dos Passos and E. E. Cummings did in 1921, according to Cummings' recollections, Telemachus and Lyaeus go to a Madrid theater and see Pastora Imperio dancing. (Dos Passos' attendance with Cummings, necessitating a long journey to Madrid, was a measure of his continuing enthusiasm for the dancer. He says he completed the book before his travel with his friend, but that Lyaeus may have something about him of a few other people he knew or saw in Spain before 1921.)[13] Watching Pastora's movements, Telemachus and Lyaeus recognize the same gesture of defiance as that exhibited by the matador Belmonte. Telemachus says he must capture and formulate that gesture; it is inconceivably important to him — though, he realizes, it is not the kind of thing twentieth-century Americans do.[14]

In the next chapter, which is written in the first person, a donkey boy declares that in America people do nothing but work and then rest to get ready for more work. Later an acquaintance tells Dos Passos that the life of Andalusia is "*lo flamenco*": "On this coast, *señor inglés*, we don't work much, we are dirty and uninstructed, but by God we live. Why the poor people of the towns, d'you know what they do in summer? They hire a fig-tree and go and live under it with their dogs and their cats and their babies, and they eat the figs as they ripen and drink the cold water from the mountains, and man-alive they are happy."[15]

A third Spaniard comments wryly that in Spain the people live, yes — but in disease, ignorance, and bestiality. He calls for education, organization, and energy — the modern world. The dilemma, which is presented but not explicitly analyzed by Dos Passos, is how to end economic deprivation without substituting for *lo flamenco* the rhythm of machines.

Spanish life versus modern industrial life — the theme is repeated in the next chapter. Having stated again that Don Quixote typifies one of the two main aspects of Spanish life and Sancho Panza the other, Dos Passos in the following chapter has Telemachus and Lyaeus encounter a lean man on a horse and a fat man on a donkey traveling together. The lean man's name is Don Alonso, and he is from La Mancha. He tells Telemachus that thousands of people never have enough to eat from the day they are born till the day they die and that even in freezing weather children sleep in doorways. That he is too old to fight, he admits; what Lyaeus took to be a lance is a fishing pole. Nevertheless Don Alonso holds to his anarchistic creed: "Many years ago I should have set out to right wrong — for no one but a man, an individual alone, can right a wrong; organization merely substitutes one wrong for another. . . ."[16] Don Alonso comments that his generation and his son's generation have set out once again to right the wrongs of the oppressed. Spain, he says in the next interlude, has never been swept clean. It missed the Reformation but was exposed to the full wrath of the Inquisition. It suffered under Napoleon, but the Revolution bypassed it. The laborers are demanding that things at long last be changed. Don Alonso believes the thinkers must clear the road and the laborers do the building.[17]

Again follows autobiography written in the first person. If Dos Passos did not find a truly revolutionary Spain in 1917, he found one two years later. The next chapter, which is a comment on what Don Alonso has just said, is based on Dos Passos' second piece for the *Liberator*. In Cordova after the war, Dos Passos said in the *Liberator*, he had sought out Francisco Azorín, an architect who had served a prison term for supporting a recent strike of farm laborers, and Azorín had taken him to see the editor of a prolabor weekly. In the editor's little office the two Spaniards had spoken to him of Cordova's past and future and had made vivid to him for the first time the misery and the aims of the impoverished working people.[18]

In the book this chapter is called "Cordova No Longer of the Caliphs." Ever since the sixteenth century, Dos Passos says here, the people in the region between the Tagus and the Mediterranean have had only one means of escape from the virtual serfdom existing in this area of huge estates — emigration to America. Recently they have learned there is another way. "As everywhere else, Russia has been the beacon-flare." The peasants now have an unshakable faith in a "new law"; it is this hopefulness that marks the difference between the present agrarian efforts and the desperate uprisings of the past.[19]

Scattered through *Rosinante to the Road Again* are essays on the Spanish novelists Pío Baroja and Blasco Ibáñez, the poets Antonio Machado and Juan Maragall, the theater in Madrid, and incidents in the nineteenth-century fight of Giner de los Ríos and his followers for academic freedom in Spain. Those on Giner de los Ríos and on Baroja are particularly important for tracing the development of Dos Passos' views of American society and politics.

The essay on Giner de los Ríos is, in fact, a comment on infringement of and assaults upon academic freedom in the United States.[20] The narrative is very similar to that in an April 1922 article in *Broom,* an *avant-garde* literary magazine published in Europe. There is one striking difference. In *Broom* Dos Passos drew an explicit moral for the United States:

And hereby hangs a moral highly applicable to our own trustee-ridden universities, if to nothing else. If we really wanted liberty of speech and thought, we could probably get it — Spain fifty years ago certainly had a longer tradition of despotism than has the United States — but do we want it?

In these years we shall see.

The moral did not specify means, but Giner de los Ríos and his followers had attempted revolution, as well as resignation of their positions, to gain their ends.[21]

A real change in Dos Passos' attitude toward Blasco Ibáñez

and Baroja occurred between 1916–17 and 1921. During the war Blasco Ibáñez had written *The Four Horsemen of the Apocalypse* and other novels which Dos Passos considered ''well-sugared pro-Ally propaganda.'' These performances as well as his seeming abandonment of Spanish and proletarian themes led Dos Passos to take a noticeably cooler attitude toward him. Blasco Ibáñez was now ''An Inverted Midas'' — one who turned everything he touched into a commonplace. It was too bad, Dos Passos said, that Americans were not reading a worthwhile novelist like Baroja instead.[22]

Revolutionary anarchism impressed Dos Passos as the rationale of Baroja's work. Baroja felt the misery of his characters deeply, Dos Passos wrote, and it was for that reason that he was so sensitive to the affirmation of the rights and duties of man that was stirring downtrodden people throughout Europe. It is noteworthy that the part André Dubois in *One Man's Initiation — 1917* assigns to the intellectual is similar to Baroja's idea of his own role as Dos Passos explained it:

He [Baroja] says somewhere that the only part a man of the middle classes can play in the social revolution is destructive. He has not undergone the discipline necessary for a builder, which can come only from common slavery in the industrial machine. His slavery has been an isolated slavery which has unfitted him for ever from becoming truly part of a community. He can use in only one way the power of knowledge which training has given him. His great mission is to put the acid test to existing institutions, to strip them of their veils. . . . it is certain that a profound sense of the evil of existing institutions lies behind every page he has written, and, occasionally, only occasionally, he allows himself to hope that something better may come out of the turmoil of our age of transition.[23]

The quotation is applicable to much of Dos Passos' own work, as is his further comment that Baroja was too deeply interested in human beings to exchange the character of novelist for that of propagandist. The intellectual's role as critic, first articulated in *One Man's Initiation — 1917*, is stressed so often in Dos Passos' writings that it is almost certain he consciously assigned this role to himself.

The revolutionary task that Baroja had assumed was probably only one source of interest that Dos Passos found in the novelist. Reading the trilogy *La lucha por la vida (The Struggle for Life)*, which Dos Passos considered Baroja's best work, one notices how the impoverished, frequently itinerant characters evoke the geography and institutions of the countryside even as they blend with them. The itinerant characters in *U.S.A.* do the same. One also notices that the final volume of Baroja's trilogy is almost a handbook of anarchistic beliefs. This volume alone would have been enough to make Dos Passos angry at the manner in which the government of the United States was treating anarchists.[24]

Dos Passos followed his trip to Spain in 1921 with a tour of the Middle East, including Turkey, the Russian Caucasus (which he entered fairly early in August), Persia (which he entered on August 26), Iraq, and Syria.[25] His course of travel suggests that despite his curiosity about the Soviets, he was concerned less with studying Communism than with exploring ancient and nonindustrial corners of the world.

He was lucky to be able to make the trip at all. The *Metropolitan Magazine* had collapsed, and without this market for his articles, he was finding himself more and more pressed for money. Stopping in Paris and there seeking ways and means of getting to the Near East, he fortunately encountered Paxton Hibben, whom he probably had met at Floyd Dell's house (though when Mrs. Hibben reminded him of their first meeting there, he said he had rarely, if ever, been at Dell's place). Hibben was one of a party of Americans who had come from New York to survey conditions in Transcaucasia for Near East Relief, an organization incorporated by Congress in 1919, after the Red Cross, because of the religious symbol in its name, had met with Moslem resistance. If Dos Passos could manage to reach Constantinople, Hibben now said, he would try to get him into Near East Relief.

In Constantinople the two Americans became good friends. When Hibben was unable to persuade N.E.R. officials at Roberts College to include his impecunious friend, he smuggled him amid an N.E.R. team onto a steamship going to Batum. Arriving in Tiflis, Dos Passos was again unable to get work with the organization, but he spent some time at the N.E.R. mission there.[26]

Although the civil war was past, starvation and repression prevailed in the Soviet Union when Dos Passos entered. As a result of invasion, war, and governmental attempts at communization, Russian agriculture, industry, and trade lay in ruins. With industrial production in 1920 at only a small fraction of its volume in 1913, the government had gradually begun a policy (short-lived and unsuccessful) of conscripting industrial workers into labor armies. Although all arable land had passed into peasant hands during the revolution, inefficiency and ruthless governmental requisitions had impoverished agriculture. (The drought of 1920 and 1921 brought famine, an estimated 5,000,000 people perishing in 1921–22.) Support for the regime was waning. Toward the end of the civil war, the Bolshevik party had denied legal existence to opposition parties and subjected its own members to restrictions and coercion.[27]

In what was probably Dos Passos' first article on life under the Soviets (an article bearing a Tiflis dateline and appearing in the August 1922 issue of the *Liberator*), he began by admitting that he knew none of the languages spoken in the Caucasus and that he had spent only about three weeks there. The article is nevertheless significant because it documents Dos Passos' early dislike of Bolshevik methods.

Everywhere in the Caucasus Dos Passos found terrible poverty. For many there was no work. The old people lived by selling their possessions one by one. They were quite unreconciled to the new government and waited for the day when it would collapse and their wrongs would be set right. The peasants could be well off, for they were able to sell their produce at a huge profit. But many of them had been so frightened by the dangers of government requisitions and by the revolutionary atmosphere that they had stopped working and had flocked to the railroads; ragged and starving, they moved aimlessly into and out of the cities. Nobody in the Caucasus from the president of the revolutionary committee down was being paid a living wage; rich and poor alike were continually coming to the Near East Relief Mission, where Dos Passos was staying, to sell anything that might conceivably have money value.

Although Dos Passos had a good word for the expansion of education and the theater under Bolshevik direction, his article was unfavorable toward the party. Communist governmental methods were in part responsible, he wrote, for the present paralysis. The idea that the state could requisition anything it saw fit at any time made the population feel insecure. The judicial system terrorized the country by its secret methods. The courts in the Caucasus were extremely moderate in many respects, but the penalty for any crime was shooting, and the accused were given little opportunity to prove their innocence. As a result, administrators feared to assume any responsibility.

The Communists, Dos Passos believed, were not numerous enough to control Russia. Throughout the country there was such a lack of men of education and ability that anyone with a bit of either who was not actually plotting against the regime was given a responsible governmental position. In the Caucasus half the administrators were non-Communists, even in the Red Army. In the government of Georgia Dos Passos could not find any Communists at all, except for the president. As a result, while the Communists in Moscow were seeking Utopia, their local officials were attempting in a confused and "non-theoretical" manner to preserve what was left of the old civilization.

The arbitrariness and terror that Dos Passos glimpsed in the Soviet Union in 1921 were certainly not what he had been speaking of soon after World War I, when he described Russia as "a beacon-flare" for Europe. Dos Passos now wrote: "My impression is that communism in Russia is a dead shell in which new broader creeds are germinating; new births stirring are making themselves felt, as always, in people's minds by paroxysms of despair. Communism and the old hierarchy of the Little Father both belong to the last generation, not to the men who have come of age in the midst of the turmoil. It is they who will recreate Russia."[28]

A detailed picture of life in those sections of the Soviet Union which he visited appears in *Orient Express*, published five years after the *Liberator* article. In this book Dos Passos' greatest strictures are reserved for Near East Relief. Perhaps influenced by Hibben, Dos Passos had called in the article for an honest relief service for the forty million people starving in the Volga basin. A passage in the book, again perhaps influenced by his friend, describes what he found instead. A private-carful of members of the N.E.R. spent their time trying to decide whether starving people or sated people were more likely to become Communists. Although the Russian government knew what the N.E.R. was about, in order to save lives it permitted the organization to decide who should live and who should die. Meanwhile, the relievers were taking advantage of the exchange value of the dollar and "pawing" rugs stolen from mosques, lamps from churches, pearls removed from the neck of a slaughtered grand duchess, and fur coats brought in by hungry old people.[29]

The book does not predict the end of Bolshevism, but Dos Passos does not seem, either when he prepared or concluded the text, to have been happy about the movement. Derogating material surfeit as he had in "A Humble Protest," Dos Passos wrote that the wind had blown Russia free of the junk for which men worked all their lives, the goods which divided the rich from the poor and made a man more honored as he became less self-sufficient. Would the end result be a life in which goods and institutions were broken to fit men, rather than the other way round? Or would it be a reversion to Things? Organization substituted one tyranny for another, John Andrews and Don Alonso had said. Could one look forward, Dos Passos asked of Bolshevism, to only "a faith and a lot of words like Islam or Christianity"?[30]

The terrorism dismayed him. In Tiflis Hibben, who was an enthusiastic supporter of the October Revolution, brought him by good-natured trickery to an international proletarian poetry festival, where he listened to recitations in many tongues and had to speak too. He delivered Blake's "Ah, Sunflower," a poem sounding a note of individuals' desires and aspirations (he had in *One Man's Initiation—1917* described Martin as reciting it to himself during a gas attack). While Dos Passos spoke, Hibben sat grinning in the front row of the theater.[31] The general atmosphere was gay, and the meeting broke up amid jollity and song. But on the way back, Dos Passos says in the book, he and his companions passed the Cheka, with its barbed wires, its pacing sentries, and its jail smell. The idyll crashed about their ears.[32]

Dos Passos' dismay was probably due not only to the Cheka's terrorizing of Social Revolutionaries and other dissidents, but also to its ferocious treatment of the revolting sailors at Kronstadt in 1921. Anarchism was strong among these sailors, who had played an important role in effecting the October Revolution. Feeling that the Bolsheviks had perverted the original ideals of the revolution, the sailors at the beginning of March demanded freedom of expression for workers, peasants, and leftists; democratic procedures in electing soviets; greater equality in the distribution of rations; and an end to forcible requisitioning and to seizure of small peasant holdings. Dos Passos would surely have considered these demands to be in the right direction. The Bolsheviks, on the other hand, declared the motives of the sailors to be counterrevolutionary and when they took Kronstadt on March 17 and 18, executed great numbers of the rebels.[33] They also instituted terror against anarchists in the U.S.S.R. Emma Goldman, who despite her opposition to Bolshevism, had sailed for Russia with enthusiasm after her deportation from the United States, refused to have anything to do with the Russian government after Kronstadt.[34]

Although Dos Passos may not have known all the details of the rebellion while he was in the U.S.S.R., he says that Kronstadt made "an immense impression" on him. It early made him mistrust Bolshevism. A friend, Mrs. Charles Walker, who in 1931 participated with him in an investigation of the condition of miners in Harlan County, Kentucky, writes: "I remember his telling me some years later that his real disillusionment had come with Kronstadt."[35]

From the Soviet Union Dos Passos went to Persia, whose pre-industrial society posed some of the same problems as Spain's. To McComb he wrote on August 27, 1921: "From Tiflis it was an instructive journey — four and a half days in a box car — cholera people dying of typhus on mats along the edge of the railway track — and endless processions of ruined villages, troops, armored trains — all the apparatus of this century of enlightenment. . . ."

His companion on the train out of the Soviet Union and in a dilapidated four-horse carriage for thirteen days to Teheran was a Persian physician, whom he recently identified as Dr. Hassan Tabataba, returning home from a German medical school.[36] The opinions of the "Sayyid" (meaning "descendant of the Prophet or of Ali, son of Abu Talib"), which were sensible but full of unconscious humor, are the highlight of *Orient Express*. The two travelers argued about industrialism. When, at a bazaar in Zendjan, the Sayyid complained about how hard the silversmiths and makers of copper kettles had to work, Dos Passos noted that he, like everyone else in the Near East, seemed to think that machines ran themselves. Dos Passos tried to convince him that the handworker might be getting more out of life than, say, the steelworker in Germany, in spite of the German's beer hall and cinema. But the Sayyid (if we may draw our metaphor from Dos Passos' college story) reminded his companion of the fate of the Almeh. He cited long lists of extortions by grandees, mujtahids, and governors. Persia had to have "fabriks" and railroads, he said; then it would be a great nation.[37]

Much of the remainder of Dos Passos' trip was melodramatic.[38] He went most of the way to Iraq by automobile, along a historic route crowded with pilgrims and caravans of coffins destined for reburial in sacred earth. The engineer of a train to Kut let him off at Babylon. From the banks of the Tigris he wrote to McComb that for two weeks he had been trying to arrange to go by caravan to Damascus, although he had been warned about Bedouin raids.

"My only real fear," he commented, "is that they will take my glasses."

Of his journalistic endeavors, he wrote his friend in amused weariness: "I am tired of wrangling for transport and paying hotelbills and interviewing bigwigs. I am utterly tired of writing articles on political questions. I have decided that journalism and I — even the so-called higher brand — don't jibe, and that I am wasting valuable time writing unpalatable idiocies, when I might be writing idiocies to me, at least, palatable. I am anxious to get back to conversation and good cookery. I shall retire to some quite [*sic*] nook and write long novels. . . ."[39]

He finally made the trip to Damascus, during the course of which he suffered hunger and the caravan experienced raids. Nevertheless the latter part of *Orient Express* contrasts placid desert existence with the more hectic life of the West. At one point Dos Passos felt that he didn't care if it took a thousand years to get to Damascus. He told the Agail people that if he had any sense, he would stay in the desert with them and never go back. They did not understand him and took his speech to be only a polite compliment. Once he explained to an Arab that, whereas on the desert people smoked kif to feel peaceful, in America they drank stimulants to make them excited. At Coney Island in New York Americans paid money to be shaken up. "Achmed decided we must be mad in the western lands," Dos Passos said, "but there must be a baraka in our madness because we were very rich."

The West, Dos Passos felt, was conquering in both Spain and the Near East. Nothing could resist Henry Ford's idea of mass production and interchangeable parts. Once again, as in his *Seven Arts* article, he raised the question of whether the rejection of capitalistic industrialism, with all the strife that the system creates, was not an abject retreat from struggle as a value of life.[40]

However such Nietzscheism might intrigue him momentarily, it never could convince him. If one was intent upon striking at human misery, he believed, capitalism and the remnants of feudalism were unbearable. But he had no desire to see the revolutionary manifestations he was describing culminate in Bolshevism. An individualist and a humanitarian, he considered the methods advocated in Bolshevism unfortunate and inadmissible even in Russia, and he anticipated the disappearance or drastic alteration of that creed.

V.

A STRAW HAT OUT OF SEASON

FOR ABOUT FOUR YEARS AFTER HIS RETURN TO AMERICA TOWARD the spring of 1922, Dos Passos devoted more attention to intellectual, artistic, and personal nonconformity than to political agitation. He settled in New York City, of which he wrote to McComb that May: "I like its fearfulness better than ever. I paint and scribble and dine in Italian restaurants and talk to bums on park benches."[1]

Like his characters Andrews and Herf, he had to earn his own living. And like Thoreau, he found necessity a boon. He writes of his financial situation: "My father made a great deal of money but he made unfortunate investments & was a lavish spender. All I inherited was my mother's house in Washington & a share in my father's farm, where I now live, in Virginia. This became involved in a complicated trusteeship so that until 1939 I was dependent (laos deo) on what I could scratch up for myself." For a while he still thought of studying architecture, but except for that, he writes, he "never considered any career in those days except travel and my own curious sort of political-literary agitprop."[2]

Between travels he occasionally sublet friends' apartments, and for some time he rented from Elaine Thayer, the future Mrs. E. E. Cummings, an apartment studio at 3 Washington Square North. Some of *Manhattan Transfer* he wrote in a room on Columbia Heights, Brooklyn, looking out at the harbor.[3] Most of the time he appears to have lived sparingly on what he earned from his writings. Both his finances and his attitude toward them are conveyed in a letter he wrote to McComb around April 1922 indicating that he saw money as a means of living and working as his spirit called, and contemplated going broke rather than getting rich: "3 soldiers has produced 8000 iron men — Never had so much in my life — though I owe almost 2500 of it. At any rate it will solve the question of the next trip to foreign parts when that question arises. Also I shant write any more damn fool little articles until I am broke again."

Before going abroad again, Dos Passos brought together his sole volume of verse, *A Pushcart at the Curb* (1922), and completed the novel *Streets of Night* (1923).[4] Most of the poems reflect his recent wanderings in Europe. Some describe erotic longings while others express the intense desire to travel that inspired his journeys in Spain and the Near East. Descriptions of European streets and landscapes predominate, and Dos Passos often uses history or classical legend to give importance or an additional dimension to his scenes. The most intensely expressed emotion in the volume is horror at the European war.[5]

Parts of *Streets of Night* he first wrote for the abortive novel "The Walls of Jericho" immediately after his graduation from college. He now rewrote this earlier material, attempting, he says, to express his feelings as an undergraduate.[6] *Streets of Night* deals with the refusal or inability of three young friends in the Harvard environment — Fanshaw, Wenny, and Nan — not merely to "take a flying Rimbaud at the moon," but to live at all. They exist in a sort of limbo (in Dos Passos' subsequent phrase, "under the bellglass"). All three are in varying degrees afraid of love or of sexual relations, and their fears, associated in the novel with fear of life itself, result in suicide for Wenny and almost certain spinsterhood for Nan. Dos Passos' picture of Nan and Wenny envying the earthy Italian immigrants all around them because these people seem to them to be really living takes on political significance when one remembers that he later cited New Englanders' fear and envy of immigrants as a factor in their prosecution of Sacco and Vanzetti.[7] Fanshaw's disgust at the immigrants makes his worship of the often-earthy Italian Renaissance a little ridiculous.

In the spring of 1923 Dos Passos boarded ship for Europe again. "Never been so happy in my life," he wrote McComb. "I dont know where I'm bound and I haven't much money but I dont care — " As soon as he felt fresh, he said, he would start a long novel "about New York and go-getters and God knows what besides." By September he was back in the city, writing and looking ahead to new journeys.[8]

Courtesy of Elizabeth Dos Passos

A traveler full of restless energy and wanderlust. "I dont know where I'm bound and I haven't much money but I dont care."

That his way of life was eccentric and his politics were subversive, conventional people and popular newspapers were ready to inform him daily. Just as business dominated American government during the decade, the ethos of the businessman dominated American public opinion. From 1923 to 1929, Frederick Lewis Allen writes (quoting Stuart Chase), the businessman was " ' the dictator of our destinies,' ousting 'the statesman, the priest, the philosopher, as the creator of standards of ethics and behavior' and becoming 'the final authority on the conduct of American society.' ' "[9] In the businessman's cosmology, there was no room for nonremunerative experiments in art or in the conduct of life. As for experiments in politics and economics, the years 1917–1920 had revealed how highly they were regarded!

James Warren Prothro has studied the ideas that spokesmen for the National Association of Manufacturers and the Chamber of Commerce held and disseminated during the decade. He writes that these spokesmen believed that society consisted of the "superior few" and the "inferior many." The two were almost distinct species. The masses were good-natured and, ordinarily, content to recognize their limitations. But they were incapable of thought. Leisure — which for them meant idleness — made the masses envious and dangerous. It led to crime, radicalism, and disintegration of character. The elite were, on the other hand, capable of thought, and they might without corruption enjoy leisure and seek luxuries.

These spokesmen held that success in all fields was measured by money. Since most money was to be made in business, the ablest men naturally entered that field, where America provided opportunities for anyone who was industrious, clever, and thrifty. Businessmen, it was said or implied continually, constituted the elite of humanity. Prothro writes:

"Elitism" in the concept of human nature is supplemented by the assumption of a material standard of values. Who constitutes the elite? The answer is simple: "A man is worth the wages he can earn." And any creation of man, be it salami or sonnets, is subject to the same test. If the most basic and permanent human motives are selfish in nature and economic in content, what more appropriate measure could be devised? The choice of a business career demonstrates the inherent worth of an individual, then, and successful experience in business molds him into a superior person. Every "100 per cent American" finds his *summum bonum* in the endless pursuit of greater material accomplishments.

According to these same spokesmen, human beings were

selfish, not cooperative; however, the business elite, while serving itself, also served society. Since business made possible individual and social fulfillment, it was thus the paramount social institution. Government aid to the elite facilitated natural economic processes, but government aid to the masses hampered these processes. To advocate the former was statesmanship; to advocate the latter was low politics. Government was, in fact, an institution secondary to business, though necessary for the protection of life and property. Organized labor was not a legitimate institution at all. It threatened business. It ought to be fought by legal and, if necessary, extralegal means! Popular government, too, threatened business, for unscrupulous politicians might corrupt the multitude. Individualism (not Don Alonso's type, but rather freedom from governmental interference in business) was, therefore, necessary, but such individualism did not imply a right to denounce the business system itself.[10]

Although these ideas probably appeared among small businessmen, farmers, and wageworkers in only diluted forms, they created an oppressive atmosphere for many serious writers and artists. Some struck back with mockery and criticism; some became expatriates, most of them going to France; a few either became political and economic radicals or were confirmed in their radicalism. Dos Passos exemplified the first and third of these tendencies, and he was very much aware of the second. He satirized the prevailing ethos in *The Garbage Man* and *Manhattan Transfer*. He gradually collected a large number of friends in Paris who thought of themselves as exiles, and, while he never considered living in that city, he used to stop there for weeks on his way to other places.[11]

Dos Passos was "the greatest traveler in a generation of ambulant writers," Malcolm Cowley declares in *Exile's Return*. "When he appeared in Paris he was always on his way to Spain or Russia or Istanbul or the Syrian desert."[12] Lewis Galantière, who first met Dos Passos in 1923, recalls that he was not around Ford Madox Ford or the *"transition* crowd" in Paris. One did not identify him with the groups meeting in cafés and all writing for the same review magazines. Among the people with whom Galantière saw him in Paris were Ernest Hemingway, Archibald MacLeish, Gilbert Seldes, F. Scott Fitzgerald, and the Mark Cross heir and painter Gerald Murphy.[13]

A traveler always, an exile never, he wanted America, but he wanted it different.

Dos Passos wanted a humanitarian cooperative economy as

a means of preserving civilization from militarism and war. He supported the antimilitarist La Follette for the presidency in 1924 but was actually in sympathy with the syndicalism of the I.W.W.[14] How did he reconcile his attraction to radical labor with his revulsion from industrialism? He thought, when he wrote of industrialism, of its capitalistic form, whose attendant evils often included the oppression and deprivation of workers. Though certainly not pastoral movements, socialism and communism promised to use industry for the workers' benefit. As Edmund Wilson pointed out forty years later:

Norman Thomas and the early Max Eastman as well as Eugene Debs were imagining an extension of democracy which would get the big "capitalist" off the "wage-slave's" neck and restore the American community to the realization of something like Walt Whitman's vision of a robust fraternal race exploring and cultivating and building and enjoying the country's resources.[15]

Unlike the Bolshevik party, the I.W.W. was an undisciplined, anarchistic group, a majority of whose members were suspicious of and impatient with any type of central authority. Its anarchism, its gusto, its indigenous character had given it tonic appeal to many Greenwich Village leftists before the World War. Dos Passos came to know many members of the colorful American organization and in *The 42nd Parallel* created Mac as a composite of several of them.[16]

Dos Passos attributes much of his political development after the war to the influence of Greenwich Village.[17] A relatively isolated section of Manhattan, the Village in the second decade of the century had grown to be a haven for writers, artists, and radicals, and had become the locus of *Masses*. Mabel Dodge Luhan has depicted some of the ferment there before the war. Labor leaders, poets, journalists, editors, and actors frequented her salon at 23 Fifth Avenue; among those coming she mentions Lincoln Steffens, Emma Goldman, Alexander Berkman, John Reed, Walter Lippmann, Max Eastman, Margaret Sanger, Jo Davidson, Mary Heaton Vorse, William Haywood, William English Walling, and Hutchins Hapgood. "They were in groups that did not meet," she writes, "yet in each of these groups would be found one or more who had some contact with those in other groups. . . . Everybody had a little knowledge or at least a fore-knowledge of all the others."[18]

The Greenwich Village Dos Passos frequented after the war was better known, more accessible, and more expensive than it had been, but sheltering men and women whose outlooks contrasted with the prevailing ideology, it kept some of its old character. Dos Passos recollects that although repelled or chilled by the pretensions, fashionable clichés, and repudiations of a family life he missed, he took to much of the prewar attitude of Greenwich Village.[19] In the face of a business ideology that saw both artists and workers as pariahs, he and other Village artists thought of laborers as allies in the battle for freedom. He declares:

> Greenwich Village met us at the dock. American Bohemia was in revolt against Main Street, against the power of money, against Victorian morals. Freedom was the theme. Freedom from hard collars, from the decalogue, from parental admonitions. For Greenwich Village art and letters formed an exclusive cult. The businessman could never understand. It was part of the worldwide revolt of artists and would be artists and thinkers and would be thinkers against a society where most of the rewards went to people skillful in the manipulation of money. . . . When artists and writers found it hard to make themselves a niche in industrial society they repudiated the whole business. Greenwich Village was their refuge, the free commune of Montmartre on American soil. *Les bourgeois à la lanterne.*[20]

In Greenwich Village during the era of progressives and muckrakers before the war, nonconformity was an edifice with many chapels. (A big top with many rings, a supercilious observer might have called it.) The war made dissent against conventional sexual morality conventional but dissent against political and economic institutions dangerous.[21] Dos Passos still thought of nonconformity as a tradition within which anarchists and communists and experimental poets all had their place.

In considering some of the sources that buttressed his admiration of nonconformity and shaped his discontent with American society, we must remember that Dos Passos possibly has read more widely than any other major American novelist of this century. Because he invariably selects from and adapts ideas rather than accepting them whole, an account of particular influences upon him must be indicative and general rather than exhaustive and specific.

Although specific evidence of his indebtedness to Thorstein Veblen appears only in the late twenties, Veblen may earlier have influenced Dos Passos' view of the state, his sympathy with I.W.W.

syndicalism, and, in a general way, his portrayal of society in *Manhattan Transfer*. It may be significant, for example, that in the early 1920s Dos Passos was using the term "predatory" in characterizing urban civilization, for that word was a key one in Veblen's vocabulary: according to Veblen, the predatory type dominated and exploited his cooperative fellows in a barbaric and business civilization.[22]

Veblen's influence was toward anarchism or socialism. The modern state, he held, "is a residual derivative of the predatory dynastic State, and . . . continues to be, in the last resort, an establishment for the mobilisation of force and fraud as against the outside, and for a penalised subservience of its underlying population at home." It is for the benefit of businessmen and, to a lesser extent, of officeholders that governments like that of the United States establish trade programs favoring their nationals, maintain diplomatic and military establishments, and engage in preparedness programs which inevitably lead to war. The gains which the controlling classes realize are commonly "no more than a vanishing percentage of their net aggregate cost to the underlying populations." "The substantial interest of these classes in the common welfare is of the same kind as the interest which a parasite has in the well-being of his host . . . " while "the service . . . rendered by the constituted authorities in the aggregate takes on the character of a remedy for evils of their own creation." If absentee ownership and the metaphysical concept of sovereignty were eliminated, a democratic commonwealth would be "an unsanctified workday arrangement for the common use of industrial ways and means." Democracies would "be in a fair way to become what they profess to be, — neighborly fellowships of ungraded masterless men given over to 'life, liberty and the pursuit of happiness.' "

Veblen looked with a certain sympathy upon the I.W.W., for he believed that some such group (but a more responsible one) would have to cooperate with technicians in seizing industry from its absentee owners. He considered the leadership of the A.F.L. a "kept class" and wrote of the A.F.L. that "at the best its purpose and ordinary business is to gain a little something for its own members at a more than proportionate cost to the rest of the community." Not the A.F.L., but unions like the I.W.W., he said, frightened the authorities. His references to absentee owners' "sabotaging" industry constituted an ironic use of a term identified with syndicalist tactics.[23]

Dos Passos says that his political thought was influenced greatly by Albert J. Nock and to some extent by the *Freeman* group as a whole.[24] During its brief existence after the war, from March 17, 1920, to March 5, 1924, the *Freeman*, says a historian of the periodical, "gave the most consistent and intense expression of any magazine of its time" to a period "when the reassertions of intellectual freedom were strongest, when political reforms seemed possible, and when a belief in cultural criticism outweighed purely aesthetic concerns." The editors, Francis Neilson and Albert J. Nock, saw in the state a coercive instrument by which a plundering class blocked economic emancipation and individual liberty. Though opposing socialism, the periodical was open-minded about kinds of industrial organization that would circumvent state control, about guild socialism, syndicalism, and the Soviets.[25]

Nock, whose editorials set the political line of the *Freeman*, proclaimed the periodical radical rather than liberal. Liberals believed, he wrote, that the state could be improved by political methods; they were "politically-minded, with an incurable interest in reform, putting good men in office, independent administrations, and quite frequently in third-party movements." Their idea of the state was "pure conjecture" while the radicals' approach was historical.[26] All states had arisen "to enable the continuous economic exploitation of one class by another," and all states, whether republican, constitutional-monarchical, or autocratic, behaved exactly alike. They monopolized crime and never moved disinterestedly for the general welfare "except grudgingly and under great pressure."[27]

Nock described Thomas Jefferson's individualistic principles, manners, delicate perceptions in matters of conduct, and strength of character as ideals for a free society. Liberals and progressives wished to encroach upon men's conduct by law, he said, but laws, whether good or bad, hampered the development of individual responsibility. "Living in America is like serving in the army," Nock quipped; "ninety per cent of conduct is prescribed by law and the remaining ten per cent by the *esprit du corps*."[28]

Such ideas may well have interested or appealed to Dos Passos, vitally concerned with nonconformity as he was in the twenties. But only after his return from the Spanish Civil War in mid-1937 did he study Jefferson's thought and become strongly attracted by it; in later years Dos Passos denounced huge centralized government in the United States and wrote extensively and appreciatively about Jefferson.[29]

Van Wyck Brooks, the literary editor of the *Freeman*, was,

with Nock, largely responsible for determining its policy in letters. With the assistance of Lewis Mumford and Harold Stearns, Brooks made the periodical virtually an organ for expressing the cultural criticism of "the college generation of 1912 and later who had taken fire from Brooks and Bourne and had found outlet and inspiration in the *Seven Arts* and then in the older *Dial.*" This group continued to write of the necessity of art's becoming an integral part of life in America as it was in Europe, of the situation of the artist in America, and of the difficulty of creation in a machine civilization. Discussions in the *Freeman* inspired Harold Stearns to edit *Civilization in the United States*, a volume in which thirty writers indicted most phases of American civilization.[30]

The group around Brooks could at the beginning of the decade still be called the *avant-garde* in American letters; but after 1922 the *Dial*, which had been turned into a literary magazine in 1920, became the periodical closest in touch with contemporary creative writers. Brooks continued to emphasize social and ethical problems, while he declared contemporary experiments in language and form "dangerously private and personal." Nock, it is true, called upon critics to stop writing about the inhospitable American culture and instead help artists create, but Nock himself was too much out of sympathy with most contemporary writers to aid them. At a time when Eliot, Joyce, and Proust were exciting attention, the *Dial*'s emphasis upon language and structure seemed more pertinent than did Brooks' stress on sociology and literary history.

Commenting on the two magazines in 1920, Dos Passos made it clear that he preferred the *Freeman*. The *Dial* he described as mostly genteel and dull. While he continued to see it — he liked some of the things he found there and he had friends among the editors and contributors — he published in it only now and then. In the separation of the types of literary interests represented by Brooks and by the *Dial*, writes the historian of the *Freeman*, American criticism lost a wholeness of vision.[31] But Dos Passos in *Manhattan Transfer* transmuted many of the themes in the sociological criticism of *Seven Arts* and the *Freeman* into experiments in form like those with which the *Dial* group was concerned.

To our survey of particular influences upon Dos Passos' social thought we must add E. E. Cummings — a frequent and most spirited contributor to the *Dial*. Dos Passos certainly appreciated and joined in his friend's call for joyful spontaneity in life. In a review of *The Enormous Room*, Dos Passos, derogating the "great

clanging, dusty machine of American life,'' praised Cummings'
fervid individual nature and the integrity and courage with which
he displayed it.[32] We must add, too, the fact that Dos Passos
shared with a number of his contemporaries an artistic seriousness,
integrity, and dedication which, for an understanding of his career,
is as important as it is intangible. Edmund Wilson, Ernest Hemingway, and Cummings were among the closest to Dos Passos in
the extensive list of his literary friends.

Before discussing *Manhattan Transfer* (1925), Dos Passos'
major work prior to *U.S.A.*, we must consider his play *The Garbage
Man* and his writings on the theater. These works help to explain
the genesis of the subsequent novel in at least three ways. First,
the theme of the play, which is the nature of American society
and the effect of the creed of success upon the happiness of individuals, is among the major themes of *Manhattan Transfer*.
Second, the play and the dramatic criticism contain some of the most
explicit evidence of Dos Passos' political and social opinions at
this time. He discussed the contemporary theater in the light of
his social views, and he resorted to sociology to help justify technical
innovations in the drama. And finally, Dos Passos' excitement
over the experimental theater of the 1920s helped to shape the
styles of both *Manhattan Transfer* and *U.S.A.*[33]

In his discussion of the *Teatro Nacional* of Madrid, published
in 1921, Dos Passos described that theater as part of the daily
life of the people. The first time he attended a play by Benavente,
he wrote, he recognized on the stage the same types of people
and the identical phrases and intonations that he found among the
audience. To understand the theater of Madrid, one had to know
the café. There playwright, actor, and audience spent their spare
time smoking, drinking, and chatting. Out of café life had developed
"a theatre of manners and local types and customs."[34] Strong
sympathy, if not intimacy, among playwright, actor, and audience
became a touchstone in Dos Passos' theatrical criticism. We may
link his long-standing revolt against preoccupation with art remote
from one's civilization to his call for theater to become a vital
part of communal life in America. The New York theater, he wrote
in the *Freeman*, had no connection with the desires and fears of
the average New Yorker; it offered plays that the producers did
not feel, the actors did not feel, and the audience did not feel.[35]

Along with Dos Passos' call for theater as communal expression went another for theater as spectacle. Probably the latter was in part due to his growing delight in seeing with the eye rather than through the mind and ought to be related to his enthusiasm for painting, architecture, and ballet.[36]

Gilbert Seldes' discussions in the *Dial* of jazz and vaudeville as popular arts must have interested him. After the war Dos Passos and John Howard Lawson, who had met as members of the Norton-Harjes Ambulance Service, engaged in long discussions of how to make the theater in this country more colorful and more American. The two turned to expressionism, a method of conveying idea and emotion that was exciting many playwrights, and considered adapting vaudeville and jazz to its requirements. Dos Passos was working on *The Garbage Man* (which he began perhaps as early as 1916 and completed around the end of 1922) at about the same time that Lawson was writing *Roger Bloomer* and *Processional*.[37] When Lawson published *Roger Bloomer* in 1923, Dos Passos contributed a foreword.

In that foreword he said that an American theater had existed in such plays as *Blue Jeans, Uncle Tom's Cabin,* and *Ben Hur,* and was being re-established by plays like Eugene O'Neill's *The Hairy Ape* and Lawson's *Roger Bloomer.* "Something approximating a national theater," Dos Passos declared, "is the most direct organ of group consciousness and will come into being, inevitable with the welding of our cities into living organisms out of the junk heaps of boxed and predatory individuals that they are at present." Two years later in an article he said that attempts to develop an American theater hadn't succeeded because, for one thing, aspirants had persisted in the view that "plays must be regarded primarily as masterpieces of literary effort, fraught with the culture of a by-gone age." Asserting that Lawson's *Processional* was the first American play of the generation frankly to abandon the theatrical convention of an invisible fourth wall, Dos Passos described it as "the straw to break the camel's back of the literary drama."[38] This play featured a procession of striking miners which was also a jazz band, and it offered routines usually associated with vaudeville.

In spring 1925 the Harvard Dramatic Club produced *The Garbage Man,* under the title *The Moon Is a Gong,* in Cambridge and Boston. True to its author's theories, the play had a theme of immediate concern to its audience: the stultification of youth by the creed of success. If the simple Fuselli had made himself ridiculous over the creed, more complicated young men were also in various ways its victims. As John Chamberlain later explained: at the time "college graduates who were otherwise quite normal and natural human animals were trying to sell insurance, bonds and advertising space on a 'service' basis when, as a matter of cold record, they didn't give two bits for the cant they were taught, with such sublime automatism, to use." The director, Edward Massey, using settings of Dos Passos' own design, arranged the play as a musical comedy.³⁹ Here we shall describe Dos Passos' first published version, which appeared the next year.

The characters in *The Garbage Man* act and speak to the music of a jazz band. At the very beginning, Tom and Jane, a boy and a girl returning from a party early in the morning, dance on the stage. When they hear the whirl of engines, they fear them, and Jane says the power of the engines is the life they drain from people. Implicitly contrasting with the engines his private symbol of freedom, Tom tells Jane that when he was a child he used to think the moon was like a gong and wish that he could climb the Flatiron Building or Jack's beanstalk and beat on the moon.

For many years Jane has spent much of her time tending her mother, an invalid. Now a figure with a stage doctor's paraphernalia appears, and Jane learns that her mother has died. The following scene, in which Jane's family gathers for the funeral, might conceivably reflect some of Dos Passos' private wounds, the relatives dancing in, gossiping, quarreling, uttering platitudes and nonsense — and one aunt expressing disapproval of Tom, whom she considers erratic and socially inferior. Jane's aunts and uncles resemble each other, and two of the cousins wear "Arrow Collar faces." The gathering of stereotypes is broken up by the colored butler, who drives the outraged and terrified relatives from the house with a rhapsodic homily describing as dead all those people who suppress their instinct for religious joy in order to carry "deir sperits in a hearse at de end o' de parade of de pomp o' de world."⁴⁰ Rather than be subject to the tutelage of her relatives, Jane runs off with Tom.

The next scene occurs at the site of a railroad accident. Jane, now Tom's wife, tells him that he has not helped her to escape from her humdrum life, and she adds that she is not interested in having children. Suddenly death appears, this time disguised as a member of the repair crew, and comments on how some of

Mourning Jane's mother. Scene from the New York production of *The Moon Is a Gong* in March 1926.

his victims had postponed living. After hearing death, Jane says
to Tom that the only thing which can be done two by two is getting
out of the ark and that she is leaving. Love is evanescent, she
tells him (much as Ellen Thatcher tells Jimmy Herf in *Manhattan
Transfer*), whereupon Tom answers (as Jimmy Herf might have
answered Ellen) that if he had not wanted to make her happy and
comfortable, he would not have "slaved all night writing damn
lies in a stinking office."[41] He adds that now he will live every
sort of life and see the world.

At Union Square in New York, a shabby man with a big
telescope on a tripod offers glimpses of the moon for ten cents.
Tom appears, ragged and hungry. And Jane, now Janet Gwendolen
(like Ellen Thatcher, an actress), enters accompanied by three young
men with "cold cream faces." Death, now a man in a frock coat
and a stovepipe hat, offers money to Tom and the younger of
two bums on the stage if they will participate in a robbery. After
Tom and the young bum have left, the old bum and the telescope
man discuss life in New York, the former describing the city's
attractions and the latter its empty reality. (This discussion is another
link between the play and *Manhattan Transfer*.)

Tom and the young bum have participated in a million-dollar
gem robbery. A "gorillafaced policeman" and a "baboonfaced
policeman" rush on the stage, kill the young bum, and pursue
Tom, who next appears on a backyard fire escape of the house
where Jane lives. He has been in the Near East and in Africa,
he tells her, but without her he has bungled everything. Jane replies
that he must not intrude upon her career. When police come, a
hard-working neighborhood woman, Mrs. Halloran, hides Tom in
her laundry basket. Looking about at the ash cans, she says that
New York certainly is a city for rubbish and garbage and that
it has been a long time since the garbage man came. Soon Jane's
intellectual and tea-drinking friends appear, as does a man in a
Panama hat, who identifies himself as a federal detective and tries
by blackmail to make her spy on them. Meanwhile, Jane's friends,
to the strains of "Tea for Two," dance and chant about spirituality,
the education of capital and labor, and the link between influenza
and morality.

Suddenly spying death in the guise of a garbage man, Jane
collapses and calls for Tom. The ark has shut one of them in
again, he declares, but he will help her get out. Jane, who for
popular success has abandoned husband and the prospect of children,

affirms that she is a helpless prisoner within the mesh of all her affairs.

Now the man in the Panama hat begins to act as Jane's publicity man, saying that a Prosperity Day parade is to come by and he wants a photograph of her watching it enthusiastically. As the parade passes, a radio voice, certainly the voice of American capitalistic industrialism, calls for total conformity and proclaims "That there shall be a list made of all dissenters knockers reds carping critics nonchurchgoers wearers of straw hats out of season nonfordowners loafers discontented persons readers of foreign languages divorcees advocates of free love the eight hour day subversive doctrines."[42]

The straw hat out of season deserves special notice, for in *Manhattan Transfer* it reappears more prominently as a symbol of nonconformity. During the postwar excitement over Bolshevism, Graham Wallas had written in the *Atlantic Monthly*: "The Chicago *Evening Post* said the other day, 'Just now, in popular parlance, a Bolshevik is anybody, from a dynamiter to the man who wears a straw hat in September.'"[43]

Tom shouts his defiance of the "voice of the machine," with its talk of straw hats out of season. "It's not for you," he says, "that the desires of men and women beat against the silver moon and temper it hard as a roaring gong by the beating of their wants." The radio voice goes on: "Lynch the slacker. Lynch the doubter. Lynch the misfit."[44] Death, now wearing an enormous sheriff's badge, attempts to arrest Tom, but he escapes by climbing the fire escape. A boy shouts that he can see him running across roofs and climbing up the slanting roof of the tallest building, dancing on a lightning rod and beating on the moon. The garbage man now seizes Jane, who, swaying her arms like a broken doll, again calls for Tom. Unaccountably together again in the last two scenes, Tom and Jane agree that despite the dynamos they will live for the fleeting today.

In *The Garbage Man* American civilization is characterized by qualities which Dos Passos was contrasting in the early 1920s with Spanish individualism, spontaneity, and passion. Human movement has been adapted to the requirements of machines. Advertising and mass journalism have shaped dress, ideas, and values to the marketing or political requirements of industrial capitalism, providing avenues for amoral opportunism. Among the civilization's many advertised and publicized commodities are fashionable artists of all kinds. Tom's references to children and the ark (as well as other references in the play to possibly sexual symbols such as the lightning rod and the moon and gong) remind us of natural values and spontaneous behavior. To the extent to which people have become uniform and manipulated, they are the "deadalive" of Dos Passos' play; people who have resisted manipulation and uniformity the civilization considers outlaws, and upon them it imposes social, economic, and legal penalties.

Unfortunately, in *The Garbage Man* the desire of Tom and Jane to live is not clearly related to contemporary American institutions. One of the difficulties is that Tom and Jane are not intended to be individuals with specific histories of their own; Dos Passos' piece is closer to the morality play, with its allegory and didacticism, than to the realistic drama. Another difficulty is that one grasps much more about how Tom and Jane feel than about what they think; for all its didacticism, Dos Passos' expressionistic play does not appeal to discursive reason.

For several years preceding 1925 Dos Passos seems to have experimented to find a form that would enable him to incorporate in a novel some of the themes that appear in *The Garbage Man*. In the final version of *Manhattan Transfer* he combined narration with imagery and symbolism — including some highly expressionistic symbolism — to present a picture whose appeal would be both discursive and intuitive. He changed the story of Tom and Jane into that of Jimmy Herf and Ellen Thatcher, and he carefully linked political and economic institutions with his characters' activities and incomes, and with their values and views of one another.

Dos Passos says that Emile Verhaeren's *Les Villes tentaculaires* and Gustave Flaubert's *Sentimental Education* were among the works which influenced *Manhattan Transfer*[45] and that the European experimental literature which had excited him during and after the war had its effects too. "Rapportage was a great slogan," he recalls. "The artist must record the fleeting world the way the motion picture film recorded it. By contrast, juxtaposition, he could build reality into his own vision." In *Manhattan Transfer* Dos Passos attempted a reportage of New York.[46]

Manhattan Transfer is an experimental novel the events of which span approximately the first twenty-five years of New York's history in the present century. It is an arresting and memorable work. A product of multitudinous artistic influences and direct experiences, it fuses character, place, image, and symbol in a many-faceted portrayal of the metropolis. The two characters most fully depicted are Jimmy Herf, a young journalist, and Ellen Thatcher, a young actress. In the course of the novel they marry. But the values and demands of the city — which blight journalism, theater, and much else that could inspire men — frustrate Herf, agitate Ellen, and finally result in her divorcing him and his quitting the city.

The form of the novel is peculiarly appropriate for a picture of New York, which is not a community where an individual is known or where his personality is a matter of moment. The story contains scores of characters — among them one or more reporters, actors, lawyers, playboys, factory workers, labor leaders, importers, bootleggers, housewives, waiters, architects, tramps, and bankers. Many of these characters appear only once, while others go through adventures that are merely tangential to the main plot of the story; scarcely more than a half dozen recur with regularity, as scenes, dissimilar in length and in the people they portray, succeed one another rapidly.

New York is still in the gaslight era at the beginning of the book. Immigrants are pouring in from rural districts and from Europe. The greater New York bill has just been passed, and real estate men are assuring customers that the value of Brooklyn lots will double within six months. Steady development in upper Manhattan indicates the continuity of Dos Passos' Manhattan with the one that Henry James depicted in *Washington Square*. Early in *Manhattan Transfer* a house agent tells a man and his wife that there is no finer location than Riverside Drive and that soon they will not be able to get an apartment there "for love or money." *Washington Square* pictures the Irish as entering in conspicuous numbers during the potato famine; now Jimmy Herf's Uncle Jeff declares that the city is overrun "with kikes and low Irish" and complains of their competition in business.

But the book has a far greater resemblance to William Dean Howells' picture of the metropolis in the 1880s, *A Hazard of New Fortunes*, than it does to James' sketch of an earlier New York. As Granville Hicks has noted, Howells used a cumbersome conventional plot, which involved the publication of a magazine, to gather together a large number of diverse characters and to reveal a city of labor strife and clashing ideologies.[47] The ideological conflicts, though not the labor disputes, have now grown sharper;

whereas the two earlier books spoke only of immigration, there is now forced emigration.

Another link appears in the status of New York. When Howells depicted Basil March leaving Boston for that city to become the editor of a new magazine, he did so because New York had become the publishing center of the nation. This development in publishing was one small aspect of the growth of New York to national pre-eminence. The characters in *Manhattan Transfer* know what New York stands for, as did the colleague who eulogized Dos Passos' father in 1917. "And dont forget this," Jimmy Herf's Uncle Jeff says to him, "if a man's a success in New York, he's a success!"[48] When the lawyer George Baldwin complains that his success seems empty to him and Ellen Thatcher asks why he doesn't go into politics, he replies (Dos Passos making Baldwin's description of power conform to that of populists and radicals), "Why should I go up to Washington into that greasy backwater when I'm right on the spot where they give the orders? The terrible thing about having New York go stale on you is that there's nowhere else."[49]

Theodore Dreiser's *Sister Carrie* is also an important predecessor of *Manhattan Transfer*. Dos Passos' novel contains many scenes like the one juxtaposing Hurstwood's begging and falling in the snow with Carrie's enjoying an apartment in the Waldorf. At the conclusion of the book, for instance, Jimmy Herf's cousin James Merivale, sitting in the Metropolitan Club, thinks of himself as a successful young man and of his cousin as a Greenwich Village misfit; Herf at the time is preparing to abandon New York. Dreiser's knowing evocations of poverty in America and his portrayal of a society in which individuals are isolated and are constantly rising or falling finds parallels in stories like that of Herf's relation to Joe Harland.[50]

In the review that was responsible for the rapid recognition of *Manhattan Transfer* as a major literary achievement, Sinclair Lewis, who had been portraying the Gopher Prairies and Zeniths of America, declared that Dos Passos had done what other writers had frequently proven could not be done: he had presented "the panorama, the sense, the smell, the sound, the soul, of New York."[51] It is difficult to imagine what impression the book makes upon readers who do not know the city; but New Yorkers who have frequently felt themselves strangers in the midst of what is by definition their home city and who have, by day and by night, walked the city to grasp its purpose and justification, are likely to agree with Lewis that Dos Passos re-created the sense and soul of the metropolis they know.

The New Yorker's relationship to strangers and casual acquaintances contrasts sharply with that enjoined in the Bible, to love the stranger as oneself. And everyone, Dos Passos shows, is to a considerable extent a stranger in the city. Uncle Jeff's complaint about business competition from immigrants is merely symptomatic of important facts: established residence brings no recognition, and long-time employment usually brings no security. Outside, shiploads of immigrants land continually, for to them the United States appears to be a land of opportunity; within, men seek jobs without success, particularly after the war, and old people beg for the price of a cup of coffee.

The ferryboat and maternity-ward scenes at the beginning of the book imply that people in New York are treated like garbage. And near the end of the book, when a seamstress is horribly burned while at work in a dress shop and her employer asks Ellen to reassure the customers in front, Ellen declares: "Madame Soubrine asked me to tell everybody it was nothing, absolutely nothing. Just a little blaze in a pile of rubbish."[52]

The history of the farm boy Bud Korpenning makes the same point only a little less directly. Korpenning is glad of the anonymity the city affords as he arrives from upstate New York at the beginning of the novel: his father, or guardian, had beaten him with chains, and Korpenning killed him. In the metropolis Korpenning wishes to get into the center of things in order to find a job; he has no idea of how far removed from people like him, and how nebulous besides, is the center of things. The acquaintances he makes are fleeting. He does find a job as a dishwasher in a lunchroom, but he flees when he imagines that a detective has entered the kitchen. A woman promises him a dollar to bring some coal into the house and then cheats him. In despair and terror he hurls himself from Brooklyn Bridge. Picking up the body a moment later, a tugboat captain curses in annoyance.

The toll that metropolitan society takes of individuals can be gauged from the histories of Jimmy Herf and Ellen Thatcher, the only characters whose childhoods the reader encounters in any detail.

The daughter of an accountant, Ellen dreams from early childhood of romance, riches, and glamor. (These are the delusive aims of a number of women in Dos Passos' works, people who never learn to link art or interesting existence with humanity and self-sacrifice.) Elaine of Lammermoor, the child imagines herself to be in one of the short stream-of-consciousness passages which Dos Passos, probably influenced by Joyce, uses throughout his novel. (He had read *Ulysses* in February 1922, while aboard ship returning from Europe.[53]) Ellen's first marriage is to the actor John Oglethorpe, who does a great deal to further her stage career. When Jimmy Herf encounters her on his visit to a girl friend in Greenwich Village, she is already an actress with a reputation. But she is unhappy, for Oglethorpe has turned out to be homosexual.

Ellen falls in love with the personable but deranged playboy Stan Emery. She finds him "humanly young" and gratifyingly different from the lawyer George Baldwin, who complains to her that the tension downtown has been wearing him out and that he needs her so that he can relax and be happy. Stan is so different that he asks why everyone is anxious to succeed. He can understand people running about to get money to live, but what can they do with success?

Success in Dos Passos' New York is, in fact, as ironic as it is resplendent. Harry Goldweiser, a rich theatrical producer, wants Ellen for the same reason as does Baldwin. Goldweiser is thirty-five, successful, but, like Baldwin, apathetic toward life. Ellen loves only Stan, but he goes off on a drunken trip to Canada with another actress and gets married along the way. After a subsequent escapade to drown his regrets, he burns himself to death.

Ellen Thatcher is dissatisfied with New York. She thinks the show in which she is appearing is bad and the acting false. "In a musical show you could be sincere," she says, voicing a little of her author's theatrical criticism. When Goldweiser tells her that the public doesn't want art, she replies: "I think that this city is full of people wanting inconceivable things."[54]

The New York of Goldweiser and Ellen reminds us by contrast of "Benavente's Madrid," where actor, playwright, and audience formed part of the same community, and we recall that Telemachus sees in the movements of Pastora Imperio the Spanish gesture. But as Ellen stands with Goldweiser in a roof garden overlooking Central Park in industrial New York, she feels like a "stiff castiron figure in her metalgreen evening dress."[55]

In an Italian restaurant (probably in Greenwich Village) before the war, Jimmy Herf and Ellen Thatcher listen to Herf's friend Martin declare that industrial civilization has given a few men an

amount of power unprecedented in modern history and that the
only remedy is through syndicalism. Herf supports Martin's indictment, which is also Dos Passos' own. But in *Three Soldiers*,
Manhattan Transfer, and *U.S.A.* there seems always, along with
the economic system, to be the individual with his own grain.
Mindful of private problems, Herf tells Ellen soon afterward that
he wishes he could blame all troubles on the system.

Ellen says that Stan made her realize there are other things
in life besides success as an actress — adding that she intends to
have and rear Stan's baby. Herf, who has been greatly impressed
by Ellen, tells her how much he admires her and is about to say
more when she rushes from him into her house. In a spontaneous
gesture, Herf kisses the steps on which she stood. In a subsequent
scene Ellen has an abortion and then takes a taxi to the Ritz.

When Jimmy and Ellen next appear together they are returning
from Europe married and with a baby, and we learn that they
have been overseas in the Red Cross together. Jimmy has written
some articles on his war experiences, but since his opinions are
unpopular, no one will publish the pieces. Ellen must take an editorial
job because he cannot find employment. When he does get a job,
it is as a reporter; the type of writing for which the world will
pay makes him miserable, and the pay is less than Ellen's. Her
love for Herf has now disappeared, and since they work at different
hours, she suggests that he rent a room somewhere.

Glimpses of George Baldwin, who is among the most ruthless
of the predatory men of affairs in the book, have already shown
him seducing a client's wife and betraying political associates. Now
a prosperous lawyer with a promising future in politics, Baldwin
again approaches Ellen. Feeling that a woman cannot be entirely
independent, Ellen divorces Herf and consents to marry the lawyer.
While Baldwin assures her that life will mean something to him
now, she feels that she has surrendered most of her desires. Such
surrender Dos Passos equates with spiritual death and rigor mortis.
Ellen senses that she will henceforth be petrified, incapable of
a spontaneous gesture.

When Herf was sixteen his Uncle Jeff had offered to let him
work his way up in the firm quite as if he were Jeff's own son,
but Herf had seen a vision of a life spent going in and out of
revolving doors and rejected such an existence with repugnance.
After graduating from Columbia, he had been disgusted with the
toadying and the violations of integrity and personality involved
in his work as a reporter. He and the chief character in *Three*

Soldiers, John Andrews, react similarly to journalism, and both find the New York environment inhospitable to art. Reading *Jean Christophe* before the war, Herf broods on the lack of creativity in the United States: "Nobody ever writes any music or starts any revolutions or falls in love. All anybody ever does is to get drunk and tell smutty stories."[56]

He has now given up his job. The only thing he finds desirable in New York is his wife: he has been obsessed by a symbolic vision of a skyscraper to which he cannot find a door and from every window of which Ellen in a gold dress is beckoning to him. But although he needs money to retain Ellen, he finds that making it gives him no gratification. Business civilization, its strains upon men and women, and its stamp upon their values are here linked to one another and related to national politics: as Herf considers his situation, he is reminded of the deported anarchists. "Pursuit of happiness . . . right to life liberty and . . . " he thinks a while later. "Go away in a dirty soft shirt or stay in a clean Arrow collar. . . . What about your unalienable right, Thirteen Provinces? . . . If only I still had faith in words."[57]

Toward the end of the book, he says that he has found the nerve to admit to himself how much he dislikes certain things. When a friend tells him of a man in Philadelphia who has been killed fighting over his right to wear a straw hat on May 14, Herf proclaims the victim a saint.[58] The fate of this martyr recurs to Herf several times as he leaves New York, much as Christian in *Pilgrim's Progress* leaves the City of Destruction.

Back from contemplating the ruins of ancient Near Eastern cities, as well as of the Russian and Turkish empires, Dos Passos could not help seeing vividly his own civilization as vulnerable. New York is, in one of its aspects, the City of Destruction, doomed supernaturally for its evil ways. References to destructive fire, which suggest the fire anticipated by Christian in *Pilgrim's Progress*, occur everywhere in the book, while less numerous allusions to the Biblical flood suggest a second source of catastrophe. Disaster is indicated in still other ways. Lady Godiva, the Saxon noblewoman who saved the people of Coventry from oppression by riding through the city clad only in her long hair, reappears in *Manhattan Transfer* debased by advertising. She wears a sign "Danderine" over her saddlecloth. ("Rings on her fingers," says Stan Emery, "And bells on her toes, And she shall cure dandruff wherever it grows."[59]

For ills more serious than dandruff, New York will apparently have to find another savior. The tramp "Jonah," coming upon the campfire of Joe and Skinny above the Hudson River, tells the two that God took only seven minutes each to destroy the tower of Babel, and Babylon, and Nineveh. Manhattan, Brooklyn, and the Bronx will go in seven seconds, Jonah says, for there is more wickedness in a New York City block than there was in a square mile of Nineveh.

Among Dos Passos' important symbols are garbage, animals and cages, and skyscrapers, as well as fire engines, floods, and the spurious Lady Godiva. Such symbols usually appear as chapter headings, either before or after they occur in the text. A number of the symbols are merely descriptive of industrialism; "Revolving Doors" indicates the monotony of industrial life and "Roller-coaster" the spurious thrills in which men seek relief. (We may contrast these two symbols with Telemachus' flamenco.) But many of the symbols portend disaster. Since these achieve cumulative effect as the narrative proceeds and since the histories of a number of characters reach unhappy climaxes in the last chapter, the effect is to indicate that apocalyptic doom is near.

But despite all the symbols of doom in the book, it is no exception to the rule that Dos Passos' fiction has always reflected the complex world rather than any simple generalization about it. It is not entirely accurate to say, as Joseph Warren Beach did, that *Manhattan Transfer* depicts a world totally without affection, moral obligation, or cooperation.[60] True, only a pecuniary bond joins employer and employees, stranger and stranger, and very often husband and wife. But the bootlegger Congo offers to lend Jimmy Herf a thousand dollars; Uncle Jeff, not a particularly kind man, does what he conceives to be the right thing for Herf after the boy's mother dies; Ellen Thatcher does have friends for whom she will do favors. Those who attempt to succeed economically, Dos Passos implies, must, like James Merivale, Harry Goldweiser, Ellen Thatcher (and even the base George Baldwin and Phineas Blackhead), contort their personalities; successful people are, hence, likely to be thwarted people. Dos Passos has merely reaffirmed a theme, not introduced one into American literature. Thoreau was almost obsessed with the same theme in the middle of the nineteenth century, and Henry James was concerned with it early in the twentieth.

Herf's concern with a Philadelphian's right to wear a straw

hat on May 14 reminds us that Dos Passos' subject is not only New York but also the nation. Most of the events in *Manhattan Transfer* are manifestations of the political, economic, and cultural history of the United States during the first quarter of the century, although they occur almost exclusively in the nation's largest city. For example:

At the beginning of the book, young Jimmy Herf, coming into New York with his mother, is conscious that she is for Parker for president (even as Dos Passos knew that his father was for Parker in 1904).

A decade later, when World War I breaks out, the French bartender Congo, an anarchist, blames industrialists and financiers. When the labor organizer Joe O'Keefe is sure that America will not help England, its traditional enemy and the oppressor of Ireland, Joe Harland tells him to read stock quotations, not history books.

Herf's friend Martin argues for syndicalism, a noticeable movement in prewar America, while Mead repeats the standard business ideology.[61]

The postwar depression, with its unemployment, is important in determining the fates of many of the characters. The war veteran Dutch Robertson cannot find work; he has no food and no place where he can go with his girl, Francie. Jimmy Herf's own marital problems are complicated because he cannot get a job.

The war over, United States business is attempting to expand its economic power, and the press is denouncing economic unorthodoxy as Bolshevik. The crooked importer Densch tells George Baldwin that America is about to take over "the receivership of the world." He warns against radicalism, rejoices in the attitude of the press toward it, and declares: "We're approaching a national unity undreamed of before the war."[62] On a ferry leaving the immigrant station, meanwhile, defiant deportees like those expelled on the *Buford* sing the "Internationale."

After demobilization O'Keefe takes advantage of the depression to organize a veterans' bonus committee associated with the American Legion. When Legionnaires a year later raid a garment workers' ball, Gus McNiel, a Tammany politician, warns O'Keefe that public sentiment is changing. Organized labor in the United States has by this time been forced into its decade-long retreat, and we hear a Jewish garment worker exhorting his girl friend to be class conscious.

Although the postwar depression is over, the economy is unstable — the import-export firm of Blackhead and Densch founders in one of the business slumps of the early 1920s.

Prohibition and violence have replaced labor and radicalism as topics of public interest. Congo and his associates fight off hijackers on a boat landing at Sheepshead Bay. Dutch and Francie, who have turned to robbery, become the subjects of a current newspaper ballyhoo, which labels the girl as "the flapper bandit." A judge, after delivering a lecture on property rights and jazz-age evils, sends Francie to prison for twenty years.

Although the war, prohibition, and the postwar depression, with its attendant unemployment, were the products of individuals and institutions, Dos Passos refuses to interpret this fact directly in *Manhattan Transfer*. He merely presents scenes chronologically and implies that it is the reader's task to furnish the historical commentary. Much of the commentary, he believed, had to bear on industrialism.

Condemnation of industrialism was a salient feature of contemporary cultural criticism; it is illuminating, for instance, to compare Waldo Frank's essay "New York," published in 1919, with *Manhattan Transfer*.[63] But Dos Passos probably found Whitman's writings at least as provocative as contemporary thought when he examined the metropolis. The East River between New York and Brooklyn, Barrett Wendell wrote, was in Whitman's day "the spot of spots where life seemed most material, most grindingly distant from ideal beauty."[64] That spot, too, Whitman said in "Crossing Brooklyn Ferry," contained perfection and furnished its part toward eternity.

Whitman wrote when America still had a predominantly agricultural economy and when business was still relatively small. One feels that Dos Passos measured the beauty of the city in his own day against the ugliness, gauged the prospect of progress against the prospect of calamity, and rendered a negative report. The beauty of Dos Passos' Manhattan lies mainly in its lights and colors, a fact that reminds us of his being a painter. One remembers "glowworm trains," and the river beneath Brooklyn Bridge glimmering like the Milky Way above, and night crushing "bright milk out of arclights." A dominant image is that of the sun painting the city. But as Blanche Gelfant has pointed out in her acute study of the imagery, the city provides its own indictment as it comes to life: Ellen gropes "continually through a tangle of gritty saw-edged brittle noise," and through Jimmy Herf's window comes "a sourness of garbage, a smell of burnt gasoline and traffic and dusty pavements, a huddled stuffiness of pigeonhole rooms where men and women's bodies writhed alone tortured by the night and the young summer."[65] It may be significant that the novel at both its beginning and its end has a ferry scene conveying no beauty or hope for the city.

Whitman viewed both New York and the nation as moral phenomena and evidence of the degree of success of democracy. His criteria for a successful democratic personality included personal independence, camaraderie, and "sane athletic maternity," woman's "crowning attribute."[66] But in modern New York, Dos Passos indicates, business demands that one sell his personality, society is atomized, and motherhood has become a horror. Still, *Manhattan Transfer* probably should not be labeled a naturalistic novel, for Dos Passos does not conclude on a deterministic note. While the masses of men react almost mechanistically to physical stimuli and to pressures for conformity, a few like Jimmy Herf preserve their personalities — at a high cost.

Manhattan Transfer was a milestone in Dos Passos' development as a novelist. Here he for the first time took society as his subject and made many of his characters both vital and interesting. The cultural and political nonconformity in Greenwich Village, the political and ideological dominance of big business during the twenties, the discussions of American civilization in the *Freeman*, and Dos Passos' interest in new techniques of literary expression were to a large extent responsible for the resoluteness with which he undertook to portray the American metropolis; and the social and political climate evoked much of the pessimism which found its way into Dos Passos' portrayal.

Despite his social theme, the years following his return from the Near East were not ones of marked political combat for him. Excitement over experimental art is the primary impression one gets from his writings at this time. At once an aesthetic triumph and a vision of social blight, *Manhattan Transfer* reflected his experiences with painting, theater, and other arts, as well as with people and print. It also reflected the stimulus of prior adventure. Stimulating, meaningful activity followed by vigorous literary work — Dos Passos had engaged in this sequence in producing two major books, and he was soon to repeat it again. Before undertaking *U.S.A.* he would be as excited about politics as he had been during the war.

VI.

"CLASS WARFARE"

DURING THE LATTER PART OF THE TWENTIES THE STRUGGLE between capital and labor became a major theme in Dos Passos' fiction, which assumed an urgent tone reminiscent of his wartime novels. These developments were due not only to his witnessing some of the industrial disputes of the decade but also to his coming to consider as more than sporadic injustices governmental interference with the efforts of workers to organize. His humanitarian fervor and idealism reached World War I pitch in the Sacco-Vanzetti case, in which he put immense effort into agitating for the defense. Condemnation to death of the two radicals in 1927 seemed to him the culmination of a "wave of repression . . . whereby the great industrial manufacturers were able to use the machinery of the courts and the police power to harass every effort to organize working people into trade unions."[1] Concluding that industrialists and financiers had so succeeded in making the law their instrument that they could prevail no matter how notorious the case, he openly wrote in favor of "revolution" in the United States.

Many employers attempted after World War I, we have seen, to destroy the gains their workers had achieved and to crush organized labor altogether. Management, through its trade groups, set up open-shop associations which proclaimed the laborer's right to work where he pleased. Unions were declared to be un-American and the open-shop program to be the "American plan." Employers used yellow-dog contracts, lockouts, and injunctions and resorted to strikebreakers, spies, and armed hoodlums to further this American plan. Some firms established company unions and attempted by various paternalistic devices to show that militant labor organization was unnecessary. In resisting the onslaught, organized labor suffered serious disadvantages: the national administrations frequently sided with management in disputes, and courts upheld yellow-dog contracts, declared boycotts illegal, interfered with minimum-wage legislation, and hampered peaceful picketing.

During the decade, employers were able to destroy some of the unions that had been established in wartime and to reduce seriously the power of organized labor. While employers were least successful in their efforts to break A.F.L. craft unions, these unions did little for the majority of workers and still less for the unskilled. It is true that conditions of work in the most thriving industries were good enough to discourage unionization. But while real wages rose and the number of hours in the work week fell for labor as a whole during the decade, not all workers or all industries shared the bounty. Estimates of unemployment in 1921 ranged from 3,500,000 to more than 5,000,000.[2] There were always at least 1,000,000 people unable to find jobs between 1922 and 1929. The textile and bituminous coal-mining industries were in economic difficulty.[3] These circumstances, combined with the deterioration of the I.W.W. and the inactivity of the A.F.L., enabled the Communists to bid for the leadership of militant labor.

The establishment of *New Masses* in 1926 helped to focus Dos Passos' attention upon questions of labor organization and leftist ideology. Besides giving him a convenient vehicle for publishing on these subjects, it probably put him into more intimate contact than he had known before with a large and varied group of radicals. At the end of 1922 the editors of the *Liberator* turned the magazine over to the Workers (Communist) party, thus ending a decade of independence for the *Masses* and the *Liberator*. Two years later the career of the *Liberator* ended, when the periodical was combined with two others to become an official Communist party organ edited by Earl Browder.[4] After the demise of the *Liberator*, Joseph Freeman and Michael Gold discussed establishing a "broad united front" of liberal and radical writers and artists around a new *Masses*. For money, they turned to Scott Nearing and Roger Baldwin, both of whom were influential in the American Fund for Public Service, to which "a Yankee philosophical anarchist" Charles Garland had given his million dollar inheritance. The Garland fund subsequently gave Freeman $27,000 with which to support the new periodical for three years, on the conditions that *New Masses* be edited by him and not be controlled in any way by the Communist party.[5]

When, after considerable delay, *New Masses* appeared in 1926, it listed as its editors Egmont Arens, Joseph Freeman, Hugo Gellert, Michael Gold, James Rorty, and John Sloan. Dos Passos and Paxton Hibben were among the sixteen members of the executive board. It was perfectly natural, writes Joseph Freeman, for Dos Passos to join in founding the periodical: "He and Edmund Wilson had been in Greenwich Village, they had known the Masses group, they were new writers, they sympathized with labor and radicalism. Dos Passos . . . was sympathetic to the Russian Revolution and to American reform. Besides, we all met socially, we were friends, this was our community. So when we sent out letters for a meeting to found the N.M., Dos got one and showed up."[6]

Dos Passos' close friends Edmund Wilson and John Howard Lawson were among the contributing editors, and some of the others were Sherwood Anderson, Van Wyck Brooks, Stuart Chase, Floyd Dell, Max Eastman, Waldo Frank, Arturo Giovannitti, Susan Glaspell, Lewis Mumford, Eugene O'Neill, Elmer Rice, Carl Sandburg, Upton Sinclair, Genevieve Taggard, Louis Untermeyer, Mary Heaton Vorse, and Art Young.[7]

Freeman says that of the fifty-six writers and artists involved in the venture, only two were members of the Communist party and fewer than a dozen were sympathizers with it.[8] Dos Passos agrees in substance, writing that most of the people concerned "could hardly have been called Marxists." "It's amusing to remember," he commented in 1956, "that in those carefree days a Communist party-member and an anarcho-syndicalist and even some sad dog of a capitalist who believed in laissez faire could sit at the same table and drink beer together and lay their thoughts on the line. It wasn't that you respected the other fellow's opinions exactly, but you admitted his right to remain alive."[9]

At the full editorial meetings, there were sharp political debates. One exchange of opinion, which found its way into print, establishes Dos Passos' views at the time. His attitude toward Bolshevik certainties was as cold as it had been in his "The Caucasus Under the Soviets" (1922). Michael Gold had called him a "bourgeois intellectual," and Dos Passos replied in an article "The New Masses I'd Like." As technology grew in America, he wrote, general ideals increasingly tended to restrict themselves "to Karl Marx, the first chapter of Genesis and the hazy scientific mysticism of the Sunday supplements." He objected to dogma, particularly the type imported from abroad. Since Columbus' time, he wrote, imported systems had been the curse of the continent. If the writers of *New Masses* explored the minds of the working class without preconceptions, they might be able to formulate a theory for action; if they approached the task with Marxist preconceptions, they would suffer the fate of finding exactly what they had been looking for.[10]

New Masses came into existence during the Passaic textile workers' strike of 1926, a long, momentous battle which gave the editorial board its first cause. The Communist party was responsible for initiating the strike. One of the party's organizers informed a Communist leader, Benjamin Gitlow, that Botany Mills of Passaic, New Jersey, had announced a ten per cent wage cut, to begin in October 1925, and Gitlow placed Albert Weisbord, a graduate of the City College of New York and Harvard Law School, in charge of organizing a strike. Gitlow estimates that seventeen thousand workers, chiefly foreign-born and unskilled, walked out as the strike spread through Passaic and its environs.[11] Since some of the mills did not shut down completely and many of the skilled workers remained on the job, the strikers undertook mass picketing; in thousands they marched past the mills, crossing the bridges between towns, singing their strike songs.

The United Front Textile Committee, the union in charge of the strike, claiming that the workers were receiving between $10 and $19 a week, demanded higher pay, shorter hours, and recognition of the union. The employers rejected all the union's demands, replying that average pay was between $15 and $23 a week, that business conditions made a wage cut necessary, and that the strike was caused by outside agitators. Asserting that Weisbord was a Communist, the employers refused to see a committee headed by him.

Until March 2, 1926, the strike was fairly peaceful. On that day the Passaic police harassed, and finally dispersed with tear gas and fire hoses, strikers who had emerged from a meeting hall a block from the Botany plant and were straggling peacefully past the mill. The next day small boys throwing stones and ice angered the Clifton police, who thereupon charged the strikers and their sympathizers on the dividing line between Clifton and Passaic, chased newspaper photographers intent on taking pictures of the scene, and beat reporters.

A crisis occurred when Forstmann and Huffmann announced on April 8 that their mill would open in a few days, and the strikers planned a strong picket line. Police and deputy sheriffs subsequently

Passaic textile strikers in February 1926. Crossing bridges between towns, thousands marched past the New Jersey factories.

halted pickets in Garfield and ordered them to walk away from the Forstmann and Huffmann mills. "The leaders refused," reported the *New York Times*, "and Sheriff Nimmo [of Bergen County] read the Riot act, a statute adopted after the Civil War, ordering the dispersal of a crowd within an hour." The police did not wait an hour. "In a few minutes half a dozen arrests were made." Justice of the Peace Louis Hargreaves, who had previously fixed pickets' bail at $500, raised it in some instances to $10,000.[12] He refused to allow stenographic notes to be made of the court's proceedings, claiming he was presiding over not a court of law but a court of martial law.

Holding that a reading of the Riot Act imposed martial law, the Garfield police banned all gatherings, even those in private halls and on private grounds. Then the sheriff of Passaic County announced that he was preparing a similar ban. The American Civil Liberties Union and the League for Industrial Democracy denied that the Riot Act established martial law. On April 14 Norman Thomas tested the Riot Act by speaking from a tree stump on ground rented by the League for Industrial Democracy. He was arrested, denied counsel, and arraigned secretly before Judge Hargreaves, who set bail at $10,000. Later Sheriff Nimmo announced that he would not permit the Reverend John Haynes Holmes to speak in the strike area; Holmes, pastor of the Community Church in New York, had planned to speak under the auspices of the American Civil Liberties Union. By mid-April it seemed the strike must collapse, for Weisbord and most of the ostensible leaders were in jail. But the strikers fought with some success in the courts, and the strike continued.[13]

That April Dos Passos journeyed to the strike area with a group of intellectuals and afterward published an account of the event in *New Masses*. With irony he described the visitors' talking of the Bill of Rights as, clad in warm overcoats, they rode in taxicabs and shiny sedans toward "the place where the meeting was going to be forbidden." The deputies politely held the doors of the sedans open, and the visitors retreated past impoverished strikers and back to New York; only one man was arrested.[14]

In Dos Passos' account of the journey to Passaic there is a feeling of guilt about being a member of the middle class, as in his wartime letters there had been this feeling over Harvard pacifists' acquiescence in the catastrophe. One can in retrospect comment further on the strike, pointing out the dangers to labor from a

Bolshevik organization more interested in its ends than in the causes it ostensibly champions. Gitlow confessed much later to the Communist party's having exploited liberals, juggled relief funds, and provoked some incidents.[15] But if we may judge by Dos Passos' disturbance over discoveries in 1931 — which we will consider in the next chapter — these tactics were not known to him, a major reason probably being that he was not seeking a beam in the Bolshevik's eye.

To understand the subsequent history of the strike, we must look at the Communist strategy. The United Front Textile Committee, which seemed to be running the strike, was an instrument of the Communist party. To prevent the A.F.L. from interfering, the party had the Committee apply for affiliation with the United Textile Workers (A.F.L.). The A.F.L., however, imposed the condition that Weisbord resign as strike leader. When it became clear that the strikers could not win, the Communist party decided to let the United Textile Workers take the responsibility for defeat.[16] Weisbord, who had avoided discussing politics at mass meetings, resigned on September 2, 1926. *New York Times* accounts gave the impression that his decision was voluntary.[17] Years later, Weisbord divulged how much had gone on behind the scenes: "The Communist Party leadership terminated the Passaic Strike in a disgraceful fashion, all the principal leaders of the Party voting that the independent union formed enter the A.F. of L., despite the fact that the communist union leaders were to be expelled. Only two members of the committee voted against, of whom the author is one."[18]

Textile industry leaders cared no more to negotiate with the A.F.L. than with a Communist-directed union. The strike dragged on and on, finally ending on a piecemeal basis. The companies yielded nothing substantial except the right of the workers to organize, and the last hold-out conceded nothing at all.[19]

The character of Weisbord the strike leader interested Dos Passos the novelist and playwright; he heard Weisbord speak, read about him, and may have met him.[20] Weisbord was, the *New York Times* reported, a "thin and frail" young man who did not look older than his twenty-five years. It added that observers attributed the duration of the strike to his personality and that the mill owners admitted his hold on the strikers was extraordinary. Gitlow, whom Weisbord antagonized during the strike, resented what he believed to be his narrowness, sectarianism, vanity, and ambition. After

Gitlow left the Communist party, he described Weisbord as "thoroughly saturated with Marxist-Leninist lore, including all the exegeses and homilies thereof." "It was not unusual for him to address ten meetings a day and be twenty hours a day on the job. . . . Fanatical in his zeal, he literally ate, slept and talked nothing but the strike and Communism."[21]

After his role in Passaic was over, Weisbord was active in organizing Communist textile unions in the South and elsewhere. He was expelled from the central committee of the Communist party in October 1929 and suspended from the party for a year that December — for, in the words of the central control committee, "maintaining an unpermissible non-communistic attitude toward the party and its decisions, taking upon himself to decide which decisions of the party he will carry out and which other decisions he will fight." In April of the next year the Communist International completely expelled him from the party. Weisbord organized a splinter group, the Communist League of Struggle, in March 1931.[22]

A character somewhat suggesting Weisbord, Walter Goldberg, appears in Dos Passos' play *Airways, Inc.* (1928) and Ben Compton in *U.S.A.* greatly resembles Weisbord in physical appearance and public character, although Compton is somewhat older and serves a term in jail for refusing to go to war. Like Weisbord, and like a number of members of the first generation of Communist leaders, Compton attends a metropolitan college. Subsequently he joins the Socialist party and studies law, though not at Harvard. Compton reads Marx carefully until Marx comes to dominate his thoughts, but he reads considerably more also; ultimately he writes a pamphlet modeled on Lenin's *What Is to Be Done?* Like Weisbord, Compton works at organizing textile workers' unions in New Jersey, and he is finally called to organize the towns around Passaic. He is an indefatigable worker and a tremendously popular strike leader, but he is also narrowly sectarian. When the A.F.L. officials take the strike out of his hands, he speaks of a sellout. Compton too is finally expelled from the party amid charges of "oppositionist" and "exceptionalism." "Well, that doesn't matter," he tells Mary French, "I'm still a revolutionist . . . I'll continue to work outside of the party."[23]

For Dos Passos the fact that Communists were leading the Passaic strike must have appeared unimportant beside the facts that low wages had been cut further and that legal authorities were violating the law in efforts to break the strike. His reaction to police and judicial tactics in New Jersey was heightened by his intense concern at about the same time with the Sacco-Vanzetti case in Massachusetts. Because he interpreted a long series of events since America's entrance into the war to be violations of democratic procedures and civil liberties, the executions of the two men appeared to him to be an ultimate indication of the depravity of America's government and its economic system. Justice was dead, wrote Edna St. Vincent Millay, and Dos Passos agreed.[24] Although he did not become personally involved until late in the course of events, it so powerfully affected his subsequent thinking that the history of the case becomes a vital part of his own.

In Bridgewater, Massachusetts, on December 24, 1919, two armed men attacked a truck which was carrying the payroll of the L. Q. White Shoe Company. They exchanged gunfire with the guards and fled. The attempt at robbery was unsuccessful, and nobody was shot.

A successful payroll robbery occurred less than four months later, on April 15, 1920, in South Braintree, Massachusetts. Two men killed a paymaster and a guard who were taking a $16,000 payroll from one building of the Slater and Morrill shoe factory to another. The assailants, with a third man who may have participated in the shooting, got into a car containing two others. Several persons observed the fleeing robbers, and a stolen car used in the flight was found two days later.[25]

Sacco and Vanzetti, two radical aliens who had been moderately active in strikes before the war and had fled to Mexico to evade the draft in 1917, were arrested on May 5, 1920, not long after the height of the red scare. The prosecution later claimed that the police had simply been looking for Italians who might be trying to get the use of a car, especially if their manner seemed surreptitious. (State witnesses spoke of the murderers as being Italian-looking.) Both Sacco and Vanzetti were carrying guns. When they were questioned, they gave answers that were incorrect or deliberately false. On June 22, at the Plymouth court, District Attorney Katzmann brought Vanzetti to trial, before Judge Webster Thayer, for the Bridgewater holdup. The prosecution's case was weak, but the defense's must have appeared weaker, for Vanzetti did not testify. He was found guilty and on August 16 was sentenced to from twelve to fifteen years for assault with intent to rob.

On May 31, 1921, Sacco and Vanzetti were placed on trial

for the South Braintree holdup and murder. Thayer again presided and Katzmann again prosecuted. At this second trial, in Dedham, the state offered eyewitness testimony to the defendants' guilt, claimed that a bullet found in the body of the murdered guard had been fired from Sacco's revolver, and alleged that the actions of the defendants at the time of the arrest showed consciousness of guilt. The state also tried to show that a cap found at the scene of the crime had belonged to Sacco and that the revolver Vanzetti had been carrying was one taken from the murdered guard.

The eyewitness testimony against the defendants appears to have been notoriously weak; it was frequently discredited and more than offset by that of the eyewitnesses for the defense. The cap was of common size and color, and the state's theory regarding Vanzetti's revolver was mere speculation; Vanzetti established a different line of ownership. On the question of whether the fatal bullet had come from Sacco's gun, two experts testified for the state. One said he was "inclined to believe" that the bullet had come from Sacco's pistol, and the other said the bullet was "consistent" with being fired from that pistol. Two experts for the defense said that in their opinion the bullet had not been fired from Sacco's gun. District Attorney Katzmann misrepresented the strength of his experts' testimony, but the lawyers for the defense did not expose its defects, and they presented their own ballistic evidence poorly. The judge failed to describe the testimony of the state experts adequately in his charge to the jury, and he probably gave a wrong impression of its strength.

In Judge Thayer's charge to the jury, he emphasized the issue of consciousness of guilt. Why had Sacco and Vanzetti been carrying revolvers and why had they lied to the police? Vanzetti claimed that he carried a revolver to protect money he used in his business as a fish peddler. Sacco said he had been planning to shoot some of his cartridges in a deserted place before leaving on an imminent trip to Italy. Both men said that, anticipating government raids, they had been seeking an automobile to remove radical literature from the homes of their friends. They claimed they had believed they were being arrested as radicals (the district attorney had not informed the two that they were suspected of murder) and said they had lied to the police to protect their friends.

Katzmann succeeded in making the defendants' radicalism a chief issue. His lengthy and sarcastic examination seemed so successful in appealing to antislacker and antiradical sentiment that the defense found it necessary to insist that one might be guilty of radicalism without being guilty of murder. The defense made a feeble effort to show by detailed chronological references to past events how the defendants' minds had been disturbed by fear not only of prosecution, but also of illegal violence and even of murder by government agents. Thayer blocked this argument, and he did not allow counsel for the defense to probe the motives of a state witness who had himself recently pleaded guilty to larceny. In his charge to the jury Thayer spoke of the jurors' service as a patriotic duty and reminded them of the heroic dead of the World War. On July 14, 1921, the jury returned a verdict of guilty.

Sacco's and Vanzetti's Italian friends came to their aid immediately after the arrests. By May 1920 these friends had organized the Sacco-Vanzetti Defense Committee, which worked singlemindedly in behalf of the defendants until the very end. For the Dedham trial the committee engaged attorney Fred H. Moore, who had defended Ettor and Giovannitti in 1912 and had done other defense work for the I.W.W. Since Sacco and Vanzetti were radicals and labor agitators, Moore used his familiar labor channels of publicity, and the case became another labor defense case. The New England Civil Liberties Committee and the liberal League for Democratic Control became apprehensive about the likelihood of an unfair trial and helped the defendants.

Between the end of the Dedham trial and November 1923 the defense presented five motions for a new trial on grounds of newly discovered evidence. The first charged that the foreman of the jury had exhibited revolver cartridges in the jury room, and this complaint was later supplemented with an affidavit that before the trial the future foreman had said, "Damn them, they ought to hang them anyway." The second motion was based in part on the discovery of an eyewitness previously known to the police but overlooked by the defense. From the seat in the getaway car where the prosecution placed Sacco, a robber had shot at this witness from a distance of a few feet, and the witness was sure that Sacco had not been that assailant. The third and fourth motions, as well as parts of the second, attempted to discredit witnesses; there were retractions and consequent re-retractions of testimony. The fifth motion offered additional ballistic evidence and an affidavit from one of the state's experts saying that he and the prosecution had deliberately misled the jury on the question of whether the fatal bullet had come from Sacco's gun. Judge Thayer denied all five motions on October 1, 1924.

Almost immediately after Thayer's decision, Fred Moore and other defense lawyers withdrew from the case, and William G. Thompson, a conservative Boston lawyer, became chief defense counsel. Attorney Thompson now undertook an appeal to the Supreme Judicial Court, the highest tribunal in Massachusetts. That court could determine whether the defendants had received a trial according to law, but it could not weigh the evidence again. Thompson charged that the trial judge had used his discretionary powers incorrectly or with prejudice. He appealed from Thayer's denial of the defense's plea that the verdict was against the weight of the evidence. He appealed too from the judge's denial of the first motion for a new trial, that part of the second motion dealing with a new eyewitness, and the fifth motion. The attorney had filed all his supporting material by November 10, 1925, and it seemed that his last major task would be to argue the briefs accompanying that material. Suddenly an event occurred which opened an entirely new line of defense.

Celestino Madeiros, like Sacco an inmate of the Dedham jail who had been found guilty of murder, wrote a note confessing his part in the South Braintree murder and exonerating Sacco and Vanzetti. Madeiros would not identify his confederates, but the defense established a hypothesis placing the guilt on the Morelli gang of Providence, Rhode Island. That gang had stolen shipments of shoes from the Slater and Morrill factories in the past; several of its members fitted descriptions given by eyewitnesses to the South Braintree crime; and one member resembled Sacco strongly. On May 26, 1926, two weeks after the Supreme Judicial Court denied Thompson's appeal, the defense submitted the Madeiros confession as grounds for still another appeal for a new trial, and in addition presented affidavits to show that the United States Department of Justice, though believing the two defendants innocent, had improperly helped Katzmann to prepare a case against them. Thayer again denied a new trial on October 23, 1926, saying that he could not find for a fact that Madeiros had told the truth.

The knowledge of Sacco's and Vanzetti's radicalism became more and more widespread between the time of their conviction and May 1926. Even before the trial Eugene Lyons had gone to Europe and interested the Italian press in the case, and Art Shields, another left-wing journalist, had written a pamphlet about it. European leftists demonstrated violently over the verdict. After the conviction civil liberties groups continued to be active in the prisoners' behalf. In spite of the conservative policies of the A.F.L., its conventions asked for a new trial in 1922, and in 1924 called the men "victims of race and national prejudice and class hatred."[26]

Dos Passos first became involved in the work of the Sacco-Vanzetti Defense Committee when an anarchist printer, Aldino Felicani, the man most responsible for organizing the defense, asked him to report a motion for a new trial.[27] There was much about the case to arouse him in favor of the defendants. His own indignation over America's participation in World War I made Sacco's and Vanzetti's unwillingness to enter the army appear creditable. From the start, radicals had linked the case with Attorney General Palmer's unlawful behavior, which had outraged Dos Passos at the beginning of the decade, and now affidavits from former Justice Department agents seemed to confirm their accusations. Dos Passos' Latin origins and his cosmopolitanism helped to make him exceptionally impatient of agitation against Italians.[28] His travels in Spain had given him some understanding of anarchism among Mediterranean peoples, and he was able to see and present the ideologies of the two defendants sympathetically.

In writing on behalf of the defendants, Dos Passos consulted with anarchists and I.W.W. men on the Sacco-Vanzetti Defense Committee. Felicani he describes as one of the "straightest" people he has ever known.[29] Although Dos Passos became more friendly with the committee than with the Communist defense, he did not participate in controversies between the two.[30]

Before Dos Passos published anything on behalf of Sacco and Vanzetti, he spoke to each of them personally. He seems to have been the member of the *New Masses* staff who visited Vanzetti in the Charlestown House of Correction in June 1926 and heard him complain about how poorly the defense's case was being presented to the public.[31] The interviews were decisive in convincing Dos Passos that the defendants were really as well as technically innocent. Thirty years later, in reviewing the case, he commented: "Any man, I suppose, is capable of any crime, but having talked to Sacco and Vanzetti themselves it's impossible for me to believe they could have committed that particular crime."[32]

Dos Passos' comment on the case in the August 1926 issue of *New Masses* bore a title reflecting his emotional reaction to the visits — "The Pit and the Pendulum." The article differed from his pamphlet of the next year mainly in its brevity. He characterized Vanzetti's anarchism as "less a matter of labels than of feeling, of gentle philosophic brooding." Four months later the official bulletin of the Sacco-Vanzetti Defense Committee carried Dos Passos' account of his interviews with the men.[33] Then in 1927 the committee published Dos Passos' 127-page pamphlet *Facing the Chair*.

Why had Sacco and Vanzetti, Dos Passos asked, been indicted for murder? He recalled as background the hatreds stirred up during the World War; the fears to which government officials had succumbed over the unsolved bombings in 1919; the sailing of the *Buford*; and the January raids. He quoted at length from the pamphlet *Illegal Practices of the Department of Justice*, which twelve well-known lawyers, including Roscoe Pound and Felix Frankfurter, had prepared in May 1920. Public opinion had demanded a solution to the South Braintree murder and robbery, Dos Passos said, and the local authorities had felt that proving reds guilty would please people. The United States Department of Justice had helped frame the two because it had been unable to secure evidence upon which to deport them as radicals.[34]

After the war, Dos Passos said, Vanzetti had gone to New York as a delegate of a group of Italian anarchists, syndicalists, and Socialists. His purpose had been to hire a lawyer and arrange bail for an Italian anarchist printer Andrea Salsedo and Salsedo's friend Elia. In New York Vanzetti had heard rumors that the possession of any literature that might be interpreted as subversive could lead not only to deportation but also to the third degree. On May 3, 1920, Salsedo had jumped or been pushed from the Justice Department's offices on the fourteenth floor of a building where he had been secretly imprisoned for eight weeks and evidently tortured. Two days later Sacco and Vanzetti had set out with other members of their group to hide dangerous literature. When they were arrested, they were carrying the draft of a handbill announcing a meeting to protest Salsedo's death; they were carrying revolvers too, probably out of a feeling of bravado, for they did not intend to let Salsedo's fate befall them.

Where, Dos Passos inquired, did the case stand? On October 23, 1926, Judge Thayer had denied motions for a new trial in a 30,000-word document that read like a personal apologia rather than an impartial decision. Quoting from affidavits as he went along, Dos Passos described the evidence presented at the hearing. The defense could, before Thayer passed sentence, he wrote, appeal to the Supreme Judicial Court on grounds of procedure. Afterward the defense could appeal to the governor for executive clemency, or to the Supreme Court of the United States on the ground that Sacco and Vanzetti had not received due process. In all these recourses, Dos Passos saw little hope. Sacco and Vanzetti, he added, wanted neither a pardon nor a commutation of sentence to life. They were entitled to complete acquittal.

Sacco and Vanzetti were symbols, Dos Passos said, of all the immigrants who had built the country's industries and had received for their work "a helot's position under the bootheels of the Arrow Collar social order"; the two men symbolized the dream of a saner society.[35]

The hardships of immigrant textile workers in Passaic were fresh memories for Dos Passos, but there were older and perhaps more haunting ones: what experiences had led him to contrast, in *Streets of Night*, the vitality of Boston Italians with the frustrated refinement of Cambridge Anglo-Saxons? Drawing force from his discontent with American industrial society, he castigated Sacco's and Vanzetti's accusers.

Although Dos Passos contended that the framing of Sacco and Vanzetti had been conscious and deliberate, he believed that to understand it completely one had to be familiar with "the psychology of frame-ups." There exists an unconscious or subconscious desire, he wrote, to incriminate people whom one dislikes. For half a century, and particularly since the assassination of McKinley, the anarchist had been a "bogey" in America. Dos Passos traced the ideals of Latin anarchists back to the hope of Christ's kingdom on earth. The hope had disappeared after the first millennium, but in modern times many Italians had looked forward to finding an ideal land in America. Those Italian immigrants who had not yielded to the system of "dawg eat dawg" (here we may recall the opportunism of Fuselli, the second-generation Italian American in *Three Soldiers*) had become anarchists.

At the Plymouth trial, Thayer had said that highway robbery was consistent with Vanzetti's ideas. If there were terrorists among the anarchists, Dos Passos asserted, their presence did not make the two terms synonymous; there had been terrorists among oppressed and despised sects since the world began. Of course, employers found it easy to think of an anarchist who organized their employees as a terrorist. Still, Dos Passos mused, there was perhaps a reason deeper than loss of profits for the hatred of Sacco and Vanzetti. "The people of Massachusetts centuries ago suffered and hoped terribly for the City of God. . . . The irrational features of this case of attempted communal murder can only be explained by a bitterness so deep that it has been forgotten by the very people it moves most fervidly."[36]

Dos Passos devoted the final fifty-six pages of his pamphlet to a chronological account of the case, including a detailed analysis of the murder trial based on his perusal of 3,900 pages of official transcript. At Vanzetti's trial for attempted robbery, Dos Passos wrote, his lawyer probably had sacrificed him deliberately. The lawyer had certainly shown criminal negligence in not permitting Vanzetti to take the stand and in not filing a bill of exceptions. Some of the testimony at the first trial was, Dos Passos added, patently incredible; moreover, several state witnesses had changed their original accounts to favor the prosecution. If Vanzetti's witnesses had been Americans instead of Italians, their testimony would have been accepted. At the second trial, Dos Passos wrote, the identification testimony had been overwhelmingly in favor of Sacco and Vanzetti, but the court had made patriotism an issue and had stressed the question of whether the defendants' behavior upon arrest indicated consciousness of guilt. Their behavior had in reality been due to "the consciousness of the dead body of their comrade Salsedo lying smashed in the spring dawn two days before on the pavement of Park Row."[37]

Dos Passos had written in "The Pit and the Pendulum" that defense attorney William G. Thompson wished to continue believing in the honesty of Massachusetts justice and in the fairness and humanity of the typical Harvard-bred Bostonian. As the facts he encountered every day made such belief difficult, Thompson wished he were out of the case. In the pamphlet, Dos Passos wrote more favorably of Thompson. It was largely due, he said, to Thompson's personal influence and his reputation for conservatism and integrity that lawyers, college professors, ministers, and newspaper readers generally were now becoming interested in the Sacco-Vanzetti case. Thayer's last denial of a new trial had helped to awaken some of the "respected" members of the community, people who had not suspected that anything but justice was meted out in the courts. The truth had to be told so that if Sacco and Vanzetti were executed, no one could plead ignorance of the facts. If they died, Dos Passos declared, in words crucial for his own history, "what little faith millions of men have in the chance of Justice in this country will die with them."[38]

The Supreme Judicial Court rejected all further appeals of the defense, and on April 9, 1927, Judge Thayer sentenced Sacco and Vanzetti to death. On June 1 Governor Fuller took the extraordinary step of appointing an advisory committee to investigate whether the trial had been fairly conducted, whether subsequently discovered evidence justified a new trial, and whether Sacco and Vanzetti seemed guilty beyond a reasonable doubt. This action was an acknowledgment of the steady growth of doubt among lawyers, newspaper editors, and other influential citizens. There was, on the other hand, widespread hostility to a review. The Massachusetts House had on April 14 defeated by a vote of 146 to 6 a resolution calling for a commission to study the case. Probably four in five, perhaps nine in ten, Boston lawyers held that nothing should be permitted to damage the reputation of the state judicial system. A majority of the people of Massachusetts believed that the major need in the Sacco-Vanzetti affair was to protect the American way of life against radicals throughout the world.[39]

The report of the Governor's committee upheld the trial and the verdict. It asserted that Judge Thayer had tried to be scrupulously fair, although he had been indiscreet in conversation with outsiders during the trial. As for District Attorney Katzmann's cross-examination, it had been justified as an attempt to determine whether Sacco's "profession that he and his friends were radicals liable to deportation was true, or was merely assumed for the purpose of the defense."[40] The report dismissed Madeiros' confession as worthless and uncorroborated, and it denied that newly discovered evidence justified a new trial. Sacco and Vanzetti were guilty beyond a reasonable doubt, the report declared, adding that their guilt rested upon a cumulation of factors, none of which was conclusive.

Upon the release of the report, Dos Passos wrote an open letter to the most prominent member of the committee, President Lowell of Harvard. The letter, remarkable for its heated tone as well as for its content, declared that Lowell was making himself and, indirectly, the university a party to judicial murder. Many people interested in the case had felt, Dos Passos wrote, that Lowell's appointment to the committee "assured at least a modicum of fair play and of historical perspective." But these people had

U.P.I.

Dos Passos among pickets in Boston after Sacco and Vanzetti were condemned to death. His aspect is still an observer's, but his hands and face convey anguish. (Or is it outrage or defiance?) Dorothy Parker walks behind him in the picket line.

been disappointed first by the secrecy of the hearings and finally by the report. He told Lowell:

. . . you are allowing a Massachusetts politician to use the name of Harvard to cover his own bias and to whitewash all the dirty business of the arrest of these men at the time of the anarchist raids and their subsequent slow torture by the spiteful and soulless mechanism of the law. They have probably told you that this was a mere local decision on a Boston murder case, but to any man with enough intelligence to read the daily papers it must be clear that somehow it has ceased being a Boston murder case. . . . Sacco and Vanzetti . . . have become huge symbols on the stage of the world. . . .

The report in its entirety is an apology for the conduct of the trial rather than an impartial investigation. Reading it, the suspicion grows paragraph by paragraph that its aim was not to review but to make respectable the proceedings of Judge Thayer and the District Attorney's office. Not in a single phrase is there an inkling of a sense on your part or on that of your colleagues of the importance of the social and racial backgrounds of the trial. Your loose use of the words ''socialistic'' and ''communistic'' prove that you are ignorant or careless of the differences in mentality involved in partisanship in the various schools of revolutionary thought.

This is a matter of life and death, not only for Sacco and Vanzetti but for the civilization that Harvard University is supposed to represent. The Sacco-Vanzetti case has become part of the world struggle between the capitalist class and the working class, between those who have power and those who are struggling to get it. In a man in high office ignorance of the new sprouting forces that are remaking society, whether he is with them or against them, is little short of criminal. It is inconceivable that intelligent reading men can be ignorant in this day of the outlines of anarchist philosophy. Instead of crying ignorance it would be franker to admit that as anarchists and agitators you hate these men and disapprove of their ideas and methods. But are you going to sacrifice the integrity of the legal system to that feeling? Are you going to prove by a bloody reprisal that the radical contention that a man holding unpopular ideas cannot get a free trial in our courts is true?

I cannot feel that either you or your colleagues have understood the full purport of your decision. If you had you would certainly have made out a more careful case for yourselves, one less full of loopholes and contradictions. It is upon men of your class and position that will rest the inevitable decision as to whether the coming struggle for the reorganization of society shall be bloodless and fertile or inconceivably bloody and destructive. It is high time that you realized the full extent of the responsibility on your shoulders.[41]

Until the very end most of the people with whom Dos Passos was working on the case were confident that Sacco and Vanzetti would obtain a new trial. The report of Governor Fuller's committee and the refusal of Justices Holmes and Brandeis to issue a writ of habeas corpus astonished them. Dos Passos (covering the action for the *Daily Worker*), Edna St. Vincent Millay, Hibben, and Lawson were among those arrested during demonstrations against the executions.[42]

Felix Frankfurter had concluded a book defending Sacco and Vanzetti by asserting that while American criminal procedure had its defects, one would be mistaken to "find in an occasional striking illustration of its fallibilities an attack upon its foundations or lack of loyalty to its purposes."[43] But to Dos Passos, reflecting upon the heavy penalties imposed under the wartime Sedition Act and conscious of current judicial and police abuses, the executions were evidence that opponents of capitalism could not expect justice in the courts. In appealing to Lowell's conservatism, Dos Passos invoked some of his own characteristics and desires; his radicalism was to a great extent conservative in its inspiration, motivated by a desire to safeguard or reclaim historic freedoms and to sustain civilization.

The Sacco-Vanzetti affair was as important in directing his interests as a creative writer as in directing his politics. The affair supplied a new impetus for his studying American society — its leaders, its myths, its ideologies, its sources of information.

Gardner Jackson, one of the leaders of the Sacco-Vanzetti Defense Committee, recalled that on the night when the report of the Lowell Committee was issued, he and Dos Passos went to see the publisher of the *Boston Herald*, Robert Lincoln O'Brien. The *Herald* had the previous year published a highly influential editorial denouncing Judge Thayer's handling of the case. Now O'Brien outraged Jackson by his urbane manner, his refusal to listen, his wisecracks. After the two had departed, Dos Passos said to Jackson, "Don't take it so hard. He's nothing but an old feather duster."[44]

"They Are Dead Now — ," Dos Passos' first literary comment on the executions, in October 1927, may appear merely to echo his remark to Jackson (and echo a theme of *The Garbage Man* and *Manhattan Transfer*) as it contrasts the physically dead Sacco and Vanzetti with their spiritually dead executioners. But Dos Passos had greatly altered his view, already a sufficiently

Arrested for picketing for Sacco and Vanzetti in front of the Massachusetts State House.

troubled one, of the spiritual solvency of most middle-class Americans.[45] He now undertook to study, analyze, and discuss their class and to make explicit judgments upon it. In *Airways, Inc.* (1928) he described the partiality of a middle-class family toward capitalism, but that play was a comparatively minor effort. For Dos Passos, the culmination of the Sacco-Vanzetti affair was *U.S.A.*, a study of the minds, characters, and fates of a dozen Americans during the first third of the twentieth century.

During the year of the executions, Dos Passos was deeply involved in theatrical work. The Sacco-Vanzetti affair helped shape not only *Airways, Inc.*, but also some of his pronouncements about American theater. Since his dramatic criticism inextricably linked politics and aesthetics, the affair somehow became connected for him with a workers' theater and the absence of a fourth wall.

While he was abroad after the completion of *Manhattan Transfer*, Dos Passos received a telegram from Lawson reporting that the banker Otto Kahn was advancing money to launch an experimental theater. Was Dos Passos willing to be one of the directors?[46] From Morocco — where we catch glimpses of him walking among the mountains, studying Arabic, and sympathizing with the Berbers' war against colonialism — Dos Passos returned to the United States in March 1926 and assisted in establishing the new theater — in addition to helping Sacco and Vanzetti and observing the Passaic strike.[47]

By February 1927 Dos Passos, John Howard Lawson, Michael Gold, and two other men, Em Jo Basshe and Francis Edwards Faragoh, had formed a producing group and leased the Fifty-second Street Theatre.[48] They hoped that their approach, repertory theater with playwright directors, would allow them to experiment with productions and to educate an audience. The New Playwrights Theatre staged two plays in the spring of 1927, Lawson's *Loud Speaker* and Em Jo Basshe's *Earth*. Since neither was financially successful, the producers economized by moving to the small Cherry Lane Playhouse in Greenwich Village.[49]

In November 1927 Michael Gold referred to the venture as a *New Masses* theater, and he told readers of the periodical that the New Playwrights Theatre had established the same goals in the drama as had *New Masses* in literature and the graphic arts.[50] Gold's article, which appealed for readers' support, probably indicated some reorientation. Though the New Playwrights differed in their aims, the group apparently began more devoted to method than to revolution. Subsequently, proclaiming the enterprise a workers' theater, they talked more than before about revolution and the nature of their audience.[51]

Dos Passos' motives for a change in emphasis are clear. He and other radicals had for some time been thinking of theater as a means of reaching a larger public than was accessible to them through periodicals. From the new methods of artistic expression, in painting, music, cinema, ballet, etc., experienced after the war, they hoped to devise ways for theater to appeal to the common man.[52] But it was no coincidence that the executions of Sacco and Vanzetti came at the end of the first season and that Dos Passos published his article "Towards a Revolutionary Theatre" for the second season.* Here Dos Passos linked good theater in America with revolution:

> By revolutionary I mean that such a theatre must break with the present day theatrical tradition, not with the general traditions of the theatre, and that it must draw its life and ideas from the conscious sections of the industrial and white collar working classes which are out to get control of the great flabby mass of capitalist society and mould it to their own purpose. In an ideal state it might be possible for a group to be alive and have no subversive political tendency. At present it is not possible.[53]

He now applied many of his previous theories about the drama to a workers' theater. By a theater, he indicated — as he had in his discussions of theater in Madrid — he meant a group of people, part of whom put on plays and the rest of whom formed the audience. When, later, he explained his insistence on abolishing the picture-

---

*An event occurring just before the executions of Sacco and Vanzetti could not have left Dos Passos feeling that radical artists — especially Jews, Italians, and other unpopular peoples — had a promising future in the United States. In June 1927 an eighteen-year-old Jewish student, David Gordon, had been sentenced to an indeterminate term, possibly three years, in the New York City Reformatory for writing and publishing in the *Daily Worker* a strongly worded, derogatory ode to America. Among the judges' questions was how long his name had been Gordon. Dos Passos wrote a protesting editorial in *New Masses* and sent letters to F. Scott Fitzgerald, Dreiser, and other friends, asking that they appeal to the parole board. "If this kid ought to be in jail," he wrote Dreiser, "we all ought to be." Dos Passos, "Lese Majeste," *New Masses*, III (July 1927), 3; undated letter from Dos Passos to Theodore Dreiser. The letter, mimeographed, was prefaced by a handwritten note and accompanied by a copy of the poem and an excerpt from the court record. Fitzgerald received the same letter and a similar note.

frame stage, he called the relationship of his aesthetics with revolution that of form with content:

The revolutionary theatre will aim to justify the ways of politics (mass action) to the individual-in-the-mass much the way the Greek theatre justified the ways of the priestinterpreted gods to the citizens of the cityrepublics. The whole scale and category of ideas is entirely different from that of the bourgeois theatres which aimed to make the private lives of wealthy or hopetobewealthy people interesting, exciting tragic or funny to them for a couple of hours after dinner.[54]

Dos Passos' three-act play *Airways, Inc.*, first published in 1928 and produced by the New Playwrights Theatre the next year, is much more realistic in technique than *The Garbage Man*.[55] Though deriving largely from the Passaic strike and the supposedly framed executions of Sacco and Vanzetti, *Airways, Inc.* gives expression to others of Dos Passos' concerns. Anti-Semitism in the play is probably the same outlet for a frustrated native Protestant majority that Dos Passos saw anti-Italianism as being in Massachusetts. The Chamber of Commerce and the American Legion are elements in a joyless capitalistic world indifferent to the requirements of such normal relationships as marriage and family life. Over the whole community hover the threat of industrial warfare without quarter and the specter of Fascism, two new concerns in Dos Passos' drama and fiction.

The leading characters are the Turners, a lower-middle-class Protestant family who live in one of an only partly completed row of one-family houses in the suburbs. Behind these houses stand the Hartshorn Mills, the Swastika Refrigerator Company, and the Universal Electric Plant. Walter Goldberg, a Jewish labor leader, is conducting a strike of textile workers at Hartshorn Mills. The Turners are involved because Goldberg is also trying to win the hand of Martha, a member of their family. Martha is a woman of almost thirty who, since the death of her mother, has been serving as housekeeper for her father and brothers. During the course of the play she summons courage to break with her family, most of whom dislike the strike leader as a radical and a Jew, and agrees to marry Goldberg.

The Turners identify their interests with capitalism, despite the fact that they are being strangled morally and economically by it. Claude, the eldest brother (obviously one of the "deadalive" in Dos Passos' works), is a man of about thirty-five from whom

"fifteen years of white-collar slavery have taken all the joy."[56]
At his American Legion post he plays pool and talks about menaces.
Claude says that he cannot marry on the $30 a week he earns
as an employee of the Chamber of Commerce; nevertheless, he
complains that the strikers, who have been receiving only $17.50,
are destroying confidence and depressing real estate values. When
Martha tells him that he does not know anything about what Goldberg
is trying to do except what he reads in the papers, Claude replies
with words the playwright intended for dramatic irony: "That's
enough, ain't it?"[57]

The youngest brother, Elmer, is a twenty-six-year-old inventor
and aviator who holds several flight records but is ignorant of everything that does not pertain directly to gasoline engines. In some
ways his situation is similar to that of Charley Anderson in *U.S.A.*
The promoters of an airline, All-American Airways, Inc., plan
to use Elmer's reputation to sell securities to the public and are
making him a top executive. Elmer, who has swallowed whole
the prevailing belief in promotion, does not know the extent to
which finance is incompatible with technology. He complains that
the promoters are not interested in aviation, but he is unable to
formulate his objections as social theory.

Dad Turner is an old man who cannot get a job in industry.
He blames the failure of his career on his once having stepped
on J. P. Morgan's toe in an elevator, for he is sure that the financier
must have pursued him vindictively through life. Instead of linking
his present plight to a need for social reform, the old man clings
to individualism and talks obsessively about how his rotary alcohol
engine will revolutionize industry. He realizes that he has lost all
status and respect at home, and early in the play commits suicide
because of this plight.

As a favor for a sick friend, Elmer agrees to drop Chamber
of Commerce leaflets over a strikers' rally. But he has had too
much to drink, and when he attempts to stunt, the plane crashes
and his spine is broken. At the same rally, a gun is slipped into
Goldberg's pocket, and he is arrested for murder.[58] He is convicted,
in spite of Elmer's testimony that he had counseled the men against
violence, and is sent to the electric chair.

Some of the characters' comments on the execution may reflect
the attitudes of Dos Passos' own acquaintances toward the killing
of Sacco and Vanzetti. An old European revolutionist who has
been living with the Turners and, like Dad Turner, has been uttering

chorus-like reminiscences, expresses ideas contrary to all that Dos Passos has stood for: "We will have an enormous funeral procession through the main streets of the city. They'll try to break it up, there'll be wounded and killed at his funeral. . . . The electric current that burned out our comrade's life must burn all softness, all tenderness out of our lives. We must be steel automatons."[59]

To be a steel automaton, to burn all tenderness out of his life — whatever Dos Passos' anger, such determination was alien and repugnant to his temperament. Such toughness is an achievement of fictional characters who appear in *The Big Money* as, in varying degrees, the "deadalive" of the left.

Martha voices utter disillusionment: "America, where I've scurried from store to subway to church to home, America that I've never known."[60] At the end of the play she is stunned and miserable, but she clings to what she considers her class. Elmer is permanently paralyzed, and his girl friend has left him for one of the promoters. Claude, having become an official of All-American Airways, Inc., boasts that the family is on "easy street" from now on.

Airways, Inc. ran for four weeks before "an audience made up largely of empty seats." The producers presented the play on a solidly built set with a spotlight illuminating most brightly the area where action was taking place at the moment; to bring the actors close to the audience, they extended the apron of the stage beyond the orchestra pit. Dos Passos later attributed the play's lack of popular success to audiences' being accustomed to the "pictureframe stage" and "Belasco realism" of Broadway.[61] But the *New York Times* and *New York Herald Tribune* critics complained far less about the setting than about the language and development. Brooks Atkinson was annoyed by a lack of realism in some of the speeches, and both he and Richard Watts, Jr., of the *New York Herald Tribune*, held that the strike and airways narratives did not converge satisfactorily.[62]

Two comments in the *Daily Worker*, by A. B. Magil and Michael Gold, were more free with praise. Magil reviewing *Airways, Inc.* found it true to life, intelligent, clear, and disciplined in emotion, though hampered by too much thematic material. He praised the play as a satire of petty bourgeois life in America and remarked that Dos Passos had gone left in the past few years and was now close to Communism.

Magil seems to have wanted the play to be entirely a weapon, and not a mere rapier either. In spite of its merits, he felt it had defects as a social drama: too much labor conflict took place off stage; not the strike, but the fact that a Jewish strike leader had fallen in love with Martha, disturbed the Turner family; and Goldberg's death was presented, not as a social tragedy, but as Martha's private tragedy. Magil noted that Martha, along with other members of the Turner family, became wealthy at the end of the play; if this was supposed to be ironical, he wrote, it failed in its intention.[63]

Michael Gold in another article dwelt primarily on the ideology of the play. *Airways, Inc.* was Dos Passos' most important work, he claimed, though he thought the author might disagree. Gold wrote that Dos Passos was growing increasingly class-conscious. In *Three Soldiers* he had described rebellion from the point of view of a bourgeois pacifist, and in *Manhattan Transfer* he had written from that of a reporter. Now, in *Airways, Inc.*, Dos Passos had begun to analyze society in Marxian terms. Each of the characters was a definite "social type," and the play dealt with the most important theme in the United States and in the world, that of the class struggle.[64]

The comments by Magil and Gold were early instances of criticism from the left which obscured facets of Dos Passos' thought even while revealing others. Dos Passos says that he read Volume I of Marx's *Capital* with interest after the war, but that he read little else by him except his historical commentary (the "Louis Napoleon stuff" interested him greatly). He does not consider himself well-versed in Marx, but says his opinions were affected by Marxism's being in the air during the twenties.[65] *Airways, Inc.* is not a Marxist play, despite the attention its author gave to Marxism during the decade. It is nevertheless in large part a satire on the American white-collar class for not recognizing their own interests as workers. The final ironic success of the Turner family does not confuse the satirical intention.

Ideas voiced by Thorstein Veblen appear again and again in *Airways, Inc.*[66] Elmer Turner is an inventor and technician who profits by serving as a pawn for promoters. Veblenite ideas of the leisure class appear when Edna sneers at Eddy for becoming a carpenter's helper and asks why he doesn't get a job "doin' clean work, like in an office?" When Goldberg explains to Martha that his experience with "the wornout laws" of Judaism helped shape his reactions to society, he is offering an argument that appeared in Veblen's essay "The Intellectual Pre-eminence of Jews in Modern Europe."[67] Still, we must not overstress even Veblen's influence, for Dos Passos attempted to describe the realities around him rather than adhere to theories.

Airways, Inc. was a turning point in Dos Passos' literary career. For the first time he used fairly recognizable public figures as characters, as he did in *U.S.A.* and in many of his subsequent novels. Goldberg is a tremendously popular leader of a textile strike in which the issues are much the same as they were at Passaic. Like Weisbord, he is close-mouthed about his politics. His co-worker Eliza Donahue may suggest Elizabeth Gurley Flynn. Elmer suggests Charles A. Lindbergh, who was pre-empting headlines during the last months of the Sacco-Vanzetti affair. After his famous flight to Paris, Lindbergh went on a good-will mission in Central America for the State Department. When Gardner Jackson heard about the mission, he wrote an open letter to Lindbergh citing American imperialism in that area. The letter, which appeared in the anti-Fascist *Lantern* a month before a contribution by Dos Passos on Italy, raised the very questions about Lindbergh that Dos Passos raised about Elmer.[68]

Another of the similarities between *Airways, Inc.* and *U.S.A.* is the portrayal of the mass mind as the result of identifiable influences. When Elmer and Mae sing "Close the doors they're coming through the windows" — a song which Dos Passos in *U.S.A.* juxtaposes with headlines about Rudolph Valentino's funeral — and when Claude gapes at the news of the drunken murder of a husband by an adulterous couple, the reader can identify elements that enter into the "Newsreel." One of the Turner sons is named after Edison, who like Valentino receives a biography in *U.S.A.* Behind popular heroes such as Valentino and Elmer himself, lurks the public relations man, a paid manipulator of opinion. He claims Dos Passos' attention in *The Garbage Man* and appears as J. Ward Moorehouse in *U.S.A.*

The theme of the rich pre-empting the sky appears in a confused form in this play. One may note, if only as a curiosity, an aerial incident during the textile strike of 1926. The day after the police of Clifton and Passaic attacked photographers and reporters, an airplane carrying a newsreel photographer swooped over the combat area in wide circles.[69] In Dos Passos' play, while real estate men participate in the plan to found All-American Airways, Inc., in order to raise land values in Florida, one of the strikers says: "Look up in the sky an' see the clouds; company don't own the clouds. Send aeroplanes up, but don't own the sky, not yet.''[70] Dos Passos returned to his airplane theme in the ''Vag'' piece that concludes *U.S.A.*

Though avoiding the business side, Dos Passos seems to have done more work than anyone else for the New Playwrights Theatre. Most interested in designing for the stage and in painting scenery, he was also active in discussing and defending the playwrights' work.[71] His defense of experimental theater now seems more strongly apposite to Stalin, who imposed ''socialist realism'' on Russia in the next decades, than to American critics.

Objecting in January 1928 to Sender Garlin's *Daily Worker* review of Lawson's *The International*, Dos Passos wrote that Garlin's comments seemed ''to be written from the same angle as those in the capitalist press, the angle of contemporary Broadway 'realism.''' The New Playwrights, he said, had their backs against the wall. At a time when theater and movies were the only arts socially and politically important, reviewers for revolutionary periodicals ought to understand the New Playwrights' technical aims and the relationship of these aims to content.[72]

In an article published at the end of the 1928 season, he cited a lack of political support as one of the problems the New Playwrights were encountering: the socialist press had called the producers ''communists in sheep's clothing'' and the *Daily Worker* had discovered deviations from Communist tenets. Another problem, he wrote, was that people demanded a ''Ritzy finish'' that was incompatible with experimentation, growth — and a low budget. Most troublesome was a circumstance that he must have seen as imperiling his entire concept of a workers' theater: experiments in thought and art in the United States, he wrote, interested only ''a few highbrows.'' The people who went to prize fights and baseball games would stand for only ''the most smoothworn routine'' in the theater.[73]

The New Playwrights offered only two plays in the early months of 1929, Upton Sinclair's *Singing Jailbirds* and Dos Passos' *Airways, Inc.* Then the producers closed the doors, citing lack of support from the various factions of labor. Dos Passos recollects that his resignation, some time before the end, was due to a need for more daylight writing hours than theatrical life allowed and to political irritation with Communists.[74] Despite his desire to write

for a communal theater, it was through books and periodicals that
he could reach his largest audiences.

Throughout the 1920s Dos Passos continued to travel abroad
frequently, and sometime during the decade he had opportunities
to observe at first hand Fascism in Italy, the continuing class warfare
in Mexico, and the development of Communism in Russia. The
two pieces he published on Italy, though quite dissimilar in tone,
show clearly that he considered Fascism a purely destructive force
which offered no promise for the future. Stimulus toward writing
his bitterly satirical report on Fascism in Savona "A City That
Died by Heartfailure" (1928) might have come from talks with
Italians during the Sacco-Vanzetti defense. (Carlo Tresca was one
of the people he met during the affair.) And he might have been
prompted further by a desire to help a friend in a good cause;
the piece appeared in the *Lantern*, the pioneer anti-Fascist periodical
which Gardner Jackson undertook to edit as an aftermath of the
Sacco-Vanzetti affair, and to which he asked Dos Passos to contribute.[75]

Late in 1926 Dos Passos was in Mexico, a land he soon described
in the Mac episodes of *U.S.A.* The country was still undergoing
revolution, as it had been when John Reed portrayed it. Indian
peasants fought landlords over their alienated commons while the
government fought Yankee corporations over oil claims. In Mexico
City Dos Passos listened to storekeepers complain that business
was bad; to American salesmen at Sanborn's store frighten each
other every day with rumors of new revolutions and soothe each
other with the thought that "eventually we'll intervene"; and to
correspondents at the bar of the Regis discuss the power of Andrew
Mellon.[76]

With Xavier Guerrero, a Mexican painter and Communist,
Dos Passos visited Morelos, the state where the agrarian leader
Emiliano Zapata had ruled. All the "dollar-minded," Dos Passos
wrote, were pointing to Morelos as an example of the failure of
the agrarian revolution. The villagers of Morelos told him the other
side of the story: since nobody could show title to the land, nobody
dared to cultivate it. Until land was redistributed in Mexico, Dos
Passos declared, Mexican politics would be unstable. Insofar as
President Calles had been able to effect land reform, the country
was united in his support.[77]

Dos Passos visited the *Secretaria* of public education to see

Diego Rivera's paintings. He seems to have gone also to the *Preparatoria*, where Clemente Orozco was working, and perhaps to the school which Roberto Montenegro was decorating. The next year he described the public murals of Rivera and Orozco. Since most Mexicans could not read, Dos Passos said, the only way to explain the revolution to them was to paint it on the wall.[78]

The Mexican revolution probably interested Dos Passos as a native phenomenon analogous to what he wanted in the United States. The revolution had not been inspired from Russia, as he carefully pointed out.[79] Perhaps the paintings of Rivera and Orozco, by suggesting how art might explain a revolution, furnished a small amount of inspiration for the New Playwrights Theatre. But it was the Bolshevik rather than the Mexican revolution that Dos Passos heard about constantly and discussed with his associates in the theater and on the staff of *New Masses*. In 1928 he needed to take a trip, for his theatrical work had been taxing. Since he had never been in Russia proper, he undertook a second trip to the Soviet Union. He embarked for Copenhagen in the late spring, visited friends in London and Paris, went by train across Germany (meeting van den Arend in Berlin), then by boat to Finland, and by train again to Leningrad.

His visit in Russia, lasting from summer till December 1928, occurred in the midst of a crucial transition in that country, not all of which was visible or predictable while he was there.[80] After the Kronstadt revolt in March 1921 Lenin's New Economic Policy, of compromise with capitalism to increase production and revive the country, superseded War Communism. Agricultural levies were replaced with definite taxes, and peasants were allowed to sell their grain; private individuals were permitted to carry on small-scale manufacturing; and a more orthodox form of internal trade and distribution of goods replaced the socialist system. These changes so revitalized the Soviet economy that by 1927 industry and agriculture reached something like their prewar productivity, and the Soviet Union seemed well on the way to a stable economy.

This was not to be. Most of the tiny holdings created during the revolution produced no surplus, and big farmers demanded more for food than the townspeople could pay. In January 1928 the government's grain purchases from the peasants fell, if we can believe Stalin, two million tons short of the minimum needed for the cities. The Politbureau thereupon ordered illegal and arbitrary "emergency measures," including raids on peasants' houses. In 1928 and even more in 1929 all but the very poorest peasants were crushed by excessively high taxes and many direct levies.

Stalin, who had achieved virtual rule two years after the end of the civil war, was in the later years of the decade attaining complete ascendancy. During Dos Passos' stay people actually introduced friends half laughingly as Trotskyites,[81] but Trotsky had been expelled from the Politbureau in October 1926, from the Bolshevik party a year later, and was to be expelled from Russia early in 1929.

About the middle of 1929 Stalin sent many thousands of agents into the countryside to liquidate the kulak class and force "middle peasants" into collective farms. The approximately two million kulaks subsequently lost their property and were barred from the collectives. Government military operations, peasants' destruction of their own property, and mass deportations followed.

Because collective farms required machinery, Stalin initiated decisive moves toward industrialization. The rewards of the revolution were astounding, Isaac Deutscher wrote of the collectivization, the industrialization, and the mass achievement of literacy; "but so was its cost: the complete loss, by a whole generation, of spiritual and political freedom."[82]

Dos Passos arrived in Russia at the Finland Station in Leningrad. Eleven years earlier Lenin had made his first October speeches in the city, and Dos Passos was amazed to find it now so quiet. He visited the museum; Smolny Institute, where Lenin had lived and worked until the government moved to Moscow; some of the palaces; the local rest institution in what had been the royal stables; the building that housed the Leningrad Soviet; the locomotive works at Red Putilov; the café under the Europskaya Hotel (a place where money still reigned but which, he was told, the police permitted to stay open so that they could know where the criminals were); and a moving picture studio. The city seemed to be "the burntout crater" of a volcano. "Things I've read about it, Dostoyevski's St. Petersburg, and the Petrograd of Jack Reed's and Ransome's despatches still are more vivid in my mind than this huge empty city full of great handsome buildings. . . . I kept wishing I'd been there eleven years before."[83]

After a summer stop in Moscow Dos Passos went on a trip down the Volga River and on an exploratory expedition in the Caucasus, then returned to Moscow. Walking about the city in

November, he found that the houses of the eighteenth and nineteenth century merchants across the river from the Kremlin interested him more than did the citadel itself. In the old markets and in the restaurants, he saw a few remnants of the business class "in their leather jackets with their beady eyes and predatory faces"; some of the business class, he learned, were being reformed in penal institutions. He went to the Grand Hotel, where the foreign correspondents seemed to him "afraid that they'll catch bolshevism and have to rearrange their lives." He visited a kindergarten, the Sanitary Propaganda Theatre, and the Writers' Resthouse outside of Moscow. Russians were not yet afraid to be seen with foreigners, and when he told people that he was an American writer, they were helpful.[84] At a village not far from Moscow where he went to see the parents of a friend, he ate bread and butter with jam and drank tea and plum brandy. Listening to the farmers there, he felt that at last he was learning the truth; they told him that they needed the progress the revolution would bring and that they and the bureaucrats had to learn to work together, though it was not easy.[85]

Dos Passos thought of himself as a reporter of the Russian attempt to reorganize society, but the scope of the attempt seemed so great that he decided to make his approach through the theater. He spoke to theater people like the Tairovs and to the motion picture directors Pudovkin and Eisenstein, and he witnessed with delight the variety of offerings by the Moscow theater in the fall of 1928.[86]

During the New Playwrights period, he had become familiar with the work of Meyerhold — *avant-garde* leader, antirealist, and central figure of the Russian theater in the decade after the revolution. Dos Passos and his colleagues probably got to know his work through the German producer-director Piscator. Meyerhold being neither in Moscow nor in Leningrad at the same time as Dos Passos, the men did not meet, but Meyerhold's *Roar China* provided Dos Passos' most exciting theatrical experience that fall.[87]

The temptation to contrast Moscow theater with New York theater was irresistible. On Broadway the primary motive of everyone except members of the technical staff and of the audience was, Dos Passos wrote, economic speculation. The audience wanted to live vicariously, "to feel themselves part of the imperial American procession towards more money, more varnish, more ritz, that obsesses all our lives." Theater buildings were crude in Moscow and the audience did not dress up, but the people went to the theater "to feel part of the victorious march through history of the world proletariat." The "intelligently directed enthusiasm" and the "immense powers of absorption" of Russian theatrical people impressed Dos Passos even more than did the institutional structure of the Russian theater, some of which had been inherited from Czarist days; but he noted with approval that every theater in Russia had a corporate existence and a permanent tradition and that around the big theaters sprang up subsidiary studios in which experimentation took place and from which new theaters developed. Not foreseeing that Stalin would stifle artistic freedom, he was optimistic about the Russian theater; it was embarking on a period of tremendous growth, he felt, while the American theater was expiring.[88]

Dos Passos probably entered Russia wanting very much, somewhere on earth, to find promise. Despite his early distaste for Bolshevism, he came with the feeling that Russia was the frontier of tomorrow and that it had been cleared of all "the instituted lies-by-common-consent."[89] Many of his experiences seemed to support his viewpoint. When he visited the locomotive works in Leningrad, he noted how everybody with whom he talked spoke of studying engineering, literature, languages. He felt more as if he were going through a college than through a factory. At the union rest home the physician, who worked eighteen hours a day, asked timidly what the visitors thought of the institution; it was characteristic of Dos Passos' demands upon human society that he was delighted by the man's sense of purpose rather than shocked by the length of his workday. At the Leningrad museum, a young non-Communist unskilled workman from the Kirghiz steppes told Dos Passos that only since the revolution had his people had books. Their young men no longer clung to Islam but were anxious to know more about revolutionary ideas and to find out what was good for the world. Europe was dying, Dos Passos wrote, doubtless referring to its economic woes and to the growth of Fascism; in Russia, on the other hand, a civilization was being born:

But the Moscow of now, the Moscow of today, the Moscow of the new order, how can you get hold of it? . . . I hear the tramp of it under my window every morning when the Red Army soldiers pass with their deep throaty singing, I see it in the kindergarten I sometimes go to see that's so far away at the end of a trolley line, I see it most among the youngsters who run the Sanitary Propaganda Theatre where

Alexandra directs the plays, energy, enthusiasm, selfeffacement (it's not at all like the Y.M.C.A.) and that fervid curiosity and breadth of interest that is the magnificent earmark of the Russian mind. I see it in the communist friends I make who are all the time working, arguing, organizing, teaching, doing office work and who, no matter how pale and haggard from overwork they are when they come home to those late afternoon Moscow dinners, are always ready to talk, explain, ask questions.[90]

Communist students from the University of Odessa, who were on an excursion to Smolny, asked: "Why can't the workers in England realize that we are working for them as much as for our-selves?" But the students did not seem interested in Dos Passos' pertinent questions about freedom of opinion and about the economic status of the peasants. Dos Passos knew "very little Russian," but enough of Communist and capitalistic jargon to realize the pitfalls among words and phrases he was encountering. The U.S.S.R. was difficult to understand, he felt, partly because visitors like himself had trouble with the languages and partly because language hides as well as reveals facts. One could drink wine over slogans and feel fine, but how did one get under the slogans?[91]

He heard disquieting stories. The Kirghiz in Leningrad said that the workers in his factory spoke as they wished, but he was vague about the consequences: "Of course if someone made a habit of talking directly against the Party, the Gaypayoo might bring pressure to bear. He wasn't sure."[92] A Russian critic whom Dos Passos visited said that people like himself who had missed the "red train" could not publish what they wished; they never knew when they would be arrested or exiled, and the Gaypayoo annoyed their relatives and children. Still, the critic preferred the Communists to the Czar, for now the censors at least gave reasons and listened to what one had to say.[93] An Englishman who invited Dos Passos to his small apartment said he had come to Russia to work because he had been full of enthusiasm for the revolution, but his stay had become a nightmare. The government had turned upon Trotskyites, old revolutionaries, and any others who got in the way. When the old revolutionary sailors had revolted at Kron-stadt, they had been handed over to Cheka agents to be butchered with excruciating sadism, he told his dumbfounded visitor. The Englishman said he could not leave the country because he could not earn enough money and because the government would not permit his wife, a member of the old Russian intelligentsia, to go with him. He was afraid to make inquiries for fear the police might arrest her. The police came at night, and they worked in secrecy.

"But the Tcheka's gone," Dos Passos exclaimed when the Englishman spoke about Kronstadt. "They had most of them shot. The terror is over."[94] It was nevertheless evidences of police terror that led Dos Passos to decline to endorse Bolshevik Russia, although he returned far more impressed than he had been in 1921. His refusal was not hostile or ringing, for he could not discern which government activities were revolutionary and temporary and which had become permanent. But he made some of his qualms public almost immediately, and he revealed others in the book *In All Countries*, published in 1934.[95]

Dos Passos added to and interpreted these accounts in *The Theme Is Freedom* in 1956: "Everything I thought and wrote that summer was based upon the notion, which Josef Stalin was immediately to prove false, that the violent phase of the Russian revolution was over, that the drive of communist fanaticism was slackening, that the magnificent energies of the Russian people would soon be set to work on making life worth living."[96]

Stalin was still, Dos Passos wrote, manipulating behind the scenes; the terror that existed had not yet become public. The intervening quarter century of history led him to stress aspects of his experience in Russia far different from those he had emphasized at the time. During his final month in Moscow, he said in 1956, he had been frightened almost every night, and the last few days he had been afraid he would not be permitted to leave. When he returned to the United States he could not or would not, he said, write the full truth about the trip for several reasons. One was that he could not immediately absorb what he had seen; he returned more puzzled than disillusioned. Another was that he feared harming the friends he had made in the Russian theater. A third was that he was afraid what he wrote might aid anti-Soviet propagandists in the West. American capitalism then seemed much more dangerous to what he viewed as the Russian experiment than did Russian Communism to American institutions.[97]

Dos Passos' attempt to report events occurring in 1928 from his perspective in 1956 may jar some readers. Some may suspect him of trying to rewrite the past, perhaps from his desire to be politically effectual in the 1950s. Many mental processes being subtle, and often unconscious, even the most honorable man is, of course, capable of deceiving himself. But Dos Passos' early comments about Bolshevik terror tend to support his reminiscences about his fears in 1928.

So also does one of his later comments. About 1937, after he had come to believe that Anglo-Saxon democracy was America's best hope, he wrote John Howard Lawson, "The old argument about giving aid and comfort to the enemy is rubbish: free thought cant possibly give aid and comfort to fascism But we've had this all out before and it is not arguable — except in matters of detail. Naturally that position was reached after considerable travel. I now think that foreign liberals and radicals were very wrong not to protest against the Russian terror all down the line. There's just a chance that continual criticism from their friends might have influenced the bolsheviks and made them realize the extreme danger to their cause of the terror machine, which has now, in my opinion, eaten up everything good in the revolution."[98]

The war made Dos Passos an opponent of capitalism. To what extent did the years 1926–28 shape his politics? The Sacco-Vanzetti affair turned him into an embattled opponent; after the electrocution of the two men, he wrote in 1957, he thought the United States somewhat worse than the U.S.S.R.[99] If we allow for his state of mind in 1927–28, the recollection is credible. He could hope that revolutionary terror in Russia would end, and he could console himself with the knowledge that liberties had been few during Czarist days; in America, on the other hand, he believed there had occurred a betrayal of liberties once possessed.

Not Bolshevism, but the purpose, enthusiasm, and creative energy that he discovered in Russian society impressed Dos Passos in 1928. It may be significant that he wrote *Manhattan Transfer* and *U.S.A.* (chapters of which he carried with him to work on in Russia[100]) following experiences abroad with what he considered artistically or spiritually creative epochs. Both books emphasize the purposelessness of society at home and the concomitant lack of creative energy in most of the characters. The industrial debacle in America following the stock market crash of 1929 seemed to indicate the economic as well as the spiritual and moral bankruptcy of capitalism; and it was during the subsequent depression that Dos Passos wrote most of *U.S.A.*[101]

VII.

DESPERATION, DILEMMA, HOPE

N AUGUST 1929 DOS PASSOS MARRIED KATHARINE SMITH, A FRIEND of Ernest Hemingway. Although an American could not have chosen a more fateful year for marriage, the depression following the stock market crash that October did not affect him much financially. The couple made Katy's house in Provincetown, Massachusetts, their headquarters and enjoyed long stays at Key West, often in Hemingway's company. Dos Passos still managed to take trips abroad; in 1932 he was in Guatemala and the next year in Spain, where he wrote several articles strongly condemning the republican government and conservative Socialists. But far more demanding of our attention were his travels in the United States, his responses to the economic sufferings he witnessed there, and the change in attitude to which he came by contrasting Nazism in Germany, Stalin's Communism in Russia and abroad, and the New Deal at home.[1]

The sentiments Dos Passos had expressed in his letter to President Lowell reverberated in his political writings during the first years of the depression. The struggle for the overthrow of capitalism would be as violent, he felt, as the capitalists made it. Though his would probably have been one of the first radical voices to denounce a triumphant left's enjoying its reprisals, he saw only workers and leftists as imperiled. In the summer of 1930 he wrote letters and articles protesting against a new repression of Communists. That year the American Civil Liberties Union was complaining that New York City police, under Commissioner Grover Whalen, were being brutal in their suppression of Communist demonstrations; Hamilton Fish, Jr., was conducting a congressional investigation into Communist activities; and Ralph M. Easley of the National Civic Federation was discussing with Elihu Root the creation of a special federal police force to combat Communism. With unemployment increasing, Dos Passos commented, the struggle of government and business against working-class radicalism seemed to be returning to the 1919 pitch. Now the arch-enemy was Communism instead of the I.W.W. Thousands of Communists, alleged Communists, and workers had been arrested in a few months for organizing labor, distributing leaflets, and attending meetings.[2]

In offering the protests, Dos Passos was concerned primarily with the role of those members of the middle class whom he saw as not compelled by their economic positions to be pro-worker or anti-worker. He asked that such people remain neutral, at least, and demand that the struggle between capital and labor proceed under the most humane conditions possible. His assumption that there existed a middle-class group with interests divorced from those of business owed much to Veblen's writings; although Dos Passos mentioned Helen and Robert Lynd's *Middletown* in presenting the idea, that book merely took note of a nonbusiness section of the middle class and stated that it received its tone from business.

In *Middletown*, that extraordinary useful survey of a middle-western town from the point of view of academic anthropology, the authors divide the American life they're studying into three groups: the Middle Class or Business Class, the Owning Class, and the Working Class. Naturally, the great majority of the Middle Class are mercenaries and dependents of the owners and even less open to feelings of humanity than the people on top. But there is a layer: engineers, scientists, independent manual craftsmen, writers, artists, actors, technicians of one sort or another, who insofar as they are good at their jobs are a necessary part of any industrial society. (In Russia this class held over, not half as much affected as people think by the revolution. . . .) If you could once convince them of the fact that their jobs don't depend on capitalism they'd find that they could afford to be humane. The time to reach these people is now, when the series of stock market crashes must have proved to the more intelligent that their much talked of participation in capital through stockholdings was just about the sort of participation a man playing roulette has in the funds of the gambling house whether he's winning or losing. . . .

The most difficult thing you have to buck is the fact that along with the technical education that makes them valuable to the community they have taken in a subconscious political education that makes them servants of the owners. . . . It's the job of people of all the professions in the radical fringe of the middle class to try to influence this middle class, that most of them would rather not belong to, so that at least some of its weight shall be thrown on the side of what I've been calling civilization. It's a tough job, but somebody's got to do it.[3]

Somebody, but who? Dos Passos had had some interesting conversations with Ivy Lee two years before, when they were staying at the same Moscow hotel. In a letter to the *New Republic*, he now mused on what a "super-public-relations" counsel like Lee or Edward Bernays could do if enough money were available to bring the middle class the message. Just what a leftist Ivy Lee should say about technicians' liberties might, however, have been difficult for a variegated committee of radicals to resolve. In 1930, Dos Passos' reminiscences suggest, he felt that civil rights were almost equally scarce in the United States and in Russia.[4] The political history of the thirties in both countries led him to alter this view. In the forties, when he called socialism a failure, Dos Passos said much about how economic organization and political liberty are entangled with each other.

During the first half of the 1930s, Dos Passos acted in accordance with the missionary program he had sketched for radical members of the middle class. He worked with left-wing groups, some Communist-controlled, in defense of the civil rights of strikers, radical agitators, and members of minority groups. In 1930 he was treasurer of the Emergency Committee for Southern Political Prisoners. The John Reed Club was sponsoring this group to help the International Labor Defense (I.L.D.) secure bail for imprisoned workers and relief for their families. Theodore Dreiser was chairman, and Sherwood Anderson, Waldo Frank, Upton Sinclair, Louis Untermeyer, Carl Van Doren, and Edmund Wilson were among the members.[5]

In 1931 Dos Passos was chairman of the National Committee to Aid Striking Miners Facing Starvation, a group including Anderson, Frank, Gold, Sinclair, Roger Baldwin, Robert W. Dunn, and Robert Morss Lovett. Dos Passos wrote an advertisement asking sympathizers to send money to buy food and tents for the striking coal miners of Pennsylvania, Ohio, West Virginia, and Kentucky. In August 1932 he published letters asking for money to help two of the defendants in the celebrated Scottsboro rape case, and listing himself as treasurer of the fund. He called the Scottsboro affair an "attempted legal lynching." Two months later he was one of the fourteen people who signed an appeal for contributions to the National Student League, a "mass" college campus organization which the Communists dominated.[6]

Dos Passos' concern with the current coal strikes led to one of his most memorable political experiences. In *The Big Money* he involved Mary French in the coal strikes and made the sufferings she witnesses one of the many reasons for her almost frenetic devotion to the radical movement. Since the strikes gave Dos Passos insight into Communism, as well as additional experience with capitalism, the story demands narration in some detail.

Miners and mine owners were waging violent war against each other in bituminous coal fields in 1931. Men had been killed or wounded in almost every coal state. The reason for the warfare was that, because the mine owners could produce twice as much coal as they could market, profits were low, unemployment high, wages pitiful. In West Virginia one third of the 112,000 miners were said to be near starvation.

Harlan County, Kentucky, where 9,000 of the 60,000 inhabitants were coal miners, became a center of violence. The mine owners there, in order to stay in business, were using their power in company-owned towns and in county government to keep wages low. The miners were desperate, for the employed were earning only $9 to $12 a week, and the idle were dependent on friends, neighbors, and charities; their children begged from strangers. Large numbers of children had neither the books nor the clothes nor the strength to go to school. The Red Cross, some of whose officials themselves operated mines, would not feed families of men whom the operators disliked.

The immediate trouble in Harlan County began when the mine owners cut wages ten per cent in February 1931. Some even made a second reduction. When the United Mine Workers of America (then affiliated with the A.F.L.) began to enroll miners in the area, the operators discharged U.M.W.A. members and sympathizers and evicted them and their families from company-owned houses. Not having money for relief and not considering the time opportune, the U.M.W.A. did not call a strike, although some miners not immediately involved in the struggle left their jobs in sympathy.

Successive acts of terror and violence followed the discharges and evictions: from among coal company guards, the sheriff swore in deputies, who rode about the county with rifles and machine guns; company property and company-owned houses were burned; miners looted company commissaries and independent stores; deputies raided miners' homes; they escorted strikebreakers, were fired upon, and returned the fire.

Grim citizens in Harlan County, Kentucky, May 1931. Dos Passos thought the town of Evarts one of the few places in the country that still had democratic government.

A pitched battle occurred after the Black Mountain Coal Company and some other firms discharged a large number of miners and began to evict their families. The discharged men met in Evarts, a town where the officials and many businessmen sympathized with the miners, and proceeded to picket the roads to the camps. This picketing led to "the battle of Evarts" on May 5, in which three deputies and one miner were killed and a number of miners were wounded. The sheriff brought murder indictments against forty-four people, including the police chief of Evarts, a wealthy Evarts merchant who had shown sympathy for the miners, and the president of the Evarts local of the United Mine Workers. The sheriff also arrested an employee of the Black Mountain Coal Company for criminal syndicalism, charging that he had been enrolling members for the I.W.W. As a result of the battle of Evarts, the governor of Kentucky sent troops into the county, where they remained until July 18.

After the battle the United Mine Workers, which had condemned violence, ceased efforts to organize Harlan County miners. But in June the Communist-led National Miners Union (N.M.U.) appeared, charging that the United Mine Workers had sold out to the operators. The sheriff continued to use the law to cow the miners, and violence continued. An Evarts department store owner who had been giving food to miners' children was charged with criminal syndicalism and forced to leave town. A deputy sheriff was exonerated after he shot and killed two men at an I.L.D. soup kitchen a mile from Harlan.[7]

Amid this industrial warfare, the I.L.D. asked Theodore Dreiser to organize a committee of inquiry to publicize the situation in Harlan County. Dreiser tried to get such men as Robert M. La Follette, George W. Norris, William Allen White, and Felix Frankfurter. When he was unsuccessful, he asked for volunteers from among the National Committee for the Defense of Political Prisoners, as the I.L.D. had originally requested that he do. Dos Passos was, not unexpectedly, one of the seven who responded.[8] The task corresponded with the program for middle-class radicals which he himself had outlined.

On November 5 the committee arrived in Pineville to investigate the "reign of terror" in the mine fields and to conduct free speech tests. The members held investigatory meetings and took testimony in Harlan and Bell counties, visited miners' huts, and conducted mass meetings.[9] Newspapermen, representatives of the press services, and agents of the coal operators went about observing the group's work.

Soon after the committee's arrival in Pineville, the members went to a room of the Hotel Continental to gather testimony. The wife of an N.M.U. organizer described how her husband had been arrested, beaten, and shot, and her home raided and searched for radical literature. An organizer told of a raid on his home and of the seizure of guns, though possession of guns was legal in Kentucky. A publisher from Virginia testified that the sheriff of Harlan County had complained of the attitude of the visitor's newspaper, and the publisher had been nicked by a bullet the next time he came to Harlan. A former miner described how his brother and another man had been murdered and he wounded at a soup kitchen in the area. Although the assailants were known, he said, no attempt had been made to bring them to justice. Later, in Harlan town, miners and their wives came to the Llewellyn Hotel to testify that they lived on beans and bread, skipped meals, and begged for clothes. Sheriff Blair told Dreiser, who went to his office, that all Communist and I.W.W. publications were illegal.

At Straight Creek, a section of Bell County which the N.M.U. had succeeded in organizing fairly well, the midwife told the visitors that babies were dying; after hearing her, the newcomers visited some of the broken huts and witnessed the truth of her testimony. At an N.M.U. meeting held in a Baptist church in Straight Creek, someone from the *Daily Worker* reminded the participants that that night was the fourteenth anniversary of the U.S.S.R. A meeting was held in Wallins Creek the next afternoon in the gymnasium of the local high school. There was no trouble despite a warning that deputies might interfere, but people became increasingly nervous as darkness fell, and many left early. The next morning, on November 9, Dreiser's committee gathered its testimony together and departed for New York.[10]

The investigation demanded personal courage of the writers. More than once situations evoked feelings in Dos Passos akin to those he had known in the war zones of Europe.[11] He had felt terror in the Soviet Union, he may have reflected, but didn't striking coal miners, steel and textile workers; alien radical printers, shoemakers, and fish peddlers like Salsedo, Sacco, and Vanzetti — and sometimes even agitating leftist writers — know terror in the United States?

After the Dreiser committee's departure, its members were

indicted for banding together "to commit criminal syndicalism and . . . promulgate a reign of terror" and for suggesting resistance to the government, but no attempt was made to extradite them. When Waldo Frank, three months later, led an independent delegation of writers into Kentucky to distribute food and test constitutional liberties, he and an I.L.D. attorney were kidnapped and beaten.[12]

Dos Passos saw as a trite pretext the refusal of the coal operators and the local judge and sheriff to let the miners organize under radical unions[13] — the U.M.W.A. had fared no better than the N.M.U. The fact that the coal industry was sick seemed to him, not an excuse for victimizing the miners, but an indictment of finance capitalism. His explanation of the industry's predicament was in accordance with Veblen's analysis of corporation finance in the United States. "Financiers skimmed the cream off the coal companies," Dos Passos wrote, "and left them overcapitalized and bankrupt."[14]

During succeeding years Dos Passos interpreted and reinterpreted his experiences in Kentucky. Some of the people he encountered there seem to have given him a glimpse of the type of independent individual he had once called upon to stem the postwar repression. The exploited class in Harlan County still possessed the traditions of the American Revolution and of pioneer days in the West, Dos Passos declared upon his return from Kentucky. Evarts (where the small merchants disliked the operators, who forced the miners to patronize company stores) impressed him as one of the few places in America that still had democratic government. The voters there, he noted, had installed a pro-miner town council the previous month by a vote of approximately 200 to 80; the men on trial for murder, most of whom came from Evarts, had the full sympathy of their townsmen.[15] These facts prevented Dos Passos from leaving Kentucky totally disheartened.

In a letter to the *New Republic* in December, he commented on his experiences. He wanted to protest, he wrote, against the tendency of newspapers to see Kentucky as necessarily more backward or barbaric than other parts of the country. Liberal editorial writers, he thought, were always deceiving themselves with geography. Contrary to their view, one could argue that slight traces of democracy existing in many regions of the South (though not, of course, applicable to Negroes) were "a last vestige of a state of mind long swamped by industrial development through the rest

of the country.'' By traces of democracy, he wrote, he meant the
Evarts vote and Bill Burnett's acquittal by a jury of small businessmen in Mt. Sterling in the first murder trial stemming from the
Evarts war. As far as Dos Passos knew, Burnett's was the first
acquittal of a worker labeled radical since the Wobblies had been
freed after the Everett shootings in 1913.

Perhaps, Dos Passos added, the Harlan cases could be used
as bases for getting other workers out of prison. If a Kentuckian
who happened to be a miner had the right to defend himself against
operator-hired thugs wearing deputy's badges, why didn't a
Washington lumberjack have a right to defend his union hall? Why
didn't a Gastonia textile worker have a right to defend a tent
colony?[16]

One young Kentucky miner had looked disappointed when
Dos Passos said that writers remained on the sidelines as long
as they could and that he himself was a sympathizer rather than
a Communist ''lodgemember.'' Actually, Dos Passos, whose views
were influenced by what veteran I.W.W. men in Kentucky told
him, soon became disturbed at discovering that the Communists
were concerned not with people but with tactics.[17] Looking back,
he said in 1957, ''I think . . . that my first real personal disgust
with the commies appeared when I saw them in action in Kentucky
in the coal strike. A conversation with Earl Browder . . . finished
the job. Kronstadt had grown dim — Harlan Kentucky brought
all those feelings back to life.''[18]

When the I.L.D. refused to aid indicted U.M.W.A. miners,
Dos Passos complained to the Communists and revealed his annoyance to his friends. One of his friends on the trip, Mrs. Charles
R. Walker, recalls his dissatisfaction well.[19] Not for him was the
proclamation of the old revolutionary in *Airways, Inc.*: ''We must
be steel automatons.''

Some years before, writing his friends to help the eighteen-
year-old poet Gordon (see note, p. 146), Dos Passos had asked
them to base their pleas on the prisoner's youth, a consideration
which he felt would impress the parole board. ''The important
thing now,'' he had urged, ''is not to complain about fair play
or freedom of speech, but to get him out.''[20] Though appalled
in 1931 by the I.L.D.'s very different concerns, Dos Passos did
not put his objections into print. As with his experiences in Russia,
there was the problem of giving aid and comfort to the enemy;
he probably felt that, since the Communists were carrying the brunt

of protest in America, no purpose would be served by attempting to discredit them. He first revealed his resentment in the final "Camera Eye" section of *The Big Money*, where he dejectedly juxtaposes memories of his Harlan experiences with memories of terror and famine in the Red Caucasus in 1921 (and probably, too, implicit references to later terror in the U.S.S.R.):[21]

the representative of the political party talks fast through the bars join up with us and no other union we'll send you tobacco candy solidarity our lawyers will write briefs speakers will shout your names at meetings they'll carry your names on cardboard on picketlines   the men in jail shrug their shoulders smile thinly our eyes look in their eyes through the bars   what can I say?   (in another continent I have seen the faces looking out through the barred basement windows behind the ragged sentry's boots I have seen before day the straggling footsore prisoners herded through the streets limping between bayonets   heard the volley

I have seen the dead lying out in those distant deeper valleys) what can we say to the jailed?[22]

In *The Theme Is Freedom* Dos Passos said more about his dissatisfaction with the Communists' behavior. The writers' committee, he wrote, really did try to hear what both parties in the industrial war had to say. Communist party members, who were trying to direct the proceedings, displayed a "scornful tolerance" toward what they referred to as the committee's "liberalism." They sneered at "perfectly sincere I.W.W. and A.F. of L. men." When the writers returned to New York, Earl Browder, the chairman of the Central Committee of the Communist Party, asked Dos Passos to go back to Kentucky and stand trial under the criminal syndicalism law. Dos Passos, agitated, refused to be a pawn; he set about the more natural task of editing the testimony which the writers had gathered in Kentucky. The next year it appeared in the book *Harlan Miners Speak*. "I still felt that the communists — by the violence of their protest and by their tireless dedication — were filling a useful function in ramming the plight of the wageworker into the public eye," Dos Passos explained, "but I was a little more wary in my dealings with them after that."[23]

Dos Passos was in Washington for the opening of Congress in December 1931. "The representatives of the sovereign wardheelers," he called the legislators. He considered all but about a half dozen of the House members contemptible: "Everywhere the close-set eyes full of small chicanery," he commented, "the pursed, self-righteous mouth drawn down at the corners, the flabby self-satisfied jowl.'' Of the Senate chamber, he wrote: ''Ever seen a section of a termite nest under glass?''

Communist-led hunger marchers had come to Washington on this occasion — not to petition, but to demand, their leader said. Although the police near the Capitol had brought out rifles, the atmosphere reminded Dos Passos of a circus. Washington was more grim six months later when Dos Passos described the encampment of nearly 20,000 members of the ''Bonus Expeditionary Force'' in rubble lean-tos at Anacostia Flats.[24]

Detroit had felt the depression so sharply that he named it ''City of Leisure.'' Thousands of unemployed men slept in shacks along the waterfront, in unoccupied buildings, some even in scooped-out holes in a sandpile. Dos Passos watched many of the unemployed listen to speakers in Grand Circus Park or lie about on the grass. A newspaperman told him that groups of men constantly went into chain groceries and seized food, but the newspapers did not print the stories, lest other people get the same idea.[25]

In June 1932 Dos Passos attended the Republican National Convention in Chicago. The gathering interested him mainly as illustrating one of the afflictions of industrialism which he had described in some detail as early as *Three Soldiers*: the power that men who control loudspeakers have over an audience's minds and emotions. Contemplating the manipulations of sound and light, he voiced some of the perplexities that were leading him to devote sections of *U.S.A.* to a scrutiny of the American mass mind:

. . . history, or the mass mind, or whatever you want to call the solution of forces and urges and hindrances we live our lives in, is becoming more and more involved with the apparatus of spotlights, radio, talking pictures, newsprint, so that the image-making faculty, instead of being the concern of the individual mind, is becoming a social business. The control of radio waves is externalizing thought and feeling to a hair-raising degree. . . . Who's going to be man enough to stand at the switchboard?[26]

At the Democratic Convention in Chicago the next month, Dos Passos noted that Franklin D. Roosevelt's ''plain sensible and unassuming speech'' was a disappointment to the crowd. The jobless men lying under bushes in Grant Park and in rows along the roadway beneath Michigan Avenue did not care about the convention, Dos Passos said. ''Hoover or Roosevelt, it'll be the same cops.''[27]

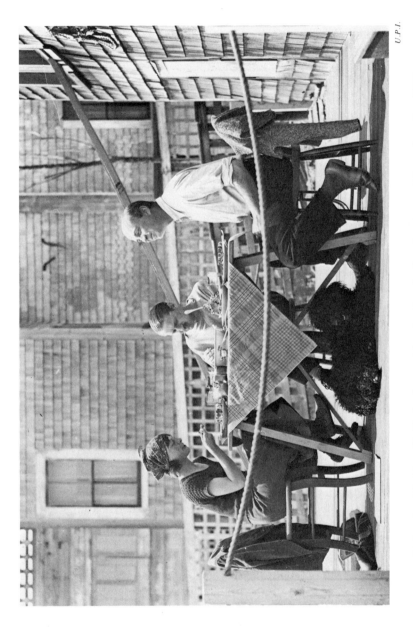

At lunch with his wife Katharine and her brother in Provincetown, Massachusetts, 1932.

His attitude toward the Socialist party was that it was "near-. beer." Describing a Socialist rally, he wrote that he thought he could detect a cloud on Morris Hillquit's face when Norman Thomas mentioned a capital levy; Dos Passos thought Thomas spoke in a manner reminiscent of the Episcopal pulpit. Dos Passos found the "forgotten man" no more in evidence at a Communist meeting than at the other rallies.[28] But the Communist party, despite its faults, seemed to him to stand for real "7½ p c" beer. "However much we may cavil at the Communists they meant [*sic*] it when they say they are fighting for socialism, i.e. the cooperative commonwealth," he asserted in a letter. In September he was one of fifty-two writers, painters, and professional people who declared that they would vote for William Z. Foster for president. Describing a Communist vote as the only effective protest against the present economic system, they urged their colleagues to join them. The fifty-two included a sizable and distinguished group of writers in that most nightmarish of depression years.[29]

At the same time that he called for support of the Communist candidate, Dos Passos distinguished sharply between a novelist's engaging in the inexact business of election-year politics and his pursuing his craft. Dos Passos' replies in 1932 to a Marxist editor's questionnaire on American writers and politics voiced his intellectual independence and his insistence upon artistic integrity. The difficulty of a writer's acting prominently as a citizen and at the same time seeking truth as a novelist, a political novelist at that, must have impressed him continually.

He wrote in the 1932 questionnaire that the United States was developing "a centralized plutocracy like that of ancient Rome." This plutocracy would inevitably collapse, he agreed, adding that a collapse would probably not occur within the ten years suggested by the questioner. Dos Passos held that Marxian writers who tried to discard the American tradition were "cutting themselves off from the continent." "Somebody's got to have the size to Marxianize the American tradition before you can sell the American worker on the social revolution. Or else Americanize Marx." He did not see how a novelist or a historian could be a Communist under the conditions then existing. "The communist party ought to produce some good pamphleteers or poets," he remarked, alluding to its insistence upon doctrinal purity. "By the way, where are they?"[30]

Dos Passos returned to the explicit defense of artistic freedom when the Communist-dominated Congress of American Writers gathered three years later. At that time he submitted a paper stressing the threat posed to the creative writer by leftist bureaucracies. The paper seems to have been suggested by Veblen's argument that an economy which makes private profit the primary consideration hampers its technicians. Dos Passos declared that a writer is a technician who "discovers some aspect of the world and invents out of the speech of his time some particularly apt and original way of putting it down. . . ." He cannot do his best work unless he has freedom from both fear and partisan preoccupation. "I don't mean," Dos Passos added, "that a writer hasn't an obligation, like any other citizen, to take part if he can in the struggle against oppression, but that his function as a citizen and his function as a technician are different, although the eventual end aimed at may in both cases be the same."[31]

The month after the presidential election of 1932, the periodical *Common Sense* appeared, listing Dos Passos as one of its contributors; edited by Alfred M. Bingham, C. C. Nicolet, and Selden Rodman, it called for the abolition of competitive capitalism by means of a "constitutional convention to adapt the principles of the American Revolution of 1776 to modern needs." In April 1933 the periodical announced its support of the League for Independent Political Action, headed by John Dewey. That organization wanted to establish "a united radical party of the common people" to achieve a cooperative commonwealth. Dos Passos' comment showed fierce preoccupation with people's distress throughout America: "Well, why not support the League for Independent Political Action? It may have more life than it seems to have shown in the past. But don't let liberal talk get you off the realities of the situation: where my bread is buttered there will my heart be. But support anything. We may be taking our last stand in the S.P.C.A. before long."[32]

For a while after the presidential election, Roosevelt probably seemed to Dos Passos, as he seemed in 1932, "the unlikeliest man in the world" to reform America. During the early New Deal Roosevelt presented himself as a combiner of interests, a harmonizer of ideologies, not a champion of liberalism.[33] Dos Passos' article "The Radio Voice," published in *Common Sense* in February 1934, epitomized his view of Roosevelt during the first years of his administration. Dos Passos portrayed the President telling a nationwide audience how he is manipulating all the controls in Washington to benefit all Americans, from unemployed workers to bankers. "Not a sparrow falleth but . . . " The audience go to bed happy. "But what about it when they wake up and find the wagecut, the bank foreclosing just the same, prices going up on groceries at the chain stores, and the coal dealers bill . . . and that it's still raining?"[34]

That same February, Dos Passos, writing in *New Masses*, described the Unemployed Convention in Washington. Following disillusionment with the New Deal, he wrote, men and women throughout the country had discovered that mass action was more effective than talk or Washington red tape. They had organized Unemployed Councils to carry furniture back into houses after bailiffs dispossessed tenants, to conduct "Sears Roebuck sales" when banks foreclosed on farms, and incessantly to demand adequate relief. Delegates from about 1,200 of the councils had now gathered in the capital to recount their successes. They would go home and report that if the unemployed did not help themselves, nobody would help them. In *Fortune Heights*, published in 1933–34, though undertaken some years earlier for the New Playwrights Theatre, Dos Passos depicted such an instance of mass action.[35]

Fortune Heights is Dos Passos' contemporary, largely anticipatory, comment in dramatic form on the early days of the New Deal. Since the play takes him further from the fanciful expressionism of *The Garbage Man* than even *Airways, Inc.* did and his course seems in conflict with his critical interests, one wonders whether the change in manner wasn't due to a need for prompt audience acceptance in a time of social crisis. Virtually abandoning expressionistic devices, Dos Passos here presented a realistic drama about a small businessman's struggle for economic success and finally for survival.

The play is a memorable one. Adherence to the single theme of the impracticability and immorality of capitalism brought a unity absent in Dos Passos' two earlier plays. But good construction alone does not make a play memorable. *Fortune Heights* seems as colorful, as American, and as relevant to its day as Dos Passos could have desired an American play to be. Most of the characters are at once individuals and familiar types. Their speech is more than phonetically accurate; apothegms and clichés fall aptly and yet casually from their lips. One of Dos Passos' most impressive achievements here is a portrayal of the mobility of the American population in the era of the automobile. He makes a highway gasoline station a device for bringing together his settled and his migratory characters.

Asked why his plays in the 1920s and 1930s were, on the whole, more politically explicit than his fiction, and whether it was by artistic design that he sought subtle nuances of character in the fiction but not in the drama, Dos Passos replied, "This was the era of agitprop. We were all very much affected by it."[36]

Fortune Heights, like *The Garbage Man*, suggests a radical morality play. Owen Hunter is the aptly named proprietor of a business consisting of a gasoline station, an automobile repair shop, a road stand, and tourist cabins. He has failed in business at least once, but he believes that at the Fortune Heights real estate development he has been let in on the "ground floor."

Owen and Florence, his wife, and Morry, an attendant at his filling station, are the major characters. Owen predicts that in a few years he will own his business completely and then perhaps earn "big money." Florence, who to earn the money Owen is investing worked at a distasteful job in a beauty parlor, feels that she cannot stand another failure. Morry declares that he himself has worked all his life and "never got anythin' by it yet."

A number of minor characters are more colorful than the major ones. Ellery Jones, the real estate operator, speaks with the usual hyperboles of members of his calling, but with some insight into his verbal extravagances. Mrs. Stead, the wife of the local banker, is egregiously casual about paying for gasoline or for the homemade preserves that Florence sells. Ike Auerbach, the motorcycle-riding boy detective who dreams of being a writer, is a fantastic creature whose counterparts attained notoriety during the prohibition era. Auerbach's disguises, his blackmailing, his informing and reward-hunting make him a caricature of man become subhuman under a fiercely competitive economic system. But there are human beings who resemble nothing so much as caricatures.

A worn, impoverished old couple, the Meakins, and their niece, Rena, come by in a Model-T Ford. Mr. Meakin relates that he worked for Ford until he unwittingly got into an argument with a company detective and that now he is too old to find work. With the Meakins are Buck and Babe, two hitchhikers clad in bold sports clothes and carrying a piano accordion and a ukulele. When the jalopy stops at the gasoline station, Buck engages in smart-alecky love banter with Rena.

Owen gives Rena a job and allows the Meakins to remain overnight without cost. He also tells Buck and Babe that they may stay till morning and offers them food. Mr. Meakin says to Owen: "If a good deed helps a man any in this world you sure ought to be on the road to success."[37] Charitable as Owen is, when he is summoned to an automobile accident he rushes to arrive before the motorist discovers that he is "next door" to a garage. During Owen's absence, Babe and Buck, after some drinking and dancing, take or borrow Ellery Jones' car. Ike, hoping to collect a reward, hurries to a telephone and reports the car stolen.

Act II depicts the onset of the Great Depression. A bum comes by and predicts that there will be an economic collapse soon: "I can see it in the fallin' off of the quality of vagrants."[38] Ellery Jones goes into bankruptcy. Owen has saved enough money to repay his loan only by selling bootleg liquor and enduring the harassments of Ike Auerbach and corrupt law-enforcement agents. But he loses the money when Buck and Babe stage a holdup — during which they kill Rena. Mr. Stead, the banker, who absconds after a visit from a bank examiner, stops at the station for gas, and, tearing his vest and coat off, impresses Owen with speeches on the position of "unaccommodated" man in America: "A man in his shirtsleeves. . . . As long as there's the nickel, there's money, society, law, wives and children, and a pain in the pit of your stomach; but when the man has no nickel, George, can he be said to exist, answer me that? Will I be alive, George, or will I be just nothing without a nickel?"[39]

Act III, "The New Deal," takes place during the presidency of Franklin Roosevelt. Representative of the rush of opportunists to the banner of the New Deal, Ellery is running for the legislature under the aegis of the administration. A sign reads: "Jones Will Make Your Troubles His."[40] The ruined banker has committed suicide; however, his widow has money of her own invested in government bonds, and Ellery is going to marry her after her period of mourning.

Morry left Fortune Heights before the robbery and was afterward unjustly imprisoned for helping to plan an "inside job." He returns just as the sheriff is about to evict Owen and his wife from their home. The Hunters have a rifle and are determined to resist. Although Morry is angry at Owen, he summons a truckload of farmers and farm hands to stop the sheriff. Eviction is not, Morry says, a private matter. When Ellery Jones comes to campaign,

Morry asks the men to beware of spellbinders, and some of the farm hands remark that they might lose their homes or starve to death before the election. Ike, who lost his government job when prohibition ended, now has a "courteous" detective agency, "in accordance," he says, "with the spirit of the New Deal."[41] He arrives with his agents, whom the sheriff has deputized. Although Owen yields, Morry and many of the men rush at the deputies. The agents open fire with their riot guns, kill Morry, and arrest the radical agitators.

At the end of the play, an agent is shown selling the roadside business to a couple who closely resemble Owen and Florence. The agent declares that the purchasers have a chance to become wealthy in a short time.

Fortune Heights contains many denunciations of contemporary capitalism from people who aid in sustaining it. A reporter who investigates the holdup and murder complains: "What do you think of a system of society where a man makes his living treading on every decent feeling he's got or his neighbors have got?" The agent who takes possession of Owen's property tells him: "I have a wife and a little girl who's sick and I've got to put my boy through college." Owen's struggles during the depression lead him to anticipate the laments of Stead, the ruined banker, and declare: "There ought to be some things you could have, even if you didn't have any money."[42] When Owen abandons the fight for his property, he says (here, in brief, is the play's message) that the way in which he was trying to run his business was immoral, and a system of "dawg eat dawg" will not do.

Since the Sacco-Vanzetti affair, Dos Passos had again and again exhibited acute concern with preserving civil liberties, tolerance, and humanity during the "class war." The rise of Hitler in Germany made him more conscious than ever before of how much freedom that might be lost the United States still possessed. The danger did not seem to him to be from foreign armies, but from the same domestic forces which had repressed labor during the past decade. If United States financiers felt themselves threatened, they seemed to him capable of imitating German industrialists and Junker landowners. "Suppose American finance had taken the trouble," he said in 1933, "to put money behind the Ku Klux Klan, to put the necessary press and advertising facilities at its disposal." Finance had not felt its power sufficiently challenged

to do this, he declared, but it might at another time. His vivid memory of the repression which had accompanied and followed World War I convinced Dos Passos that the surest way to domestic Fascism was through another foreign war. For monopoly capitalists, war was, he believed, a financial necessity and an ultimate means of obliterating domestic opposition.[43] To forestall war and Fascism, left-wing unity appeared to him to be vital, but his concern for it led him to a dilemma.

Herbert Solow recalled something of Dos Passos' behavior on the National Committee for the Defense of Political Prisoners in the early thirties. Solow became a member of this committee later than Dos Passos and ultimately left as a Trotskyite. About November 1932 he and other anti-Stalinists began to broach their points of view within Communist-dominated organizations, first in executive committee, then among the members. Between that time and 1934, Solow sensed that Dos Passos was ambivalent in his sentiments toward the Communists. A good friend of Carlo Tresca, Dos Passos seemed to have some kind of attachment to the I.W.W. and anarchism. He sat glumly through the Communists' talk about "Social Fascism" and a "united front from below," and showed no enthusiasm for the party line. Because he believed in unity of the left, he confined his criticism of the Communists to private talk; but he seemed always to be postponing a reckoning.[44]

The current party line, formulated in 1928, declared Social Democratic parties to be Social Fascist, and cooperation or contact between Communist and Social Democratic leaders to be contaminating. This line appears to have resulted, Isaac Deutcher wrote, largely from Stalin's tactics in consolidating his power. In subduing the followers of Bukharin in the International, Stalin probably saw in the hard party line an international corollary to radical collectivization and industrialization in Russia. During the course of the first five-year plan, he probably attached little significance to Comintern activities and was, moreover, "completely unaware of the significance and destructive dynamism of nazism." As Hitler attained power, Stalin's policy (against which Trotsky inveighed) helped to paralyze the German left.

When in 1935 Stalin sought an alliance with the West against Germany, he changed the line and inaugurated the era of the Popular Front.[45] But by that time Dos Passos had watched Stalin too long to be impressed with either his goodness or his wisdom. The novelist's growing wariness of the Communists in the 1930s came,

ironically, when increasing numbers of American intellectuals, turning leftward because of the depression and Nazism, were falling
under their influence.[46]

Dos Passos' first public controversy with the Communists
occurred because he believed they were undermining the very unity
he was trying to buttress. The dispute developed after the Communists broke up a meeting that trade unions staged in cooperation
with the Socialist party on February 16, 1934. A mammoth affair
at New York's Madison Square Garden, the meeting was a protest
against Dollfuss' armed attack on the Austrian left. Among the
participating groups were the International Ladies Garment Workers
Union; the Amalgamated Clothing Workers of America; the Cap
and Millinery Workers International Union; the Workmen's Circle;
and the Forward Association.[47] The scheduled speakers were Mayor
Fiorello La Guardia of New York; Matthew Woll, vice-president
of the American Federation of Labor; Dr. John Haynes Holmes;
and many officials of participating trade unions and socialist
organizations. Algernon Lee, of the Rand School, presided.

Before the meeting began, a number of Communists outside
the Garden distributed handbills denouncing LaGuardia and Woll
as Fascists. Most of the Communists came in two marching sections,
with a band and red flags. Many members of the sponsoring unions,
too, marched to the Garden in ranks. Ushers admitted the Communists, directing them to the upper balconies, but compelled them
to surrender their literature and temporarily to yield their banners.
This led to arguments and fist fights, and the Communists broke
through the line of ushers in the lobby and took seats as close
as possible to the platform. While they waited for the meeting
to open, they chanted: "We'll hang Matthew Woll to a sour apple
tree" and "Socialists and Communists unite."

Neither Algernon Lee nor any of the speakers was able to
make himself heard above the hecklers' jeers. Fights broke out
everywhere. After David Dubinsky finished his address, Clarence
Hathaway — one of the men directing the Communists — leaped
to the platform. While Communists in the balcony tried to aid
him by hurling down chairs, Hathaway was pounded with fists
and still other chairs and was ejected. Thereafter almost none
of the speakers was able to shout above the chants: "We want
Hathaway." Both La Guardia and Woll canceled their speeches
when they heard of the riots. Algernon Lee finally adjourned the
meeting with a request that the audience rise and sing the
"Internationale."[48]

After the disruption of the meeting, John McDonald and Elliot Cohen drew up an "Open Letter to the Communist Party" protesting the incident. Solow recalled that the letter was signed by a group of people just coming out against the Communists; for others like himself it seemed inexpedient to become involved. Dos Passos was one of the twenty-five people who signed, and he may have had, he recollects, something to do with framing the letter. Although it was prepared for submission to the *Daily Worker*, the letter ultimately went to *New Masses*, which published it in an editorial with the caption "To John Dos Passos."[49]

The editorial asserted that Dos Passos, one of the best-known contributors to the periodical, certainly found himself in queer company. While a few of the signers were honest but misguided, most of them were ambitious quacks. The editorial referred Dos Passos to a previous pronouncement on the fracas and elaborated upon it.[50]

The Socialists kept repeating, *New Masses* declared, that they had not invited the Communists. How could they explain the fact that they had invited Woll, who was acting president of the National Civic Federation, and La Guardia, the "wage cutting, strikebreaking mayor" whose police had only the day before ridden down workers? Socialists at the entrance to the Garden had frisked the Communists for literature as if they were dealing with thugs. Inside, the Socialists had made speech after speech, not against Dollfuss or Hitler, but against the Communist party. The periodical quoted Hathaway's declaration that he had gone to the platform merely "to propose to the chairman that I be permitted to make a one-minute appeal for perfect order in the meeting."[51] The reason, the editorial continued, that the Socialist leaders refused to form a "united front from above" (of the leaders) with the Communist party was that they objected to the Communists' criticism of their policies. The Communists, who reserved the right to criticize, had therefore tried to effect a "united front from below" (with the masses, despite their leaders) at Madison Square Garden.[52]

Dos Passos answered the editors of *New Masses* in a letter which they published on March 27:

My reason for signing the letter you printed in your issue for March 6 was the growing conviction that only a drastic change of policy and of mentality can save the radical movement in this country from the disastrous defeats suffered in Italy, Germany, Austria and Spain. By radical movement I mean the whole trend, in politics, social organization and in men's minds, in the direction of a workers' and producers' commonwealth, of which the Communist Party in this country is politically the most advanced outpost. I do not, as you know, pretend to be either a political economist or an industrial worker; as a writer I think it is my business to let my work speak for itself and keep my mouth shut the rest of the time. What happened in Madison Square Garden was shocking to me because it indicated the growth of unintelligent fanaticism that, in my opinion, can only end in the division of the conscious elements of the exploited classes into impotent brawling sects, and in the ruin for our time of the effort towards a sanely organized society. It seemed only common honesty to join in this protest, particularly as the men and women who signed the letter (which I had understood was to be sent to the Daily Worker) represented much the same group with which I put my name to a campaign endorsement of the Communist candidates for the last presidential election.[53]

Like the letter to *New Masses*, some of Dos Passos' correspondence with his friend Malcolm Cowley indicates that he was too independent in thought and act, too individualistic and humanitarian to cooperate with the Communists except when as a free man he was furthering ends of which he approved.

Thus his letters show how different from the I.L.D.'s handling of imprisoned Kentucky miners was his effort in November 1934 to help the Spanish etcher Luis Quintanilla. Hearing that the artist faced sixteen years in prison for taking part in a revolution against the Spanish republic, Dos Passos and Ernest Hemingway arranged for a show of his work in a New York gallery. Dos Passos wrote Cowley, a *New Republic* editor, that he hoped to get Quintanilla recognition as Spain's best etcher and thus make possible an effective petition for clemency. The action might lead to a protest about the government's methods in crushing the rebels. Through a misunderstanding, Cowley transformed Dos Passos' letter into one for the correspondence column of the *New Republic* and moreover allowed the printed letter to go into politics. Infuriated, Dos Passos wrote Cowley that, Spain being on the edge of a military dictatorship, the letter might cost Quintanilla his life. Later, apologizing, he said that Hemingway and he felt they had said too much about the revolution in their catalogue for the show. "After all," he wrote, "the aim in this business is to get the guy out and not to testify before the Lord."[54]

Extolling Hemingway as a literary craftsman, Dos Passos, in a letter to Cowley written at about the same time, lashed out at ''inkshitters'' who were attacking Hemingway in the pink magazines. Some rising doubts about commitment in a class war were more easily expressed in private correspondence with a friend than in public. '' . . . people aren't all black and white — or Communist and Fascist,'' Dos Passos continued; '' — when there's shooting going on, you have to take sides — I suppose. Though I'm not as sure of it as I was a few years ago — (I was always in the ambulance anyway).''[55]

Stalin's policies had led Dos Passos by May 1935 or before to change his mind about the Communists' constituting the most advanced outpost of the American radical movement. Instead, he now saw them as a liability. In a letter discussing the paper he had sent to the First American Writers' Congress, he wrote Cowley that the Communists were not capable of doing anything but provoking oppression. The great issue now, he wrote, was to defend the classic liberties. Cowley had written Dos Passos that politicians in a revolutionary society were right in wanting to suppress free speech to attain their aims. The writers, Cowley added, ought to fight hard for free speech. As the writers fought, there would be a dynamic adjustment. To Cowley's assertion that the situation was improving in Russia, Dos Passos merely replied that he did not think it was improving in America. The comrades were merely parroting changes in Russian mood and opinion, thus more than ever revealing their impotence.[56]

The altercation over the Communists' behavior in the Garden marked the end of Dos Passos' relationship with *New Masses*. The dissociation may have been due to the periodical's changing soon thereafter from a Communist-oriented magazine, which it had been since perhaps 1928, to something resembling a party organ.[57] For the next few years Dos Passos published most of his articles in *Common Sense*, the *New Republic*, and *Esquire*. His sole contribution to *New Masses* after the Garden controversy appeared in the December 1936 issue as one of a number of statements commemorating the founding of *Masses* twenty-five years before, and his article revealed his dissatisfaction with the current periodical. The era after the war, he wrote, had not favored the former disorderly methods of running *Masses*. ''For labor organization and the growth of social ideas the time was one of defeat, sectarianism, and retraction.'' As a ''sort of literary supplement to the *Daily Worker*,'' he said, *New Masses* had published a great deal of distinguished material and had done much to educate the United States in Marxian thinking. But he did not think that it would prove to have had the fertilizing influence of its predecessor. America was now, he held, "on the upward surge of a new democratic wave." If the monopolists and their supporters broke that wave before it reached its height, they would probably kill the American experiment. Dos Passos hoped that the democratic upsurge would enable *New Masses* to escape from its "narrow sectarian channel."[58]

America seemed to him to be growing more democratic, humane, and spiritually vital while Europe deteriorated. Nations far beyond the United States in the arts and in many forms of social legislation had succumbed to brutal class war or to Fascism. Writers could no longer speak of European culture with the awe that had characterized some of the articles in *Seven Arts* and the *Freeman*. Although the burden of Dos Passos' articles for the past three years had been that "it could happen here," by September 1936 he had decided that "it" was not happening under Roosevelt. In an article explaining the milieu and work of the German artist George Grosz, who had emigrated to America, Dos Passos declared:

But now in the last few years Europe . . . instead of being the land of liberty and art young middlewestern highschool students used to dream about, has become so stifling to any useful and rational human effort that suddenly the tables are turned. In the arts as in science America has become the refuge of the traditions of western European culture.

One can't help wondering whether we'll muff our opportunity. . . .

Anyway there's a Chinaman's chance that we may come to something. The fact that firstrate men who can't live in their own countries feel that they can breathe here makes you feel good about the country. The fact that George Grosz, the great visual satirist of our time, has come to live here, has taken out papers and considers himself an American makes you feel good about the country.[59]

Dos Passos' comments on Grosz appeared about two months before Roosevelt's re-election as president, and his dispraise of *New Masses* appeared a month after the re-election. As he subsequently wrote, 1936 was the time of Roosevelt's greatest glamor. The New Deal by then seemed a fulfillment of the hopes of many progressive reformers. Congress had between January and August of 1935 adopted more permanently important measures than in any previous session: social security; Wagner's National Labor Relations Act; holding company, banking, and tax bills; and a relief law which led to organizations like the Federal Theatre and the NYA.[60]

To Dos Passos, who had vividly depicted immigrant industrial workers and intellectuals and artists as victims of an Arrow Collar social order, another fact must have seemed significant: the New Deal was recognizing hitherto subordinate groups as having a legitimate place in the American commonwealth. "When Roosevelt took office," William Leuchtenburg writes, "the country, to a very large degree, responded to the will of a single element: the white, Anglo-Saxon, Protestant property-holding class." Although the New Deal neglected many Americans who lacked strong organizational spokesmen, it "achieved a more just society by recognizing groups which had been largely unrepresented," among them "industrial workers, particular ethnic groups, and the new intellectual-administrative class."[61]

Before the presidential election of 1936 the *New Republic* polled ninety-seven Americans who, it believed, had in general taken a progressive political position. Of the sixty who replied, forty-seven were for Roosevelt, nine for Norman Thomas, three for Earl Browder, one for Alfred Landon. Many of the supporters of Roosevelt, including Upton Sinclair, Archibald MacLeish, Theodore Dreiser, and John Chamberlain, wrote that they were voting for him as a lesser evil. Dos Passos — who did not participate in the poll — voted for Roosevelt with enthusiasm. He was impressed by the Wagner Act, the new controls over the economy, and the sense of belonging that the New Deal had brought even to depressed groups.[62]

The years between the executions of Sacco and Vanzetti and the emergence of promise in the New Deal must have been indeed discouraging for Dos Passos. Estranged from his government, distressed by economic depression in the United States, bitter about Americans' allowing a "centralized plutocracy" to develop; upset by the victory of the Nazis in Germany, and convinced that industrialists and tories in Europe and America, to maintain their economic power, were capable of taking the steps to Fascism; increasingly disquieted by reports of terror in Soviet Russia — Dos Passos held to his conviction of the intellectual's duty to his civilization, and sought to act responsibly. As ever, his practice was to decide upon a course of action, but also to review his decision when a situation changed.

Responsibility in the early 1930s seemed to call for left-wing unity to prevent Fascism. Though his trip in 1928 had left him with significant reservations about Russia, Dos Passos at the beginning of the decade worked with left organizations some of which were Communist dominated. But the Communists' callousness toward individual Kentucky miners in 1931, Stalin's hard line on unity of the left in the United States and abroad, and Stalin's terror in Russia left him increasingly perturbed.

As for the powerful trilogy taking form meanwhile, Dos Passos saw most of the period when he was working on it as part of an era of retreat or of desperate crisis for militant labor; the New Deal he at first described as ineffectual but deceptive and likely to distract attention from the need for socialism. His tone in *U.S.A.* was affected strongly by these views as well as by his involvement in and deep concern for the radical movement. The New Deal's achievements led him to alter his opinion about the progress of centralized plutocracy in the United States. Against the threat of American monopolistic capitalism, he could now see the country's heritage of individual liberty as a chief hope, but the situation still appeared critical. The events of four decades of his life culminated in an outstanding work of literature.

VIII.

U.S.A.

WE CANNOT REGRET ALL THE POLITICAL ACTIVITIES THAT kept Dos Passos from singleminded concentration on *U.S.A.* Unless it is psychologically necessary, there is nothing desirable about a writer's being encompassed by his art, and one reason for many a reader's interest in *U.S.A.* is that in it Dos Passos showed that he was not thus contained. Given his working patterns, the distractions were often also stimuli, and they beyond doubt added immensely to the range, vitality, and immediacy characterizing Dos Passos' epic work. He planned it as a single novel in 1927 or 1928, but it outgrew his initial conception, became a trilogy, and kept him busy until April or May of 1936. The first part, *The 42nd Parallel*, was published in 1930, *Nineteen Nineteen* followed in 1932, and *The Big Money* came out in 1936. The three parts were published in one volume as *U.S.A.* in 1938.[1]

The 42nd Parallel, or rather large parts of it, portray a prewar America still possessed of a confidence and an independence that were the heritage of frontier days. The title derives from a climatological note reprinted at the beginning of the first edition. Certain general storms "follow three paths . . . from the Rocky Mountains to the Atlantic Ocean of which the central tracing roughly corresponds with the 42nd parallel of latitude. . . ."[2] Thus the title seems symbolically to refer to the waves of populist discontent and labor rebellion which brought the specter of free silver to New York and spread rumors of social revolution in Lawrence, Cambridge, and Boston. It was in the West that the populist movement arose, that the I.W.W. first became well known, and that the most revolutionary groups within the Socialist party were located during the prewar years.

Continuing the portrayal of the United States, *Nineteen Nineteen* describes the disaster which, in Dos Passos' view, World War I brought; and *The Big Money* depicts a spiritual bankruptcy among the great majority of Americans during the decade of material prosperity following the immediate aftermath of the war. Yet broad though these concerns are, their treatment provides only one of the dimensions in *U.S.A.* No other well-known work of fiction studies so large a variety of Americans. None ranges so widely through the physical United States; events occur in every section of the country, in locations too numerous to list here, and everywhere in the narrative the national landscape in seen. *U.S.A.* presents tangible people in a real world during specific eras.

The subject of the trilogy is twofold: the moral development of its twelve main characters, and more than thirty years of American history as they fall within the consciousness of these people. The characters are presented in fifty-two sections of fictional narrative, wherein, though each section is devoted to one of the twelve, they encounter one another — and, of course, minor characters, who abound throughout the narrative. In *Three Soldiers* and *Manhattan Transfer*, Dos Passos had explored moral and psychological factors confronting sensitive individuals living in American society, and in *Manhattan Transfer* he had also dealt with an extensive group of characters, including factory workers, businessmen, and politicians. But the form of his prior novel had precluded his tracing the moral development of more than one or two of his people. While the intermingling of plots proclaims *U.S.A.* a descendant of *Manhattan Transfer*, Dos Passos is able in the long trilogy with its many fictional sections to give virtual case histories of all the principal characters.

His approach, tone, and form were affected by many literary works. The trilogy was probably influenced by the books of Cervantes, Fielding, Baroja, and by other writings about man encountering adventure on the road. *U.S.A.* also possesses some of the "earthy" quality that Dos Passos has always admired in Chaucer. Defoe's characteristic blending, in literal narrative, of historical and geographic fact with fiction may have had some effect on the style. The list of other possible literary influences is long, including Joyce's narrative innovations, Rabelais' humor, Swift's satire, and Gibbon's historical perspective. *U.S.A.* is not the work of a proletarian, but of a Harvard-educated middle-class radical familiar with many lands, tongues, and literary traditions.[3]

It is also the work of a boldly experimental writer, a fact we most readily notice from the auxiliary devices supplementing the narrative. The social, political, and economic history through which the fictional characters are living is recounted partly through three devices: "Newsreel," "The Camera Eye," and the biographies of representative men of the eras. Relatively short installments of these three are interspersed among the sections of fiction.

In all three auxiliary devices, the juxtapositions, spacings, and typography are, like Dos Passos' interweaving of sections, means of achieving a dynamic text. Some of the experimental European literature, besides Joyce's, that had stimulated Dos Passos in the past decade helped suggest techniques. "The Italian futurists, the Frenchmen of the school of Rimbaud, the poets who went along with cubism in painting," he has recalled, "were trying to produce something that stood up off the page." In *U.S.A.*, begun when he was greatly interested in the film technique of montage, his impulse toward reportage, furthermore, came to a head. "I felt," he has said, "that everything should go in."[4]

Such inclusiveness is apparent in the narrative as well as the auxiliary sections, and goes far beyond variety of landscape and character. For instance, Dos Passos creates fictional people who are not only socio-political but also biological beings, their impulses interacting constantly and dramatically. He presents numerous tragic and comic aspects of life, thus helping to give the narrative power and interest beyond that of the political theme.

The "Newsreel"'s most obviously give the impression of everything having gone in, although there has been, of course, painstaking selection. Composed of newspaper headlines; stanzas of popular songs; and fragments of articles, editorials, and advertisements, they reveal what historical events were taking place at the time of the action in nearby narrative and "Camera Eye" sections. As the "Newsreel"'s represent the storms, tides, currents, eddies, and vagaries in human existence, they contribute to the tragic and comic dimensions of the trilogy. They also help to describe the mass media of information which determine most Americans' view of their civilization.

The period that Dos Passos describes in *U.S.A.* coincided with the rapid development of radio and the motion picture and with the emergence of propaganda as a science. Many radicals were inclined to attribute to the power of the mass media the indifference or hostility with which the great majority of the population regarded leftist programs. *U.S.A.* explains contemporary society partly by the fact that many men lack moral perception and moral integrity; nevertheless, Dos Passos' trilogy stresses the insidious and debilitating influence of the mass media.

The "Newsreel" is excellent satire. Usually Dos Passos permits society, with its perverse values and practices, to condemn itself:

Girls Annoyer Lashed in Public
SINGS FOR WOUNDED SOLDIERS; NOT SHOT AS SPY
GARY CALLS ROMANTIC PUBLIC RESPONSIBLE FOR
EIGHT HOUR DAY
Society Women Seek Jobs in Vain as Maids to Queen
RADICALS FIGHT WITH CHAIRS AT UNITY MEETING[5]

Sometimes the "Newsreel" is roguishly contrived. In one section, classified advertisements repeating the cry "OPPORTUNITY" occur between verses of a song:

Oh tell me how long
I'll have to wait

Do I get it now
Or must I hesitate

Oh tell me how long[6]

Sometimes headlines are ironical merely in the context of the trilogy:

MARQUIS OF QUEENSBERRY DEAD[7]

From time to time public attention is shown to be concentrated upon particular events, such as America's entrance into World War I. But only those members of the public who were sophisticated enough to recognize significant items amid the preceding confusion could have understood such climactic occurrences. These embody earlier themes as do fugues.

"The Camera Eye" is a series of impressionistic views of Dos Passos' life describing events which have helped determine his opinions, presenting experiences upon which he has drawn in

writing *U.S.A.* and earlier works, and containing significant clues
to his personality. Here Dos Passos appears to present accurate,
though not all-embracing or coherent autobiography. Sometimes
he gives details without regard for time sequence or seems to omit
details and explanations to safeguard individuals' privacy. Selectiv-
ity is nowhere more apparent than in the fact that he mentions
Spain only fleetingly. Perhaps he believed that talk of his love
for Spain might needlessly complicate for the reader his concern
with the United States.

Many sections of "The Camera Eye" are rewarding to the
uninitiated reader, but only a reader familiar with Dos Passos'
life can approach a full understanding of the text. In section 1,
Dos Passos as a little boy is careful not to tread upon grass blades
(his concern seemingly indicating early compassionate feelings).
Immediately he and his mother, mistaken for Englishmen in the
Low Countries during the Boer War, almost suffer violence themselves.

Dos Passos, Sr., appears in sections 2, 4, 15, 16, and 28,
and is mentioned in 3 and, probably, 18. In section 2, Dos Passos'
father toys with the mother's Southern sensibilities by asking her
what she would do if he were to invite a Negro to the table. Dos
Passos' mother is, in section 16, "feeling well for once"; the father
speaks of law reform and politicians, and probably voices some
opinions that went into his books and pamphlets. Section 28 refers
to Dos Passos' coming home from Harvard to learn of his mother's
death, and also shows him returning from Spain a year later upon
learning of his father's death. Sections 29 through 42 describe some
of his experiences during America's entry into and participation
in World War I and during the period following the war.

Several sections of "The Camera Eye" require particular notice
here. Section 43, describing Dos Passos' return to the United States
from Europe after the war, seems Whitmanian in its insistence
on personality as a test of democracy. What good were the sufferings
in the European war, Dos Passos asks,

> if today the crookedfaced customsinspector with the
> soft tough talk the burring speech the funnypaper antics of
> thick hands jerking thumb
> (So you brought home French books didjer?)
> is my uncle[8]

Section 46 describes the temptations and doubts that Dos Passos
faced in considering his vocation as a novelist and a political journal-

ist. Speaking in a crowded hall in New York, and outdoors in Union Square, he wants to explain that "doubt is the whetstone of understanding," but he finds it difficult to avoid offering shibboleths to his radical audience.

Section 47 describes the manner in which Dos Passos was drawn to his explorations and to his writings. Referring to the continuing tension between cerebration and commitment, the section helps to explain his employment of the term "The Camera Eye":

> hock the old raincoat of incertitude (in which you hunch alone   from the upsidedown image on the retina painstakingly out of color shape words remembered light and dark straining
> to rebuild yesterday   to clip out paper figures to simulate growth   warp newsprint into faces smoothing and wrinkling in the various barelyfelt velocities of time)[9]

Sections 49, 50, and 51, the last three, comment on Dos Passos' feelings and activities during the Sacco-Vanzetti case and the Harlan miners' strike. For installments of "The Camera Eye," they are unusually coherent. With the "Newsreel" and the account of Mary French in Boston, sections 49 and 50 make the executions of Sacco and Vanzetti the climax of the trilogy. Strangers have appropriated, fenced, and marred the continent, Dos Passos cries. (In all three final sections he indicts American industrialists and their supporters.) Strangers have altered the definitions of words our ancestors spoke. Dos Passos anticipates a major theme of George Orwell's *1984* when he asks: "without the old words the immigrants haters of oppression brought to Plymouth how can you know who are your betrayers America"[10]

Some twenty-seven short, factual biographical sketches appear in *U.S.A.* Dos Passos has said these are "meant as illustrative panels, portraits of typical or important personalities of the time, intended to interrupt, and by contrast to give another dimension to the made-up stories which are the body of the book, much as the portraits of saints illustrated and reinforced the narrative in the *retablos* of early church painting."[11] It must be said that only a fraction of Dos Passos' subjects are in any sense offered as saints.

The biographies contain some of the most effective writing

in the trilogy. Actually partisan essays in history, they are more vigorous, less subtle, than the narrative proper. In them Dos Passos' combatant's passion is given further range. We recall his quoting from "Ode to the West Wind" in 1916, and his demanding new Shelleys; amidst thunder and lightning, a primordial voice now reaffirms that good is white and bad is black. The biographies aim, not to depict human life in its manifold complexities, but to impose single impressions. Thus, while they are very successful as a group, they are in fact as well as intention ancillary to the narrative. One of their purposes is to allow Dos Passos to portray important members of the owning class, virtually absent from the fiction, and a more inclusive end is to furnish extensive historical background for the narrative. A biography of Henry Ford, for example, follows a narrative section in which Charley Anderson's brother faces ruin as Ford victimizes his dealers. A biography of Isadora Duncan precedes and a biography of Rudolph Valentino follows the introduction of the show girl and actress Margo Dowling into the narrative. The biography of Thorstein Veblen helps the reader to understand the society depicted in the entire trilogy.

In *The 42nd Parallel* appear biographies of four leaders of political and economic dissent during the quarter century preceding World War I: the I.W.W. syndicalist William Haywood; the Socialist Eugene V. Debs; the Progressive Robert La Follette; and the populist William Jennings Bryan. Dos Passos presents the first three as heroes, the fourth as an opportunist. The biographies of Haywood, Debs, and La Follette display a lack of concern over doctrinal details and a general approval of the prewar radical "movement." La Follette was more reactionary by Marxian logic than were the representatives of the major parties, since he was attempting to preserve small business. But Dos Passos never accepted the Marxian theory of history for the United States, much less translated the theory into morals. He praises La Follette for his integrity and his combativeness. The senator is battered when he resists the oncoming of the war, in the course of which Haywood and Debs are broken and the movements which they champion destroyed. After the war La Follette is "an orator haranguing from the capitol of a lost republic."[12] Nevertheless, the tribute to him at the conclusion of the biography is one of the most striking passages in the trilogy.

The remaining biographies of *The 42nd Parallel* are of businessmen, industrialists, and scientists: Andrew Carnegie, Thomas Edison, Minor C. Keith, Luther Burbank, and Charles Proteus Stein-metz. Dos Passos describes Keith as a buccaneer and blackguard. The others, with the exception of Steinmetz, are men who invent and create without realizing that as inventions alter society, political and economic institutions change; thus, Edison, who did at least as much to alter communications as anyone else during the era, "never worried about mathematics or the social system or generalized philosophical concepts." [13]

In a book review condemning American industrialists for obtuseness rather than for villainy, Dos Passos had in 1929 stated explicitly why he honored Steinmetz. "Steinmetz felt every moment what his work meant in the terms of the ordinary human being," he had written. "Steinmetz was not of the temperament to cash in on anything." [14]

Almost all the biographies in *Nineteen Nineteen* provide impor-tant comments on World War I. Three are devoted to men who helped (or appeared to Dos Passos to have helped) bring America into the war: Theodore Roosevelt, the Morgans, and Woodrow Wilson. Dos Passos portrays Roosevelt, so vivid a figure both to the novelist and his father, as very much a charlatan. Roosevelt stands for a dangerous triad: righteousness readily revealed, easily recognized, and heroically pursued. The biography appears to assign to his foreign policy a role in preparing the United States for war.

In one of the most masterfully written of the biographies, Dos Passos describes the House of Morgan as thriving best in war and financial panic. The House of Morgan was a thoroughly conventional villain for the left in the early 1930s, and without any action on its part it could be an ironically influential one. J. P. Morgan had lent money to aid a reorganization of Harper and Brothers, which published *The 42nd Parallel*. Although the loan had been retired, Harper felt that it ought not to be a party to an attack on Morgan. To Dos Passos (who a few years before had jested about the consequences of stepping on Morgan's toe) the biography must have seemed too central a comment on the war to forgo. Though unhappy about leaving his editor and close friend Eugene Saxton, he changed his publisher to Harcourt, Brace and Com-pany. [15]

It is noteworthy that the sketch of Woodrow Wilson is the fourteenth of the twenty-seven biographies in *U.S.A.* (twenty-eight, if we count the concluding piece "Vag"), and occurs midway through the trilogy. "Meester Veelson" is Satan in Dos Passos' epic. Serpentine features are actually attributed to him, though only by a fictional character. In a narrative section of *Nineteen Nineteen*, Richard Ellsworth Savage sees the President's face thus: "It was a grey stony cold face grooved like the columns, very long under the silk hat. The little smile around the mouth looked as if it had been painted on afterwards. . . . A terrifying face," Savage says, "I swear it's a reptile's face, not warmblooded."[16]

The biography of Wilson stresses his Calvinist upbringing and describes him as at once ambitious, ruthless, and self-righteous. Dos Passos says that Wilson did not will the war, but yielded to the financiers and Anglophiles. He betrayed liberalism and neutrality, and then he betrayed his own Fourteen Points.

Three biographies deal with radical writers with whose careers Dos Passos was in sympathy: John Reed, Randolph Bourne, and Paxton Hibben. We have already said something about their influences on Dos Passos' own career. *U.S.A.* does not apportion admiration among the three according to their specific beliefs, just as it does not do so for Haywood, Debs, and La Follette. Dos Passos presents Reed, Bourne, and Hibben as rebels or reformers and as men of unusual integrity. Reed and Bourne he pictures as full of joy and vitality, qualities which often carry a moral connotation in his work. Hibben he dubs a Hoosier Quixote (the term, coming from the author of *Rosinante to the Road Again*, is complimentary). All three suffer in the war or in the reaction that follows: "the war," Dos Passos explains, "was a blast that blew out all the Diogenes lanterns." Bourne's biography contains a refrain from his anarchistic work "The State": "War is the health of the state." The aphorism impressed Dos Passos greatly. He uses it in the biography of Wilson, and he was one day to use it in criticizing Franklin Roosevelt.[17]

Dos Passos met John Reed only once and never met Randolph Bourne.[18] But he became a good friend of Paxton Hibben. While Hibben was more enthusiastic than he about the new Russia, the two friends agreed on most issues. Like Dos Passos, Hibben was never a Communist. "He was too much of an individualist . . . ever to have worked successfully with any organization exacting unquestioning obedience of its members," Suzanne La Follette has written. "It was his misfortune to be misunderstood and distrusted alike by conservatives and radicals."[19]

The three final biographies of *Nineteen Nineteen* discuss war victims. Two are devoted to men the I.W.W. considered martyrs of the "class war," Wesley Everest and Joe Hill.[20] The last biography (if we may call it one) considers the career of the Unknown Soldier.

In *The Big Money* Dos Passos' selection of subjects for biographies helps to indicate a collapse of political and economic reform movements. Each of the two prior volumes contains several biographies of political rebels, but *The Big Money* devotes only one, Veblen's, to such a figure. Dos Passos describes Veblen as an unhappy man who died feeling that his hopes for economic reorganization had been defeated. In a magnificent image, Dos Passos declares Veblen's memorial to be "the sharp clear prism of his mind."

Only against Comstockery and Victorian ethics, Dos Passos felt in 1936, had there been an advance in freedom since the war.[21] Perhaps it was for this reason that he included in *The Big Money* a sketch of the erratic life of Isadora Duncan. We must go beyond the biography to appreciate her importance as a symbol. Joseph Freeman writes that among radicals and liberals she was deemed both the greatest living dancer and the symbol of the body's deliverance from mid-Victorian taboos: "Isadora Duncan was not a dancer merely; she was a sublime cult. Her language of motion foretold the time when life would be 'frank and free,' when it would proceed under the sky with happy fearlessness of faith in the beauty of its own nature."[22]

Following this biography of a genuine artist comes "Adagio Dancer," an account of Rudolph Valentino. Dos Passos treats the motion picture star almost sympathetically but describes with skillful satire the manner in which newspapers, popular celebrities, and would-be-celebrities cashed in on the hysteria attending Valentino's death.

The biography of Frank Lloyd Wright is peculiarly related to Dos Passos' own life; Dos Passos, who had planned to study architecture, became one of the leading structural innovators among modern novelists. Wright has sought to apply new materials, skills, and inventions to human needs, Dos Passos says. But man's needs include social reform.

Perhaps in spite of himself the arrogant draftsman, the dilettante in concrete . . . has been forced by the logic of uses and needs, by the lifelong struggle against the dragging undertow of money in mortmain, to draft plans that demand for their fulfillment a new life. . . .

His blueprints, as once Walt Whitman's words, stir the young men. . . .[23]

In the biographies of Frederick Winslow Taylor, Henry Ford, and the Wright brothers, Dos Passos again stresses how little insight manufacturers and technicians have had into the needs of the society they have been creating. Taylor, who saw nothing undesirable about men becoming cogs, erred in believing that industrialists would let him increase wages as he made gears turn more rapidly. The Wright brothers created a machine that the world was unprepared to use sanely. Ford's biography offers a particularly ironic example of "cultural lag": one of the creators of mass production and hence of the modern American economy, Ford clings to his mother's precepts and thinks that the Great Depression is due to people's gambling and getting into debt.

In the biography of William Randolph Hearst, the penultimate biography (if we exclude "Vag"), Dos Passos turns to the waxing threat of Fascism. Since the twenties he had been taking sporadic notice of Fascism, and was increasingly apprehensive about industrialists' inflicting it on the United States. Through Hearst's control of newspapers and through his power in Hollywood, Dos Passos says, he is poisoning the minds of the least responsible portion of the public. Hearst admires Hitler's Reich, like Hearst's empire "the lowest common denominator come to power out of the rot of democracy."[24] An empire of the lowest common denominator, Dos Passos might have added, is at the antipodes of Walt Whitman's vision of America.

After he has recorded news of the stock market crash and of the depression, Dos Passos offers the final biography, that of Samuel Insull. "The Camera Eye (51)" concludes with a preposition while the Insull biography begins with its object:

we have only words against

POWER SUPERPOWER[25]

Here perhaps (as in the biography of Frank Lloyd Wright) is a hint of optimism. The Insull Empire falls in the stock market crash, though it falls only to bankers. So much, then, for power super-power? When the Roosevelt administration — which was renewing Dos Passos' hope in American government — extradites Insull and places him on trial, the leading businessmen gather around him.

The magnate does not, even in bankruptcy, lose citizenship in his "nation."

Vag, dispossessed of everything, including the expectations in which he was reared, belongs to the other nation. *U.S.A.* concludes with an account of this anonymous young man. Abased and hungry, he seeks a "hitchhike" on the road, while overhead a transcontinental airplane carries the wealthy to their destinations.

In the narrative sections constituting the body of *U.S.A.* Dos Passos skillfully interweaves the lives of twelve people who are under the pressures of contemporary society, and in so doing he reveals their responses and allows the reader to make comparisons among their characters. The twelve principals are:

Mac (Fainy McCreary), a printer, I.W.W. member, and convinced revolutionary. He escapes from a distressing marriage to a woman with middle-class ideals, but lacks the dedication to remain in the revolutionary labor movement.

Charley Anderson, an air force hero during the World War, an aircraft designer and would-be capitalist afterward. Anderson is a man of marked physical appetites. Early in life he adopts some revolutionary beliefs, but he has neither real convictions nor strong ethical scruples.

J. Ward Moorehouse, a public relations executive. A man of limited talents and sensibility, he capitalizes on most events, public, private, or intimate, and achieves formidable business success.

Janey Williams, a stenographer who comes from an impoverished middle-class family in Washington, D.C. As Moorehouse's secretary she finds the respectability and prestige she desires.

Joe Williams (Janey's brother), a merchant seaman, neither educated nor shrewd and aggressive. In both peace and war, his is the lot of a victim.

Richard Ellsworth Savage, a poet and aesthete at Harvard College and later J. Ward Moorehouse's assistant. Expediency brings him to abandon both his pacifism and his verse.

Eleanor Stoddard, an "arty" woman from Chicago, who establishes an interior decorating business. The daughter of an office worker in the stockyards, she yearns for and coldly pursues elegance, wealth, and social position.

Eveline Hutchins, Eleanor's partner before the war, and later a well-known Greenwich Village hostess. A restless, promiscuous woman, who has a group of radical friends, she seems largely concerned with leading an interesting life.

Ben Compton, a radical Jewish strike leader. A dedicated and strong-willed revolutionary, Compton goes to prison for refusing to enter the army, directs strikes for the Communist party after the war, and is finally expelled for not accepting party discipline.

Mary French, a Vassar student who rejects ''society'' for social work and radical activity. Intelligent, kind-hearted, and idealistic, she continues her radical career despite repeated disappointments in public and private life.

Daughter (Anne Elizabeth Trent), an erratic Texas girl who, during a textile strike in New Jersey, learns something of the cruelty of industrial conflict. In France with Near East Relief after the war, she is seduced and abandoned by Richard Ellsworth Savage.

Margo Dowling, a resolute show girl, of mean origins, who with some dissimulation and much luck, achieves Hollywood stardom.

Of these twelve characters, all but four are at some time sympathetically interested in pacifism or labor organization, while three are active radicals. The careers of most, to some extent all, of them help to explain the signal apathy of the middle class toward social reform and toward such seeming outrages as the executions of Sacco and Vanzetti. None of the twelve characters is shown suffering real economic privation. American society was thriving enough before the depression to allow them all to become reasonably comfortable, and Dos Passos was not concerned primarily with describing a physical class struggle; he was attempting to describe the process by which Americans develop a point of view toward events.

Dos Passos believed that finance-controlled industrialism had destroyed not only rural landscape, but also valuable moral and political principles. For such a belief an ample number of precedents existed. The period following the Civil War had for many writers been one of disillusionment as they witnessed the unprecedented and unholy passion for money which accompanied industrial expansion. Dos Passos thought that the World War had continued the spiritual degeneration which had become apparent during the Grant administration. He saw America's entry into the war as the moral and political debacle of his own generation. The war had, he held, destroyed democratic movements that had arisen to combat financier-

directed industrialization. It had fostered an unprecedented conformity. After the executions of Sacco and Vanzetti, and at about
the time that he was beginning work on *U.S.A.*, Dos Passos commented bitterly:

> The sudden gusher of American wealth in the last fifty years has
> boosted into power — into such power as would have sent shivers of
> envy down Alexander's spine — a class of illassorted mediocrities, who
> have not needed even much acquisitive skill to get where they are. Aping
> them is a servile generation of whitecollar slaves and small moneygrubbers
> and under that, making the wheels go around, endless formless and disunited
> strata of workers and farmers kept mostly in an opium dream of prosperity
> by cooing radios, the flamboyant movies and the instalment plan. In
> all that welter there is no trace of a scale of values. The last rags of
> the old puritan standards in which good was white and bad was black
> went under in the war. In the ten years that have followed the American
> mind has settled back into a marsh of cheap cosmopolitanism and wisecrack-
> ing, into a slow odorless putrescence. The protest that expressed itself
> in such movements as the I.W.W. and the Non-Partisan League has pretty
> well petered out.[26]

"Can anybody still really remember the different taste, the
Western free taste of the United States before the war?" Dos Passos
asked a number of years later, while he was still at work on *U.S.A.*
He liked the I.W.W. for its savor of fresh air and open roads,
for its remoteness from middle-class timorousness, as well as for
its economic program. "Can anyone really remember the free curiosity, the need to know what different jobs were like," Dos Passos
continued, "the careless throwing up of one job and moving to
another, the working man's sense of freedom in the United States
before the war?" Then people were still "moving west . . .
looking for a frontier, a place where a man could live as he chose,
exactly in accord with the clamor of the still small voice of stiff-
necked protestantism."[27]

Industrialism had wrought tremendous changes in the past half
century, but as a novelist Dos Passos had to describe not abstractions
but human beings. He began *U.S.A.* with the idea of writing a
series of primarily fictional reportages covering a long period.
Although he was always more interested in historical panorama
than in the theories of any political sect, he recalled decades later,
he began while writing *The Big Money* to see the elemental passions,

such as the urge for power, as better explanations of human behavior than economic determinism. Ideologies and creeds began to appear as masks for these elemental passions.[28]

We find some confirmation of Dos Passos' recollections in two of his critical comments of the time, though these comments are literary, and the Jeffersonian turn is many years away. It is, in fact, for their overall literary import to the trilogy that the two comments are mainly significant. As *U.S.A.* grew, Dos Passos seems to have debated whether he ought to consider his criterion of success to be the description of an era or the creation of character. He defended the first standard in 1928:

> The only excuse for a novelist, aside from the entertainment and vicarious living his books give the people who read them, is as a sort of second-class historian of the age he lives in. The "reality" he misses by writing about imaginary people, he gains by being able to build a reality more nearly out of his own factual experience than a plain historian or biographer can. I suppose the best kind of narrative would combine the two like Froissart or Commines, or Darwin in "The Voyage of the Beagle." I think that any novelist that is worth his salt is a sort of truffle dog digging up raw material which a scientist, an anthropologist or a historian can later use to permanent advantage. Of course there's Chaucer and Homer and the Edda, but that's all way over our heads.[29]

In 1934 Dos Passos declared portrayal of character the mark of a good novelist and referred to the description of an era as a minor achievement.

> The business of a novelist is, in my opinion, to create characters first and foremost, and then to set them in the snarl of the human currents of his time, so that there results an accurate permanent record of a phase of history. Everything in a novel that doesn't work towards these aims is superfluous or, at best, innocent day-dreaming. If the novelist really creates characters that are alive, the rest follows by implication. A record of his time is fairly easy to establish for any writer with the knack of honest observation and a certain amount of narrative skill. It's the invention of characters, which is work of an entirely different order from the jotting down of true-to-life silhouettes and sketches of people, that sets the novelist apart from the story-teller or commentator.[30]

The nature of this biography has made it necessary to emphasize historical events. We have examined Dos Passos' political development and, in so doing, have encountered historical occurrences which he was to portray in *U.S.A.* In the discussion that follows we shall have more to say about the historical sources for the events and characters portrayed. But to confine our attention to political biography and history would be inadvertently to misrepresent Dos Passos' achievement in *U.S.A.* Perhaps the major subject of the trilogy (particularly of *The Big Money*) is moral choice and human limitations.

The lives of the characters in *U.S.A.* are, of course, influenced immensely by the history of the era. World War I, the central event in the trilogy, draws Anderson, Moorehouse, Savage, Janey Williams, Eleanor Stoddard, and Eveline Hutchins to Europe; it hurls Joe Williams from port to port and from ship to lifeboat. The power of the state-at-war intimidates Anderson and Savage, while the lure of big money later takes the two from inherently valuable work to stock market manipulation or to the worst kind of verbal manipulation. The same wartime drive for conformity which helps to silence these two men speeds Ben Compton to prison. Strikes reflecting the obverse side of the prosperity of the twenties help to explain why Mary French works with the Communist party. Amid the hokum and ballyhoo of the decade, Margo Dowling, a tough little girl who thinks about everything except the problems of acting, becomes a cinema idol.

But if the careers and personalities of Dos Passos' people are demonstrably influenced by social, political, and economic forces, they are not determined by these forces. On the one hand is the world, yes; but on the other is character. Some individuals merely drift. Others set sails to speed with the winds or to struggle against them. The traits that bespeak how an individual will cope with the world include intelligence, independence, and compassion.

To stop even here would be to do *U.S.A.* an injustice; the grandeur of the trilogy arises from its describing far more than a society and its various types of denizens. *U.S.A.* also describes certain rules under which human life always has been lived. One rule is that character constitutes a large part of fate and that one is at every moment molding his character. Suddenly life is almost over, and one has and is what one has lived.

It would be a mistake to think of most, or perhaps any, of the characters as having betrayed very great gifts. Much of the pathos in *U.S.A.* is due to the impossibility of conceiving of such people as Mac, Eveline Hutchins, or Moorehouse as being impressive under any circumstances. Still, most of the characters suffer from having violated themselves. The author makes the extent of a character's sufferings depend in large part on that character's former horizons. (Dos Passos' old concept of the "deadalive" flits about *U.S.A.*, although he does not allow it to impede realistic characterization.) Eleanor Stoddard suffers not at all, but Moorehouse, despite all the satire introducing him, does suffer somewhat.

"And to think once upon a time I was planning to be a songwriter." He smiled. Dick smiled too and held out his hand. "Shake hands, J. W.," he said, "with the ruins of a minor poet."
    "Anyway," said J. W., "the children will have the advantages I never had. . . ."[31]

The pictures of Ben Compton and Mary French are thrilling evidences of Dos Passos' insight into human fate. When one is struggling for a better world, even as when he is struggling for big money, he may resort to stratagems and suffer wounds. Such experiences shape character. However deep Mary's compassion and however altruistic her and Ben's goals may be, the two emerge as contorted human beings. Mary is so hardened by social conflict and private misfortune that she loses much of her original breadth and generosity. Compton very early in his career strives to become a "well-sharpened instrument." Such a transformation was certainly repugnant to Dos Passos; the metaphor is not only mechanical, but is also reminiscent of Ellen Thatcher's feeling herself "frozen in a single gesture." It is, then, the spiritual welfare of the characters in *U.S.A.* that gives the author and the reader concern.

Of the twenty narrative sections in *The 42nd Parallel*, the first seven and the seventeenth are devoted to the story of Mac, about a decade before and after 1900. Mac is the oldest of the major characters who are radicals. Perhaps it is a loss that the early sections, instead of considering a number of major characters, treat one. But the seeming remoteness of Mac's era is probably the point that Dos Passos is trying to establish. He has set a working-man in the "snarl of the human currents" of the West in the first decade of the century. Both Mac's story and the story of Charley Anderson, a younger man, convey something of the adventurousness that Dos Passos believed characteristic of American life before the war.

Mac, born about 1877, is of Irish descent. His father is an invalid who works as a night watchman in Middletown, Connecticut. Mac's mother takes in washing. The fates of his parents, like the fates of many of the characters in the prior novel *Manhattan Transfer*, are implicit but unmistakable criticisms of contemporary capitalism. When the employees at the mill where Mac's father works go on strike, the management dismisses Mr. McCreary and hires guards from a detective agency. Mac's family curses the management and the strikers — "furreners" — alternately. Mrs. McCreary takes in more and more wash, and one day she dies of overwork.

Mr. McCreary, unable to pay his debts, takes his family to Chicago, where his brother-in-law has a printing shop. In Chicago, McCreary vainly seeks a job for years, and then dies. For ten years Mac lives with his uncle, a radical Irishman who decries capitalists and priests. After Mac finishes school, he goes to work for him. When the uncle supports a strike in the trade, the other master printers buy up his outstanding bills and force him into bankruptcy. Mac must find new employment.

Doc Bingham, a charlatan book salesman ("sole owner and representative of the Truthseeker Corporation") browbeats the boy into going on a selling tour with him. The salesman reminds one of the King and the Duke in *The Adventures of Huckleberry Finn*. He has a stock of books that includes *The Queen of the White Slaves, The Popish Plot, Dr. Spikenard's Short Sermons for All Occasions*. From among this stock he moralistically dispenses appropriate volumes to traveling businessmen and farmers' wives and sons. As he sells, he utters platitudinous sentiments, quotes Shakespeare, and seeks opportunities to sleep with the wives. The episode is not merely hilarious; it is Chaucerian. Bingham lives, the American countryside lives, the language lives!

Later Mac meets Ike Hall, a youth who is wandering about to see the world. The conversation in which each discovers that the other is a socialist conveys some of the flavor of western radicalism. Mac and Ike talk about *Looking Backward, The Appeal to Reason*, Hearst, Marx, and revolution. The two subsequently wander through the Northwest, taking temporary jobs as they go.

In San Francisco Mac gets a job in a print shop owned by an Italian anarchist and becomes engaged to a girl named Maisie. After the San Francisco earthquake destroys the print shop, Mac goes to work for the *Bulletin*. At a lecture by Upton Sinclair, he meets Fred Hoff, a young man who tells him about the newly formed I.W.W. Hoff is going to Goldfield, Nevada, to see what he can do to help in the miners' strike. He tells Mac that the I.W.W. will publish a paper there and that Mac should help, rather than print lies about the working class. Mac fills out an I.W.W. card and subsequently goes to Goldfield.

As soon as Mac gets off the train there, he is accosted by a khaki-clad man who asks him his business. To get into the town, Mac must feign an excuse. Here once again, as throughout the narrative, is implicit social commentary. When Mac reaches the newspaper office, Fred Hoff tells him that the I.W.W. has the restaurant workers and some of the miners out on strike. The Western Federation of Miners has become "yellow," he says, and the A.F.L. has brought in a scab organizer. Mac and Fred Hoff report Big Bill Haywood's exciting revolutionary speech when Haywood comes to town. But Mac stays in Goldfield only a few months, for Maisie has written that she is pregnant.

Mac marries Maisie, gets a job in a print shop in San Diego, and buys a bungalow on payments. Maisie's behavior is in the pattern of an industrial society stimulated by advertising. She constantly asks for new house furnishings and annoys Mac because he is not earning as much as her brothers, who are in business. She burns Mac's radical papers and causes him to lose touch with the I.W.W. One day, as Mac is on his way to a vaudeville theater with Maisie, he witnesses an incident in a free-speech fight: a young man has chained himself to a lamp post and is reading the Declaration of Independence. At the vaudeville show, Mac observes that Maisie is "completely happy . . . like a little girl at a party."[32] She is a model recipient of the culture satirized in "Newsreel." Mac walks out of the theater in disgust, but he cannot find I.W.W. headquarters.

Unemployment, medical bills, and moving expenses bring the family into considerable debt. After a violent argument about money, Mac leaves Maisie and goes to Mexico. In Mexico City a native girl makes life so pleasant for him that he becomes the contented proprietor of a bookstore. He originally intended to join Zapata's rebels, but now when he hears that they are about to enter the city, he flees to Vera Cruz with the girl and her family. Mac does not appear again in the trilogy.

Western radicalism and the I.W.W. are explored also in the single Charley Anderson section of *The 42nd Parallel*. In Anderson's story, as in others in the trilogy, are depicted too the increasing urbanization of the United States and the decline in the importance of religion. Charley's mother runs a railroad boardinghouse in Fargo, North Dakota. She insists that he attend church on Sunday and read a chapter of the Bible every day. Nevertheless, Charley, like many another similarly reared youth of his generation, grows up irreligious. His first break with home occurs when he spends a summer vacation in Minneapolis working in his brother's garage. (The fact that the German father-in-law of his brother is a socialist provides one more element in Dos Passos' portrayal of western socialism before the war.) After Charley finishes high school he goes to the Twin Cities, gets a job as a machinist's assistant, and begins a night-school course that will prepare him to study civil engineering.

While in a hospital Charley meets a dispossessed farmer from Iowa. The farmer says that Wall Street bankers want to bankrupt farmers and seize the country. His talk about Henry George, La Follette, the Non-Partisan League, and the Farmer-Labor party gets Anderson interested in politics.

Anderson soon grows unhappy because he has traveled little and accomplished nothing. After losing his job he abandons an unfaithful girl friend and goes to Milwaukee, where he spends an unhappy week "pearldiving" in a lunchroom. Monte Davis, a fanatical, pathetic I.W.W. man who works there, persuades everyone to walk out because the I.W.W. is conducting a free-speech fight. Anderson has by now himself become an advocate of revolution.

Charley encounters Monte Davis again in Chicago and goes with him to an I.W.W. meeting in front of the Newberry Library. Then, after some luckless wanderings in the Midwest and the South, he travels by jalopy to New Orleans and by steamboat to New York. On the boat he encounters Doc, a Floridian who is preparing to sail for France with a volunteer ambulance corps. Doc does not believe in shooting white men, but he wants to see the war before it goes "bellyup"! He persuades Charley to enlist too.

The United States has just declared war. In New York every building has its flag, and hysteria is growing rife. In a German restaurant a band plays "The Star-Spangled Banner" continually — "settin' up exercises," Doc complains. A group of patrons who refuse to rise are assaulted by other diners and then arrested.[33] At a restaurant on the lower East Side, Charley hears Ben Compton say there will be a revolution if the government tries to impose conscription on the country. Charley sits down with Compton and a Minnesotan who is a reporter for the Socialist *Call*. He has almost decided to stay in the city when the two tell him there is not much chance for a man to work his way through engineering school unless he has some money saved. The final scene in *The 42nd Parallel* depicts Charley Anderson aboard a ship sailing for France.

It is clear that Dos Passos in *The 42nd Parallel* attempted to explore what one historian has described as the heyday of American Socialism. Dos Passos depicts socialism, syndicalism, and other varieties of economic radicalism as integral parts of American life before the war.[34]

In answer to the question of how he came to meet I.W.W. members like Mac, Dos Passos writes: "Met some in Greenwich Village bars in 1920 etc but learned most about the wobblies from a highly articulate fellow named Gladwin Bland I knew in Mexico . . . [in the mid 1920s]." He mentions also meeting and occasionally still corresponding with Slim Martin.[35] (A friend of Eugene O'Neill, Martin suggested some of the atmosphere and dialogue of *The Hairy Ape*.[36])

As a picturesque organization with a native revolutionary tradition, the I.W.W. interested Dos Passos both as novelist and as political commentator. Its considerable dramatic qualities have been stressed by the author of a formal history of the union:

An organization which sang in deep-throated tones songs of sardonic humor and savage mockery; which evolved a vituperative cant of its own; whose picket lines were a thousand miles long; whose tactics of battle in free-speech fights and in the harvest fields were unexpected and bold; which laughed with inimitable, grim humor — such an organization cannot be completely understood unless some attention is given to its romantic side.[37]

Dos Passos' trilogy does portray this side: the language (bindlestiff, scissorbill, etc.), the personalities, and the songs. *U.S.A.* tells the stories of particular people, moreover, not of conventions and schisms. By examining the history of the strike at Goldfield, we can see how here, as everywhere else in the narrative, historical material that is not a vivid part of a character's experience is ignored.[38]

It was at Goldfield, Nevada, that the I.W.W. first applied notably its principles of revolutionary industrial unionism. The Western Federation of Miners had a strong industrial union there, and the I.W.W. had a thriving mass union containing workers of all occupations. The A.F.L., with only craft locals of carpenters and typographers, was weak. During 1906 and 1907 bitter fights occurred between W.F.M.–I.W.W. people and the mine operators. These were due mainly to attempts by the W.F.M. and I.W.W. to supplant craft unionism in Goldfield.

According to a W.F.M. account, the dispute began in a controversy of the Tonopah *Sun*, supported by the A.F.L. locals, with the I.W.W.–W.F.M. When the *Sun* attacked the I.W.W., the I.W.W.–W.F.M. boycotted the paper, and the newsboys, who were I.W.W. members, refused to sell it. The *Sun's* attempt to use strikebreaker-newsboys failed. An I.W.W. official, Vincent St. John, has written of this strike period as a kind of golden era of the I.W.W.[39]

Very little of this background appears in *U.S.A.*, but how well the story of Mac the printer dovetails with the history of a strike that began when the I.W.W. boycotted a particularly obnoxious newspaper!

Dos Passos found much to admire in the I.W.W. Why, then, did he make Mac, the principal I.W.W. character in the narrative, so vacillating a revolutionary? Our answer probably is that Dos Passos' "warping newsprint into faces" meant groping for men's traits as well as their ideals. In his lack of dedication, Mac suggests a typical I.W.W. member. He certainly does so after Goldfield. There were more Macs than Fred Hoffs and possibly more sympathizers like Charley Anderson than members like Mac. The I.W.W. regarded itself as a revolutionary, not a business, union; however, the American economy contained sufficient lures and American society a sufficient host of Loreleis to keep the number of dedicated revolutionaries small.[40]

Almost all Dos Passos' fiction from *One Man's Initiation — 1917* to *U.S.A.* is concerned with the role of deliberately manufactured opinion in America. The propaganda that helped to bring the United States into the war in 1917, the hysteria that prevailed during the conflict, and the antilabor campaign after the war — all made the planned and paid-for manipulation of thought seem to Dos Passos crucial in current history.

Although J. Ward Moorehouse is an important figure in all three volumes of *U.S.A.*, sections devoted to him appear in only *The 42nd Parallel*. The fact is significant. In each of the narrative sections of the trilogy, Dos Passos tells the story partly in his own language and partly in language which the subject himself might employ. This dual account, the main narrative one, must be distinguished from quotations and from material that is clearly labeled as thought.[41] The story of J. Ward Moorehouse is savagely satirical. And one of the ways in which Dos Passos achieves his satire is to make the reader privy, by means of narrative style, to the banal thoughts of Moorehouse, and later, after Moorehouse has become an institution, to depict him only through other people's eyes.

No other satire in the narrative is at once as direct and as wanton as that devoted to Moorehouse; if Dos Passos sees himself as a rebuilder of venerable words, he sees Moorehouse as their mutilator. For a moment the satire threatens to explode the tonal range of the book, remarkably broad as that range is: Moorehouse was born on the Fourth of July, and his mother asked the nurse about firecrackers as a prenatal influence! After Moorehouse's father, a railroad station agent, is injured in an accident, Moorehouse is forced to leave the University of Pennsylvania and go to work for a real estate firm. He learns that he has a business asset in his "pair of bright blue eyes" and his "engaging boyish look"; he reads *Success Magazine* and is careful to dress with utter conventionality.

Moorehouse marries the daughter of a wealthy physician although he knows that she is pregnant by another man. The couple go to Paris, where Moorehouse gets a job interviewing American businessmen for the *New York Herald*. "This was his meat," writes Dos Passos, depicting Moorehouse's trite mind, "and enabled him to make many valuable contacts."[42] Moorehouse is of the temperament to cash in on anything. Discovering, after his return to America, that his wife is misbehaving, he demands not only a divorce but money as well.

The Homestead strike leads writers and progressive congressmen to attack the steel industry. Now an advertising and promotion man, Moorehouse capitalizes on the situation by suggesting that steel companies "educate the public by carefully planned publicity extending over a term of years."[43] When an information bureau is set up, he becomes an executive. Moorehouse subsequently marries an heiress, establishes an agency of his own, and turns his attention to capital-labor relations, which he views as an "unexploited angle."

Moorehouse makes himself an intermediary between financiers and industrialists, such as those who appear in the biography sections of *U.S.A.*, and the public. In addition to advancing the specific business interests of his clients, who include "Marigold Copper" and "Southwestern Oil," he combats the ideas of muckrakers, populists, and socialists. When America enters the war, Ben Compton remarks that his sister, a stenographer for Moorehouse's firm, said the clients were paying Moorehouse to disseminate prowar propaganda.

During the war Moorehouse is both director of publicity for the Red Cross and a member of Woodrow Wilson's Public Information Committee. At the peace conference he represents American oil companies seeking to prevent the British from appropriating Near Eastern oil resources. Apparently to illustrate the tawdriness and utter irresponsibility of so august an institution as the Moorehouse firm, Dos Passos, in the third volume of the trilogy, exhumes Doc Bingham. The philandering bookseller is by the 1920s the proprietor of a huge patent medicine concern. Moorehouse fights for and gets its account, promotes Bingham products, and bribes congressmen to defeat a pure food and drug bill.

Examination of historical sources for Moorehouse's career and activities is both possible and enlightening (although the story and descriptions of any illegal deeds are fictitious). The public relations man Edward L. Bernays writes that the muckrakers originally drove businessmen to employ "whitewash." ("Whitewash" is Bernays' own term, which he distinguishes from "publicity based on information and disclosure.") First those businessmen whom muckrakers had attacked and then other businessmen initiated programs of concealing or defending their activities. "Engineering of consent on a mass scale was ushered in in the 1914–18 period," says Bernays, recalling that he like his colleagues "found new public relations horizons being opened by the requirements of the war." The war led directly to an expansion and refinement of propaganda for peacetime.[44]

Moorehouse's public career is in many ways similar to that of Ivy Lee; Dos Passos, in fact, acknowledged a probable influence. When Lee "was a young New York newspaper man thirty-odd years ago," the *New York Times* wrote after his death in 1934, "there were numerous press agents in town who promoted theatres and stage stars, but there was no specialist in publicity who conferred on terms of equality with the boards of directors of great corporations. His life spanned that change, and he had much to do with the change."[45]

After several years as assistant to the president of the Pennsylvania Railroad, Lee, in January 1915, became publicity counsel to John D. Rockefeller, gaining this position through work for the multimillionaire's son, John D. Rockefeller, Jr. A major stockholder in the Colorado Fuel and Iron Company, the son was a severely harassed man when in 1914 he first summoned Lee to his aid. Violent outbreaks had attended a year-old strike by Colorado miners. At Ludlow, militia firing into tents had killed seven men, two women, and eleven children. Pickets led by Upton Sinclair and "Sweet Marie Ganz" demonstrated before the younger Rockefeller's offices at 26 Broadway, driving him to his estate at Pocantico Hills. I.W.W. men pursued him even there.[46]

Lee's publicity work on his behalf so outraged the reformer-journalist George Creel (later chairman of the wartime Committee on Public Information) that he attacked the Colorado Fuel and Iron Company. Lee subsequently had to make some discomfiting admissions before a Commission on Industrial Relations. In a bulletin of his, the annual wages of strike leaders had been represented as their pay for only nine weeks; one man receiving $4,052.92 had been listed as getting $32,000.[47]

Lee worked as publicity counsel to John D. Rockefeller until April 1916, when he established a business of his own. He remained Rockefeller's adviser, however, and his firm enjoyed Standard Oil's patronage. During World War I, Lee (like the fictitious Moorehouse) served as unsalaried publicity director for the Red Cross. His clients during a career which ended only in 1934 included the Copper and Brass Research Association, the Bethlehem Steel Company, and the Guggenheim and Chrysler interests.[48]

Moorehouse's client Bingham bears some resemblance in his showmanship and product line to Bernarr Macfadden, the picturesque hawker of "Physcultopathy" and the *New York Evening Graphic*. "Like so many other big New Yorkers," Henry F. Pringle declared of Macfadden in 1928, "he has recently engaged a press agent. Having first considered engaging Ivy Lee, he later turned to Edward L. Bernays, only slightly less renowned in the public relations field."[49]

Nineteen Nineteen is concerned, not with soldiers in combat, but with Americans at home or behind the lines. Only in the story of Joe Williams do we encounter the war from the standpoint of a man who is shot at and ordered about. And even Williams, as a merchant seaman, lives and travels in a civilian as well as a quasi-military world.

We must consider the life of Joe Williams together with that of his sister Janey, for the history of the pair is a comment on the development of social classes in America and the relationships among them. The Williamses live in Georgetown. The mother is an old resident who links the dilapidation of the section with the decline in her family's fortunes. The father is a former towboat captain with a poorly paid job in the government patent office. Two events which Dos Passos presents in a matter-of-fact manner seem upon a rereading of the narrative to be portents, since the role of the school in determining social status in America has for many decades been crucial.[50] Joe has to leave high school at the end of one year and go to work; Janey takes the commercial course, learning stenography and typewriting.

Janey's fear of contamination from plebeians appears due to her family's precarious middle-class status. She comes to the Moorehouse firm suspicious of labor and is relieved when she discovers that Barrow does not resemble her conception of a labor leader. Because Joe looks like a workingman, Janey prevents him from visiting her at an apartment that she is sharing with friends. She never doubts that Moorehouse is doing more valuable work than Joe, no more than she doubts that civilization is threatened in Europe rather than in the mining fields of Colorado.

Joe's conviction that the war is entirely crooked is the direct result of his experience as a sailor, not of ideology. He remains a fairly conventional lower-middle-class Southerner, with the passion for baseball that Dos Passos had in 1916 jocularly associated with American immaturity. When during the war two men in a saloon praise the I.W.W., Joe says that such "stuff was only for foreigners, but if somebody started a white man's party to fight the profiteers and the goddam bankers he'd be with 'em."[51] When he becomes a second mate, Joe resolves to be prudent; deciding that Janey is probably right about the war's being for civilization, he buys a Liberty Bond. His death in a fight over a French prostitute whom he discovers dancing with a Senegalese officer was prepared in the South many years before. John Chamberlain's remark about Joe as a simple man who "might have been content in a different society under his own vine and fig tree" provides an apt epitaph.[52]

Henry James in his short story "The Jolly Corner" described an expatriate, Spencer Brydon, returning to his native New York to seek out the self he might have been if he had remained at home and worked for conventional success. Brydon stalks a *Doppelgänger* in the house where he was born, but when he finally confronts his ghostly double, he collapses in revulsion and terror.

No *Doppelgänger*, Richard Ellsworth Savage lacks Dos Passos' intelligence, imagination, and energy, as well as integrity; but Savage shares enough of his author's biography to suggest that whatever other sources Dos Passos may have drawn upon, he sketched an *alter ego*. The absent father, here shamefully absent, in prison, and the mother who must be protected have counterparts in Dos Passos' own life. At Harvard, Savage is a poet, an aesthete, and a member of the staff of the *Monthly*. He is a pacifist, he becomes excited about Woodrow Wilson's election in 1916, and he joins the Norton-Harjes volunteer ambulance corps. His letter to a friend condemning the war as crooked is almost identical in theme with the letter that got Dos Passos into trouble, and his fate when censors take notice of the letter is identical. After Savage is ordered home, he considers going to Spain to write "flaming poems and manifestoes, calling young men to revolt against their butchers. . . ."[53] But in the United States a lawyer whose solicitude for Savage is vaguely homosexual exacts from him a promise not to talk about peace until after the war. Savage being the grandson of a general, the lawyer is able to get him a commission in Ordnance. After his return to Europe, Savage dismisses the fate of wartime dissenters with the observation: "Well, that comes of monkeying with the buzzsaw."[54]

Miserable because he has no prospects after the war and feeling that he must help his mother financially, Savage accepts a job with Moorehouse, saying that he will be able to continue a writing career in his spare time. His tendency being to regard his muse as ornamental and opportunistic, it is significant that he never does continue. His talk at business conferences with Moorehouse is false and cynical. On one occasion, when he detects an oily note in his conversation with a young employee and his girl, he suddenly stops speaking. But by the end of the trilogy, when he is in actual charge of the firm, he has adopted cant as his normal conversation.

In *The Theory of the Leisure Class* Veblen speaks of the leisure and luxury that upper-class women enjoy as symbolizing the prowess of their mates. However acute his observation may be, it is concerned mainly with the male's attitude. Even a chattel wife in a barbarian culture sought more than her husband's image when she looked into the mirror. In the America depicted in *U.S.A.* it is frequently the woman who, through conspicuous consumption, wages the battle for status, her husband remaining passive or suffering distress.

The marriages of Mary French's mother and father and of

Mac and Maisie are between predatory females and peaceable men. Dos Passos' repeated portrayals of such marriages are consistent with, though not mere reflections of, certain sentiments of the revolutionary left. The young anarchist who makes a radical of Ben Compton voices such feelings when he declares that women are "the main seduction of capitalist society."[55]

The chief women characters in *U.S.A.* are Eleanor Stoddard, Eveline Hutchins, Janey Williams, Mary French, Margo Dowling, and Anne Elizabeth Trent, or Daughter. Of Mary and Daughter we shall speak later. Eleanor, Eveline, and Janey all admire J. Ward Moorehouse. (Jimmy Herf in *Manhattan Transfer* and the journalist Jerry Burnham in *U.S.A.* comment bitterly, we may note, upon the extent to which women are attracted to men with power.[56]) Janey, a plain woman, becomes attached to Moorehouse but can achieve no more than to identify herself with his firm as she turns spinster. Eleanor uses Moorehouse, as she uses everyone else. Eveline gives herself to Moorehouse to win him, but she is subsequently worsted in the rivalry by Eleanor and snubbed by Janey.

Eleanor and Eveline are more dissimilar than their close association and their interest in art might seem to indicate. Another of Dos Passos' aesthete types, Eleanor identifies art with absence of vulgarity and with prestige rather than with respect and sympathy for human beings. She spends her life pursuing wealth and social position, using and discarding people as she proceeds. "When she was small she hated everything," Dos Passos writes in introducing her. "She hated her father. . . . He worked in an office in the stockyards and came home with the stockyards stench. . . ."[57] She would dream that her mother was a society lady and lived with her in Oak Park. Her treatment of her father is analogous to, though nastier than, Janey's treatment of her brother. Eleanor's friendship with Moorehouse in New York, where she establishes her interior decorating service, is a business asset. She and Moorehouse apparently do not have adulterous relations until the two are in France together; neither can survive scandal, and for Eleanor cohabitation, like patriotism, is a stratagem, not an instinct.[58] After the war Eleanor does well in business and marries an exiled Russian aristocrat; Moorehouse, discomfited, predicts that the husband will "eat her out of house and home." To Dos Passos Eleanor's fate must have seemed the most empty and ludicrous imaginable.

Eveline is a more complex person. Her impulse to engage

in sexual relations is much stronger than her ability to love, and she indulges freely, if selectively, before and after her marriage. Somewhat interested in pacifism before the war, she has a group of radical friends afterward, but she is neither a reflective nor a dedicated individual. Her behavior is due to her being as much concerned with leading an interesting life as with becoming rich and socially successful. Being the daughter of a Unitarian minister, she has enjoyed some of the advantages of which Eleanor Stoddard dreamed. She is confident of her social status and feels no need to walk tiptoe.

For Eveline, as for Eleanor, Savage, and even Moorehouse, the war offers an opportunity to escape from financial troubles, moral restrictions, or boredom. Eveline enjoys her stay in Europe, to which she goes as Eleanor Stoddard's assistant in the Red Cross. Don Stevens, whom she likes, is frequently with her at night. At the end of the war, realizing that youth is going, she contrives a marriage with Paul Johnson, a soldier perhaps five years her junior.

On the ship returning to America, Eveline invites Charley Anderson to come and visit her and Paul. Soon she is committing adultery with Charley. Later Eveline becomes noted for having the most interesting people in New York at her cocktail parties. She tells Savage that she has decided upon a divorce, adding that she likes someone very much and wishes to make some sense out of her life. Eveline, whose clothes have taken on a last-year's look, attempts desperately to get support from Savage or Moorehouse for a play that the newspaper columnist she wants has written. She is unsuccessful, and the columnist becomes engaged to someone else.

At one of Eveline's cocktail parties, which people as diverse as Margo Dowling and George Barrow attend, Mary French notices that Eveline is tired and nervous. The narrative section of *The Big Money* ends with a friend hysterically calling Mary the next day to say that Eveline is dead, apparently from an overdose of sleeping medicine. Her death, like the apartment house fire in Thomas Wolfe's *You Can't Go Home Again*, symbolizes the disastrous conclusion of a decade consecrated to hedonism.

Like Wolfe and Fitzgerald, Dos Passos could and did depict the twenties as a party. But he alone among the major writers of his generation developed as an important theme the economic ills of industrialism during the decade. These ills, we have seen, were chronic for unskilled, unorganized immigrant workers and for many workers in the depressed industries. Dos Passos' account of economic hardships during the twenties found a sympathetic hearing in the depression-stricken thirties.

The early story of Ben Compton is told in *Nineteen Nineteen*. Ben's father is a Jewish immigrant who repairs watches in a jewelry store. When he becomes ill, the Comptons lose their house in Flatbush. Possessing the sense of family solidarity reputedly widespread among Jews, Ben intends to enable his parents to retire and his sister to give up her job and marry; to accomplish these aims, he plans to study law and then go into business.

One summer while Ben is helping to run a canteen in a construction camp, he meets a young Italian anarchist who makes a radical of him. When Ben returns home to matriculate at the City College of New York, he joins the Socialist party. He also reads Marx's *Capital* at the library on Sunday afternoons and goes to lectures at the Rand School. He is studying to be a "wellsharpened instrument." ("I think," Dos Passos says of his narrative here, "the 'wellsharpened instrument' phrase first appeared in a speech or article of Lenin's — it was much used in Marxist discussion of the role of the intellectual."[59])

At a Cooper Union lecture Ben meets Helen Mauer, who was arrested and blacklisted during the Paterson strike and now works at Wanamaker's department store. Helen speaks disparagingly of the socialists and approvingly of the syndicalists. After a dispute with his father over Ben's remark that he has transferred his devotion from his family to the working class, Ben leaves home. He lives with Helen in Passaic, taking a job in a mill there. When a strike occurs, Ben and Helen serve on the strike committee, and Ben discovers that he is a good speaker.

It is worth noting how Dos Passos writes about strikes. Georges Sorel, the syndicalist philosopher, made the memorable assertion that the general strike is the proletarian myth — which he described as "a body of images capable of evoking instinctively all the sentiments which correspond to the different manifestations of the war undertaken by Socialism against modern society."[60] The fact that he was led to ascribe such importance to the general strike indicates the marked connotations that the mere word "strike" may have among leftists. Although Dos Passos does not depict any strikes as portentous events, he views them as more than humdrum aspects of collective bargaining. In *U.S.A.*, as in the play *Airways, Inc.*, strikes provide a means of examining American society and studying character.

An illustration may be found in the story of Anne Elizabeth Trent, daughter of a Texas attorney. The encounter of this ebullient girl with New York radicals is as comic as her consternation at the obscenities of industrial warfare is sobering. Webb Cruthers, an anarchist whom Daughter has met at the Columbia School of Journalism, takes her to see the textile strike that Ben Compton is directing. Subsequently she reproaches Cruthers for having run "like a deer" after making an impromptu speech; she finds his "revolutionary tactics" as ludicrous as she finds his attempt to initiate her into free love unimpressive. The mill guards, she says, were the only people who looked like white men to her. When Cruthers again takes her to New Jersey and she sees a policeman kick a woman picket in the face, Daughter knocks the policeman down and is jailed. However, her superficial and conventional judgments of people (Sacco and Vanzetti would not have impressed her as white) later lead to her mistake in loving and trusting handsome, accomplished Captain Savage.

When Ben Compton is sent to jail for six months as a result of strike activities, the newspapers describe him as a well-known socialist agitator. In jail he meets an I.W.W. member who advises him to get a red card and go to the West Coast if he wishes to learn about the labor movement. Ben is among the many participants in a free-speech fight in Everett, Washington, whom deputies kidnap and beat horribly (the description of the beating is among the most vivid parts of the trilogy). He returns to New York to raise money for seventy-four I.W.W. members who have been jailed in Everett, charged with murder.

While Ben is in New York studying law and making speeches about the Everett massacre, the Russian revolution occurs and the United States enters the war. Dos Passos masterfully describes the rejoicing of Jews upon the Czar's overthrow, the disappointment in Wilson of his pacifist supporters, and the changes which the war induces in American society. When Ben hears that the Maximalists have taken power in Russia, he decides not to flee to Mexico, despite the likelihood of his indictment under the Espionage Act. His and Savage's actions make us recall the letter to McComb in which Dos Passos contrasted, with the behavior of certain East Side Jews in 1917, the decorous radicalism of Harvard men. Arrested while making an anti-war speech to greet the "triumphant" Russian workers, Ben refuses to escape all trouble with the law by heeding his draft call. Having monkeyed with the buzzsaw, he is sentenced to twenty years in prison. After the armistice the sentence is reduced to ten years, and Ben goes to the federal penitentiary in Atlanta.

Mary French grows up in Colorado. Her father is a physician who lost his wealth through a bad investment. Instead of attempting to reassemble a fortune, he works for years among impoverished coal miners. Mary's mother, who is preoccupied with attaining social position and wealth, constantly berates her husband for having ruined her life. Mary often catches herself wishing that her mother would die. Once her parents have a terrible argument because her father says that he will vote for Debs. Two or three years later, when Mary is a junior at Vassar, Mrs. French divorces her husband.

Mary majors in sociology at Vassar and spends a summer vacation doing settlement work at Hull House. Her outlook resembles that of her father, to whom she is deeply attached. She possesses more intelligence and sympathy than her mother. She reads a great deal, the books that influence her being the same ones that influenced hundreds of left intellectuals before the war: Upton Sinclair's *The Jungle*, Ernest Poole's *The Harbor*, Herbert Croly's *The Promise of American Life*. On one occasion, Mrs. French tells Mary that she owes it to her parents to make a social debut. Mary, revolted by this talk, goes to her room and opens Veblen's *The Theory of the Leisure Class*.

After her father dies Mary leaves college and goes to Hull House, where she does social work for three years. Later she moves to Pittsburgh and tries to get a job in industry. Unsuccessful in this attempt, she becomes a reporter for the *Times-Sentinel*. The steel strike of 1919 is about to begin, and the editor asks Mary to write a feature about paid red agitators and well-compensated workers. The editor is not a radical's caricature but a good-natured person motivated as much by conviction as by expediency. Nevertheless, when Mary submits what seems to her to be a true report, he fires her. She then does publicity work for the strikers.

When the strike is near collapse, Mary accepts a job as secretary to George Barrow, a sometime A.F.L. official who has come to Pittsburgh with a Senatorial investigating committee. She believes the job may enable her to free some of the imprisoned strike leaders.

Dos Passos had the same general dislike of the A.F.L. that

Veblen and the I.W.W. had, and his attitude may have motivated the comical portrayal of Barrow as a shifty-eyed individual preoccupied with sex but unable to get himself satisfactorily married.[61] The A.F.L.'s accepting capitalism and the war explains many of Barrow's activities. When he had visited Hull House after the war, Barrow had defended labor's participation in the conflict, telling Mary that labor could, as a result, get "anything." He now tells her he has Judge Gary's word that the steel trust will not discriminate against any strikers and that experts are working on the technical problems of an eight-hour day. Mary's knowledge of conditions in the steel industry may influence legislation, he says. When the strike ends disastrously and Mary learns that the steel firms are blacklisting large numbers of workers, she shouts: "We're just laborfakers."[62] She has been living with Barrow, but she refuses to marry him; instead she goes to New York and has an abortion.

In New York Mary writes an article for the *Freeman* and gets a research job with the International Ladies Garment Workers Union. When she hears that Ben Compton, who has just been released from prison, needs a place where he can find rest and avoid federal detectives, she brings him to a rich friend's apartment. After Mary and Ben have been together for a week, they decide they are in love.

Compton goes to New Jersey to lead some textile strikes, and Mary helps with strike publicity after work. They are together whenever he comes to New York. Finally they decide to marry, and she becomes pregnant. But when the Communists call upon Ben — as they had, in historical fact, called upon Weisbord — to organize the textile workers around Passaic, Ben says that having a baby will impair Mary's usefulness to the movement; there will be time for a baby after the revolution. The two have their first quarrel. Mary finally yields, has an abortion, and sets to work for the strike committee. Compton's attitude indicates how immediate an event revolution seemed to Communists at this period.

His attitude indicates, too, how much he has divested himself of basic human feeling (abortions in *The Big Money*, as in *Manhattan Transfer*, are symptoms of social and spiritual maladies). The denial of human ties, whether by capitalist "comers" like Moorehouse or embattled revolutionaries like Compton, is no accidental element in the narrative. Like Eleanor's use of her father or Eveline's use of Paul Johnson, the Communists' use of people as means indicates a spiritual vacuity in American society. And was it not, for Dos Passos, this spiritual vacuity, quite as much as the capitalistic system, that was responsible for social evils?

During the textile strike Compton all but ignores Mary. After A.F.L. officials assume direction and settle it, Ben and Mary again quarrel. Soon thereafter, Mary leaves for Boston to do publicity work for Sacco and Vanzetti with a newly formed liberal committee. Dos Passos' experiences during the Sacco-Vanzetti affair furnished background for his portrayal of some of the defense's activities; it is outside a police station, to which Mary has been taken for carrying placards to pickets, that she meets the Communist Don Stevens, who subsequently becomes her lover.

Stevens, a minor but significant character, is the only person other than Ben who is shown emerging as a member of the Communist party. An I.W.W. man like Ben, he first appears at a Greenwich Village tea Eveline attends in prewar America. When the United States enters the war, he joins Friends' Relief. In Europe Eveline finds him excited by the success of the Bolsheviks in Russia and by reports of mutinies in the different armies; he refers mysteriously to underground forces with which he is in touch. He is arrested by the American Army of Occupation in Germany.

In *The Big Money* Stevens' attitude toward Sacco and Vanzetti is almost as callous as that which Dos Passos describes the Communists as taking toward imprisoned miners in 1931. It is not an attitude that Dos Passos in 1927 saw as characteristic of Communists. After the last motions of the lawyers have failed, Stevens, accompanied by Mary, who by then has totally yielded initiative to him, tries to organize a demonstration. When trade union officials, socialists, ministers, and lawyers say this will lead to violence and may discourage a last-minute commutation, Stevens says: "After all they are brave men. It doesn't matter whether they are saved or not any more, it's the power of the workingclass that's got to be saved."[63] Mary becomes hard, bitter, and frenetic as public and private calamities heap up, but she at no time seems capable of adopting Stevens' attitude.

Stevens' secret trip to Moscow after the conclusion of the Sacco-Vanzetti affair suggests the existence of a shadowy world of sinister intrigue whose center is the Russian capital. His return with an English comrade as wife, without his having given notice or explanation to Mary, is an ignoble fruit of an enterprise the other fruits of which are never revealed. The era of Stalin, which was beginning at about the time of this trip (and of Dos Passos' trip to Russia), stilled debate and tightened discipline within the Communist party. Ben Compton says of Stevens: "Now he's in with the comintern crowd. He'll make the centralcommittee when they've cleaned out all the brains."[64] Stevens, on the other hand, accuses Compton of thinking that the party is a debating society.

The difference between the treatment of Communists in the narratives of *Nineteen Nineteen* (1932) and *The Big Money* (1936) is due to the political history of the period Dos Passos was depicting as well as to Dos Passos' own development. We cannot disentangle the two factors. Anything that caught Dos Passos' attention for almost a decade may have influenced the trilogy.* ("Everything that happened affected it," Dos Passos writes. "The idea was to write a novel which should take place 'now' instead of 'once upon a time.' "[65]) Though Stevens' excursion reflects Dos Passos' observance of Stalin's political maneuverings up to 1936, we must note that Stevens is not an attractive figure even in the second volume. Ben Compton, who is more intelligent, more forthright, and more courageous than the spurious pacifist, seems destined to act more independently.

Granville Hicks has complained of a "notion, circulated by Edmund Wilson and by Dos Passos himself, that *U.S.A.* was conceived under the influence of Veblen rather than Marx." "It is only in *The Big Money*," Hicks says, "written after Dos Passos had begun to be disillusioned with the Communist party, that Veblen supplants Marx."[66]

The general question of whether *U.S.A.* or any of its volumes is Marxist appears to call for a definition of Marxism. But perhaps

---

The 42nd Parallel in the assembled trilogy is considerably revised from its first edition, and a few of the changes require notice here. Dos Passos altered the conclusion of William Haywood's biography from: "Russia was a worker's republic; he went to Russia and was in Moscow a couple of years and died there and they burned his big broken hulk of a body and buried the ashes under the Kremlin wall" to "Russia was a workers' republic; he went to Russia and was in Moscow a couple of years but he wasn't happy there, that world was too strange for him. He died there and they . . . " From La Follette's biography Dos Passos eliminated a comment in parentheses, "With the death of the 65th Congress representative government died in this country, if it had ever been alive," and from the description of La Follette as "an orator haranguing from the capitol of a lost republic that had never existed," he excised the last four words. (*The 42nd Parallel*, pp. 97 and 378 in the 1930 edition and pp. 96 and 368 in the assembled trilogy.) The changes in the two biographies appeared earlier in a Modern Library edition of *The 42nd Parallel* as a single volume, which Potter's bibliography dates November 10, 1937.

an observation will serve better: Marx has so affected historiography that to apply the term "Marxism" to anything less than a conscious and extensive use of his ideas is misleading. *U.S.A.* certainly contains ideas with which professed Marxists, though by no means they alone, would agree. One such idea is that technological changes alter social institutions. Nevertheless, between the time Dos Passos wrote his revolutionary letter to Lowell (1927) and the time he spoke about Americanizing Marx (1932), he remained skeptical of dogma.[67] He attempted to base his portrayal of American society upon observation. The class struggle that he depicts in *The 42nd Parallel* and *Nineteen Nineteen* is not the Marxian one; the middle class is shown maintaining its economic status. ("Vag," a section of *The Big Money*, reflects Dos Passos' actual experiences with the depression, not a belated embracing of Marx's ideas.) Neither *The 42nd Parallel* nor *Nineteen Nineteen* is an optimistic work, although Marxism is an optimistic social philosophy.

Seeking to distinguish between the influences of Thorstein Veblen and of Marx is in some respects a vain undertaking. Veblen shared several basic ideas with Marx, although he usually added substantial modifications. Veblen held that American law was on the side of capital. He held, also, that the goods and services making up the livelihood of the nation would fall short of current needs by a widening margin. But Veblen ascribed the impoverishment of society, not to "surplus value," but to the modern system of credit. Joseph Dorfman writes:

Veblen's formulation of the inherent contradiction of modern capitalism is that credit must be continually expanded in order to keep the industrial system going in the face of property rights and industrial efficiency. This expansion necessitates sabotage, labour troubles, and increased labour costs, which in turn necessitate further credit expansion, trading on a thinner equity of tangible assets, until the assets disappear.[68]

Dos Passos may have portrayed one aspect of this process when, in *The Big Money*, he described how financiers watered airplane stock and then drove their employees unconscionably in order to survive.[69]

A major difference between the economic analyses of Marx and Veblen is that Veblen approached history from the standpoint of Darwinian evolution. He consequently rejected the concept of surplus value as metaphysical, although he probably believed the idea of socialism well founded:

And, as bearing on the Marxian doctrines of exploitation, there is on Darwinian ground no place for a natural right to the full product of labor. What can be argued in that connection on the ground of cause and effect simply is the question as to what scheme of distribution will help or hinder the survival of a given people or a given civilisation.[70]

Unlike either Hegelian or Marxian evolution, Darwinian evolution has no predictable and beneficent goal. Veblen's ultimate pessimism about the likelihood of eliminating finance capitalism and establishing socialism was based on his belief that if progress was possible, so also was retrogression.

Not all nations or civilisations have advanced unremittingly toward a socialistic consummation, in which all divergence of economic interest has lapsed or would lapse. Those nations and civilisations which have decayed and failed, as nearly all known nations and civilisations have done, illustrate the point that, however reasonable and logical the advance by means of the class struggle may be, it is by no means inevitable. Under the Darwinian norm it must be held that men's reasoning is largely controlled by other than logical, intellectual forces; that the conclusion reached by public or class opinion is as much, or more, a matter of sentiment than of logical inference; and that the sentiment which animates men, singly or collectively, is as much, or more, an outcome of habit and native propensity as of calculated material interest. There is, for instance, no warrant in the Darwinian scheme of things for asserting *a priori* that the class interest of the working class will bring them to take a stand against the propertied class. It may as well be that their training in subservience to their employers will bring them again to realise the equity and excellence of the established system of subjection and unequal distribution of wealth.[71]

It is not clear whether any theoretical source helped to produce the considerable gloom in *The Big Money* and the tone of desperation in which the volume concludes. Nor is it clear whether any such source increased Dos Passos' regard for true conservatism as Nazism spread in Europe. If such a source does exist, however, it may very well be Veblen.

We have already discussed Veblen's view of national sovereignty, his dislike of the A.F.L., his defense of the I.W.W., his hope for peaceable change but growing despair of attaining it. We have mentioned too Veblen's allusions to the predatory businessman.[72] We could with reason have referred also to Veblen's description of the pecuniary character of modern democracies, for Veblen's words are suggestive of the banker Stead's laments in

Fortune Heights and of the social criticism in "Vag."[73] According to the principles of Natural Rights, Veblen commented sarcastically, the man without means has no rights to economic goods. "A numerical minority — under ten percent of the population — constitutes a conclusive pecuniary majority — over ninety percent of the means. . . ." The common man matters only as he is, in the roles of laborer and consumer, an element in the businessman's investment.[74]

If the predatory businessman in his most hirsute state does not appear in the narrative portions of *U.S.A.*, other phenomena possibly suggested by Veblen do. Hollywood has apotheosized conspicuous consumption, and middle-class women in America consider labor, though not business, to be demeaning. There is a far more important link, however, between Veblen's thought and *U.S.A.* Implicit in the Charley Anderson story is Veblen's fundamental belief in the incompatibility of technology with capitalist finance. Veblen thought of engineers and other technicians as holding in trust a heritage of knowledge belonging to all mankind. Being a small, strategic group of industrial leaders, they could, he believed, carry out a social revolution with the help of the workers. Unfortunately, according to him, most of the technicians still thought of the industrial system "as a contrivance for the roundabout process of making money." The younger ones had, partly through witnessing the wartime productive effort, become aware of the waste involved in the control of industry by investment bankers. But there was "assuredly no present promise" of the technicians' turning their insight and common sense to an attempt to alter society.[75]

Charley Anderson differs from most engineers in at least two respects: early in life he sympathizes with the I.W.W. and revolution, and after the war he enters airplane manufacturing, not merely as an engineer drawing wages, but also as a corporation executive interested in profits from the stock market. Although Anderson returns from Europe as an airman with a reputation, he finds himself reduced to a last dime during the postwar depression. He tells Paul Johnson that he does not say the reds are wrong — "but, Jesus, we got our livin's to make."[76] (As in the stories of Mac and of Mary French's father, it is not indigence but women's reaction to it that makes men miserable; just as Rosalind in F. Scott Fitzgerald's *This Side of Paradise* rejects Amory because he is not earning enough, Doris Humphries rejects Charley Anderson.) Anderson's status as a war hero more than his promise as an aircraft designer enables him to acquire stock in industry, and after he has joined the business community, he, like Savage, adopts its ethics and cant. Occasionally, and with some eloquence after his financial disaster, he speaks of himself as primarily a mechanic and designer. He wants the big money, however, and he knows that technical knowledge alone will not gain it for him.

In a letter which he wrote soon after he became an outspoken opponent of the Communists, Dos Passos minimized the effect of Marx on his work and stressed the continuing influence of Whitman: "I read him [Whitman] a great deal as a kid and I rather imagine that a great deal of the original slant of my work comes from that vein in the American tradition. Anyway, I'm sure it's more likely to stem from Whitman (and perhaps Veblen) than from Marx, whom I read late and not as completely as I should like. The Marxist critics are just finding out, with considerable chagrin, that my stuff isnt Marxist. I should think that anybody with half an eye would have noticed that in the first place — "[77]

Whitman's influence indeed pervades *U.S.A.*, although it is most explicit in *The Big Money* and in the sketch "U.S.A.," which introduces the trilogy. The sketch is somewhat reminiscent of "Song of Myself," which portrays Whitman as going everywhere in the country and identifying himself with every type of individual. In the sketch "U.S.A." Dos Passos' "young man" seeks, not mystical identification, however, but knowledge: ". . . muscles ache for the knowledge of jobs . . . he must catch the last subway, the streetcar, the bus, run up the gangplanks of all the steamboats, register at all the hotels, work in the cities, answer the wantads, learn the trades, take up the jobs, live in all the boardinghouses, sleep in all the beds."[78]

In *The Big Money* "The Camera Eye (46)" describes Dos Passos thinking of Whitman as he considers how to achieve the original promise of American democracy: ". . . I go home after a drink and a hot meal and read (with some difficulty in the Loeb Library trot) the epigrams of Martial and ponder the course of history and what leverage might pry the owners loose from power and bring back (I too Walt Whitman) our storybook democracy."[79]

For Whitman, democracy entailed much more than an annual resort to the ballot box. When he published *Democratic Vistas* in 1871, the labor problem in America was far less acute than it was to be between the presidencies of Grover Cleveland and

Herbert Hoover. Although Whitman referred to ''that problem, the labor question, beginning to open like a yawning gulf, rapidly widening every year,'' he nevertheless wrote that he saw little reason to fear for the material welfare of the United States.[80] He was apprehensive about her moral well-being. If America was not to prove to be ''the most tremendous failure of time,'' the institutions of the country had to permit average citizens to develop healthy and admirable personalities — and these citizens had to rise to the opportunity. He declared: ''The purpose of democ- racy . . . is . . . to illustrate, at all hazards, this doctrine or theory that man, properly train'd in sanest, highest freedom, may and must become a law, and series of laws, unto himself, surrounding and providing for, not only his own personal control, but all his relations to other individuals, and to the State.''[81] America had thus far not achieved its purpose, Whitman held:

With such advantages at present fully, or almost fully, possess'd — the Union just issued, victorious, from the struggle with the only foes it need ever fear, (namely, those within itself, the interior ones,) and with unprecedented materialistic advancement — society, in these States, is canker'd, crude, superstitious, and rotten. Political, or law-made society is, and private, or voluntary society, is also. In any vigor, the element of the moral conscience, the most important, the verteber to State or man, seems to me either entirely lacking, or seriously enfeebled or un- grown.[82]

Dos Passos' criticisms of American society, though rooted in his own observations of his own era, are remarkably similar to Whitman's criticisms. The political and economic history of the United States during the twenties (particularly the Sacco-Vanzetti affair, which he interpreted as characteristic of that history) led Dos Passos to believe that the moral state of the middle class was most unhappy. But he was too perceptive to neglect examination of radical as well as conservative society and private as well as public life.

As a result, *U.S.A.* offers, in addition to much vivid history, a provocative moral vision. It portrays, among other human experi- ences, the evil of abusing men for private or political ends, the vanity of separating art or meaningful life from the needs of fellow men, and the costs and consolations of individual integrity.

Evaluating *U.S.A.*, some critics have complained that more Americans were morally solvent than the trilogy indicates. But artists' visions are not sociologists' samplings; Dos Passos' trilogy by no means depicts utter moral bankruptcy; and the critics might seriously reflect upon the question of how many men are, even in the best eras, morally solvent. The critics should remember too that *U.S.A.*, while sometimes broadly comical and often tragic, is frequently satirical. Satire has traditionally emphasized its objects' shortcomings in order to present a righteous ideal.

Varied in tone, possessing the scope and some other features of an epic, and written not by an idealistic novelist merely, but by a highly intelligent, well-schooled, cosmopolitan artist, *U.S.A.* seems likely to survive any disagreement over ideology. It will probably intrigue, instruct, and delight generation after generation of readers. Its characters are recognizable and tangible; their lives are moral histories; and for the American the landscape is an old friend, a lifelong friend, inviting him to travel or to linger.

NOTES

CHAPTER I: FATHER AND SON (PAGES 1–19)

1. Jack Potter, *A Bibliography of John Dos Passos* (Chicago: Normandie House, 1950), pp. 34, 36, 42, 46–47.

2. Dos Passos, *U.S.A.: The 42nd Parallel* (New York: Modern Library [1939]), pp. 13–14, 57–58, 173–74 (secs. 2, 6, 16, respectively, of "The Camera Eye"). The Modern Library edition (which lists 1937 as the final copyright date) contains the trilogy in a single volume. References to *The 42nd Parallel, Nineteen Nineteen,* or *The Big Money* will be, unless otherwise identified, to that volume. It is far more available in libraries than the first edition of the assembled trilogy, *U.S.A.* (New York: Harcourt, Brace and Co. [1938]), which also gives 1937 as the final copyright date.

3. Communication from Dos Passos, quoted in Georges-Albert Astre, *Thèmes et structures dans l'oeuvre de John Dos Passos,* I (Paris: Lettres Modernes, 1956), 29; letter from Dos Passos to M.L., April 20, 1964; *New York Times,* January 28, 1917, sec. 7, p. 3; *The 42nd Parallel,* p. 166 (sec. 15 of "The Camera Eye"). The quotation is from Henry Wollman in his "John R. Dos Passos," *Case and Comment,* XXIV (July 1917), 163–65.

4. Wollman in *Case and Comment.*

5. *New York Times,* January 28, 1917, sec. 7, p. 3.

6. John Randolph Dos Passos, *A Treatise on the Law of Stock-Brokers and Stock-Exchanges* (New York: Harper and Brothers, 1882).

7. Wollman in *Case and Comment;* H.W. Howard Knott, "John Randolph Dos Passos," *Dictionary of American Biography,* V, 388–89; *New York Times,* January 28, 1917, sec. 7, p. 3.

8. Letter from Dos Passos to M.L., August 12, 1964. On the love affair, see Dos Passos, *The Best Times* (New York: New American Library, 1966), p. 19. Dos Passos gives the place of his birth in *Portraits and Self-Portraits,* collected and illustrated by Georges Schreiber (Boston: Houghton Mifflin Co., 1936), p. 23.

9. The circumstances of his stay abroad are from Dos Passos, *The Best Times,* p. 8. The chronology of his childhood is from his letter to M.L., August 12, 1964. Potter, *Bibliography,* p. 67, gives the boy's name at Choate, and a letter from Dos Passos to M.L., July 12, 1966, confirms and dates his father's marriage.

10. Letters from Dos Passos to M.L.: August 12, 1964, on his relationship to his parents; July 12, 1966, on the nature of his mother's illness.

11. Dos Passos, *The 42nd Parallel,* pp. 13–14, 24–25, 28–29, 108–9, 166–67,

206–7, 223–24 (secs. 2, 3, 4, 11, 15, 17, 18 respectively of "The Camera Eye"). Compare "The Camera Eye (18)" with Dos Passos, *Chosen Country* (Boston: Houghton Mifflin Co., 1951), p. 28.

12. Dos Passos, *Chosen Country,* p. 26.

13. Ibid., pp. 49, 157.

14. Ibid., pp. 25 and (for the quotation) 21.

15. Ibid., p. 26. Compare with this passage "The Camera Eye," passim, in *The 42nd Parallel.*

16. For a more detailed exposition of John Randolph Dos Passos' ideas than can be given in this book, see Melvin Landsberg, "John R. Dos Passos: His Influence on the Novelist's Early Political Development," *American Quarterly,* XVI (Fall 1964), 473–85.

17. Wollman in *Case and Comment.*

18. The pamphlet contains no date or place of publication and no publisher's name.

19. John Randolph Dos Passos, *A Defence of the McKinley Administration from Attacks of Mr. Carl Schurz and Other Anti-Imperialists* (n.p.: n.n., 1900).

20. The book was published in New York by G. P. Putnam's Sons.

21. Letter from Dos Passos to M.L., June 26, 1956; Dos Passos, *The Best Times*, p. 8.

22. Dos Passos, *The 42nd Parallel*, pp. 173–74 (sec. 16 of "The Camera Eye").

23. John Randolph Dos Passos, *The Results and Responsibilities of Our Representative Democracy* (n.p.: n.n., n.d.).

24. Idem, *Observations of John R. Dos Passos upon the Question of Direct Primary* (n.p.: n.n., 1909).

25. Idem, *Some Observations on the Proposition to Elect United States Senators by the People* (n.p.: n.n., 1911).

26. Idem, special article on desirable reforms in the administration of New York state criminal law, *New York Times*, March 1, 1914, sec. 5, p. 4; *New York Times*, February 8, 1914, sec. 2, p. 4; letter to the editor, *New York Times,* February 7, 1915, sec. 8, p. 1.

27. Letter to the editor, *New York Times*, January 4, 1914, sec. 2, p. 14.

28. John Randolph Dos Passos, *The American Lawyer: As He Was—as He Is—as He Can Be* (New York: Consolidated Law Book Co., 1919). The book first appeared in 1907.

29. Idem, *Commercial Trusts* (New York: G.P. Putnam's Sons, 1901); idem, *Commercial Mortmain* (New York: Bench and Bar Co., 1916).

30. Idem, *Equality of Suffrage Means the Debasement Not Only of Women But of Men* (New York: National Association Opposed to Woman Suffrage, n.d.), p. 6. Dos Passos writes that this pamphlet appeared after 1910, perhaps in 1912. Letter to M.L., October 4, 1965.

31. Letter from Cyril F. dos Passos to M.L., June 16, 1957; letter from Dos Passos to M.L., February 1, 1957.

32. John Randolph Dos Passos, *Trend of the Republican Party*, pp. 76–77.

33. Dos Passos, "A Humble Protest," *Harvard Monthly*, LXII (June 1916), 118.

34. See p. 34 below.

35. John Randolph Dos Passos, *Commercial Trusts*, p. 121.

CHAPTER II: HARVARD (PAGES 20–43)

1. M.L. interview with E. E. Cummings, October 22, 1956; letters from Dos Passos to M.L., February 1, and September 23, 1957. The quotation is from a letter from Dos Passos to M.L., December 12, 1964.

2. M.L. interview with E. E. Cummings. Mitchell is quoted in Charles W. Bernardin's "John Dos Passos' Harvard Years," *New England Quarterly*, XXVII (March 1954), 22. For Dos Passos on his childhood in Washington and Virginia, see "The Camera Eye," passim, in *The 42nd Parallel*.

3. M.L. interviews with Chandler Post, spring 1956, and Kenneth Murdock, May 3, 1956.

4. The first quotation is from Dos Passos, *The Theme Is Freedom* (New York: Dodd, Mead and Co., 1956), p. 152; the second is from a letter from Dos Passos to M.L., June 26, 1956.

5. Dos Passos, *The 42nd Parallel*, pp. 301–303. The quotation here differs slightly from the one in the 1930 edition.

6. Dos Passos, *The Best Times*, p. 25.

7. Harvard University furnished a list of courses. For curriculum requirements, see the *Harvard University Catalogue*, 1912–13, 1913–14, 1914–15, 1915–16.

8. Van Wyck Brooks, *Scenes and Portraits: Memories of Childhood and Youth* (New York: E. P. Dutton and Co., 1954), pp. 97–122.

9. Dos Passos, *The Best Times*, pp. 23–24.

10. Dos Passos, "The Almeh," *Harvard Monthly*, LVI (July 1913), 172–79.

11. Dos Passos, "The Honor of a Klepht," *Harvard Monthly*, LVII (February 1914), 158–63.

12. Dos Passos, Review of *Brittany With Bergère* by William M.E. Whitelock, *Harvard Monthly*, LIX (March 1915), 200; idem, Review of *Small Souls*, by Louis Couperus, *Harvard Monthly*, LIX (February 1915), 169; idem, "Conrad's *Lord Jim*," *Harvard Monthly*, LX (July 1915), 151–54.

13. Dos Passos, "An Interrupted Romance," *Harvard Monthly*, LX (June 1915), 119–22.

14. Dos Passos, "The Poet of Cordale," *Harvard Monthly*, LIX (December 1914), 77–82.

15. Dos Passos, "An Aesthete's Nightmare," *Harvard Monthly*, LX (May 1915), 77–80.

16. *Harvard Crimson*, May 18, 1915, p. 4.

17. Bernardin, "John Dos Passos' Harvard Years," *New England Quarterly*, XXVII (March 1954), 8.

18. Dos Passos, "Malbrouck," *Harvard Monthly*, LIX (March 1915), 192–94.

19. Dos Passos, "Romantic Education," *Harvard Monthly*, LXI (October 1915), 1–4.

20. Dos Passos, "The Shepherd," *Harvard Monthly*, LXI (January 1916), 115–21.

21. [John Dos Passos], "Les Lauriers Sont Coupés," *Harvard Monthly*, LXII (April 1916), 48–51. On the death of Dos Passos' mother, see the *New York Times*, May 18, 1915, p. 13.

22. Dos Passos, "Incarnation," *Harvard Monthly*, LXII (May 1916), 89.

23. Samuel Eliot Morison, *Three Centuries of Harvard, 1636–1936* (Cambridge: Harvard University Press, 1936), pp. 437–38.

24. M.L. interview with E. E. Cummings. Charles Norman's biography of Cummings describes in detail the history of the volume of verse, published by Laurence J. Gomme in 1917. Charles Norman, *The Magic-Maker: E. E. Cummings* (New York: Macmillan Co., 1958), pp. 56–71.

25. Dos Passos, Reviews of the *Catholic Anthology* and *Georgian Poetry, 1913–1915* in *Harvard Monthly*, LXII (May 1916), 92–94.

26. Paul Frederick Brissenden, *The I.W.W.: A Study of American Syndicalism* (Studies in History, Economics and Public Law, LXXXIII, Whole No. 193. New York: Columbia University, 1920), 283–98; *New York Times*, September 30, 1912, pp. 1–2; October 1, 1912, pp. 1, 3; *New York Tribune* for 1912: September 30, pp. 1, 2; November 27, p. 6; October 12, p. 6.

27. Letter from Dos Passos to M.L., June 26, 1956, speaks of his reaction to industrialism. On Veblen and industrialism see Thorstein Veblen, *The Theory of Business Enterprise* (New York: Charles Scribner's Sons, 1904), pp. 302–73; Joseph Dorfman, *Thorstein Veblen and His America* (New York: Viking Press, 1934), passim.

28. Dos Passos, "A Humble Protest," *Harvard Monthly*, LXII (June 1916), 116.

29. Letter from Dos Passos to M.L., June 26, 1956; Stefan Zweig, *Emile Verhaeren* (London: Constable and Co., 1914), pp 81–106; P. Mansell Jones, *Emile Verhaeren: A Study in the Development of His Art and Ideas* (Cardiff: University of Wales Press Board, 1926), pp. 86–96.

30. Dos Passos, "A Humble Protest," *Harvard Monthly*, LXII (June 1916), 115–20.

31. Letter from Dos Passos to M.L., June 26, 1956, cites the *New Republic* as an influence; another, March 26, 1970, specifies the domestic reforms in which Dos Passos was interested; Charles Forcey, *The Crossroads of Liberalism* (New York: Oxford University Press, 1961), passim; *New Republic*, 1914–16, passim. The comment "major rallying ground" is on p. 200 of Forcey's book, and the quotation about Croly is on p. 36.

32. *New Republic*: I (November 7, 1914), 9–10 (for quotations and next two sentences); I (December 5, 1914), 3; V (November 27, 1915), 79; II (March 20, 1915), 163–64.

33. *Harvard Crimson*, November 8, 1912, p. 1.

34. Letter from W. B. Harris, *Harvard Crimson*, February 17, 1913, pp. 1, 5. The reply is on p. 2.

35. *Harvard Crimson*, April 28, 1914, pp. 1, 5, 6.

36. Ibid., January 22, 1914, p. 1, and April 17, 1914, p. 5.

37. Arthur S. Link, *Woodrow Wilson and the Progressive Era, 1910–1917* (New York: Harper and Brothers, 1954), pp. 177–78.

38. *Harvard Crimson* for 1915: March 15, p. 2; March 16, p. 2; March 19, p. 2; March 20, p. 2; May 29, p. 2; December 10, p. 4.

39. Ibid., March 8, 1915, pp. 1, 5; Walter Lippmann, "Legendary John Reed," *New Republic*, I (December 26, 1914), 15–16; Ernest Sutherland Bates, "John Reed," *Dictionary of American Biography*, XV, 450–51; Granville Hicks, *John Reed: The Making of a Revolutionary* (New York: Macmillan Co., 1936), pp. 24–182.

40. Letter from Dos Passos to M. L., June 26, 1956.

41. Dos Passos, Review of *Insurgent Mexico* by John Reed, *Harvard Monthly*, LIX (November 1914), 67–68; idem, Review of *The War in Eastern Europe* by John Reed, *Harvard Monthly*, LXII (July 1916), 148–49.

42. *Monde* (Paris), January 18, 1930, p. 3.

43. Morison, *Three Centuries of Harvard*, pp. 450–51; *Harvard Crimson*, December 22, 1915, p. 4.

44. *Harvard Crimson*, December 21, 1915, p. 1; May 26, 1916, p. 2; June 16, 1916, p. 1.

45. Ibid., February 24, 1916, p. 1; December 18, 1915, pp. 1, 7 (for Angell's views); Graham Aldis, "The Pacifist's Perplexity," *Harvard Monthly*, LXI (February 1916), 161–63.

46. M.L. interview with E. E. Cummings; letter from Dos Passos to M.L., February 1, 1957. The comment on Wilson's brand is based on Dos Passos' letter.

47. Letter from Dos Passos to M.L., July 20, 1956.

48. [John Dos Passos], "Summer Military Camps: Two Views. I," *Harvard Monthly*, LX (July 1915), 156. Dos Passos identified this contribution in a letter to M.L., September 23, 1957.

49. Dos Passos, "The Evangelist and the Volcano," *Harvard Monthly*, LXI (November 1915), 59–61.

50. Robert Herrick, *The World Decision* (Boston: Houghton Mifflin Co., 1916), passim; A. K. McComb, Review of *The World Decision* by Robert Herrick, *Harvard Monthly*, LXII (March 1916), 24–26; D. P. [John Dos Passos], "The World Decision," *Harvard Monthly*, LXII (March 1916), 23–24.

51. "My state of mind was far more pacifist than socialist. At that [the Harvard] period it was the anti-war agitation of the Socialists that attracted me." Letter from Dos Passos to M.L., June 26, 1956.

52. Dos Passos, "A Conference on Foreign Relations," *Harvard Monthly*, LXII (June 1916), 126–27.

CHAPTER III: THE WORLD WAR (PAGES 44–76)

1. Letters from Dos Passos to M.L., June 11 and June 26, 1956; David Sanders, "Interview with John Dos Passos," *Claremont Quarterly*, XI (Spring 1964), 91; Dos Passos, *The Best Times*, p. 26.

2. Letter from Dos Passos to M.L., June 26, 1956.

3. Letter from John Randolph Dos Passos to Eliot Norton, November 12, 1916. Houghton Library (Harvard).

4. Dos Passos, "Against American Literature," *New Republic*, VIII (October 14, 1916), 269–71. Compare Henry James' comments on Nathaniel Hawthorne's America. Henry James, "Hawthorne," in *The Shock of Recognition*, ed. Edmund Wilson (Garden City, New York: Doubleday, Doran and Co., 1943), pp. 459–60.

5. Frederick J. Hoffman, Charles Allen, and Carolyn F. Ulrich, *The Little Magazine* (Princeton: Princeton University Press, 1946), pp. 86–90. See editorial in *Seven Arts*, I (November 1916), 52–53.

6. Letters from Dos Passos to M.L., June 26, 1956, and February 1, 1957.

7. See Waldo Frank, "Emerging Greatness," *Seven Arts*, I (November 1916), 73–78; idem, "Valedictory to a Theatrical Season," *Seven Arts*, II (July 1917), 356–67; Randolph Bourne, *History of a Literary Radical*, ed. Van Wyck Brooks (New York: B. W. Huebsch, 1920), including "This Older Generation" on pp. 107–27. See also Gorham B. Munson, *Waldo Frank* (New York: Boni and Liveright, 1923), pp. 14–16; Louis Filler, *Randolph Bourne* (Washington, D.C.: American Council on Public Affairs, 1943).

8. Link, *Woodrow Wilson*, pp. 224–25, 233–44. The quotation is on pp. 241–42.

9. Bernardin, "John Dos Passos' Harvard Years," *New England Quarterly*, XXVII (March 1954), 25–26. The quotation is Bernardin's.

10. Dos Passos, "Adlai Stevenson: Patrician with a Mission," *National Review*, II (October 27, 1956), 11. The elder Dos Passos supported Hughes. Dos Passos, *The Best Times*, p. 28.

11. Arthur K. McComb, "Art and Industry," *Harvard Monthly*, LXII (June 1916), 121–23.

12. Letter from Dos Passos to Arthur K. McComb, August 7, 1916. The letters, running from 1916 to perhaps 1936 (they are only partially dated by Dos Passos), are in the Library of the American Academy of Arts and Letters, along with some commentary by McComb. Though sometimes able to correct McComb's dating, I have found it a fair guide.

13. Letter from Dos Passos to McComb, August 26, 1916.

14. Ibid., August or September 1916.

15. Ibid., n.d.

16. Ibid., August 7, 1916.

17. Ibid., November 16, 1916.

18. Ibid., January 4, 1917.

19. The date of his leaving for Spain is given in a letter from John Randolph Dos Passos to Eliot Norton, November 12, 1916. The facts of the elder Dos Passos' death and the son's return are stated in letters from Dos Passos to M.L., June 11 and June 26, 1956. Addendum: the date of Dos Passos' sailing for home, and a few other dates below, are from his letters to Walter Rumsey Marvin, which I saw after this book was written and in the process of publication.

20. Dos Passos, *Nineteen Nineteen*, p. 104.

21. The views of the periodical were exemplified in a long article by John Reed, "At the Throat of the Republic," *Masses*, VIII (July 1916), 7–8, 10–12, 24. See also Max Eastman, "Who Wanted War?" *Masses*, IX (June 1917), 23.

22. *New Republic*, I (January 30, 1915), 5 (includes quotation); "Who Willed American Participation?" *New Republic*, X (April 14, 1917), 308–10.

23. Letters from Dos Passos to M.L., June 11, 1956, and February 1, 1957.

24. See Link, *Woodrow Wilson*, pp. 180–81.

25. Dos Passos, draft (n.d.), University of Virginia Library. Statements confirmed in a letter from Dos Passos to M.L., October 4, 1965.

26. Dos Passos, draft (n.d.), University of Virginia Library.

27. Letter from Dos Passos to McComb, January 4, 1917. A letter from Dos Passos to M.L., June 26, 1956, speaks of Eastman.

28. Letter from Dos Passos to McComb, n.d. Dos Passos dated the letter roughly and described the circumstances in a letter to M.L., October 4, 1965.

29. Letter from Dos Passos to Charles Norman, n.d., quoted in Norman, *The Magic-Maker*, p. 75.

30. Dos Passos, *The 42nd Parallel*, pp. 349–50 (sec. 26 of "The Camera Eye"); letter from Dos Passos to M.L., September 23, 1957.

31. Letter from Dos Passos to McComb, n.d. Dos Passos' explanation about Sessions is from his letters to M.L., December 1965 and January 3, 1966.

32. Letter from Dos Passos to McComb, June 20, 1917.

33. *New York Times*, June 1, 1917, pp. 1, 2; June 5, 1917, pp. 1, 2; John

Reed, "Militarism at Play," *Masses*, IX (August 1917), 18–19 (compare sec. 26 of "The Camera Eye" in *The 42nd Parallel*); M.L. interview with E. E. Cummings. The quotation from Hillyer's poem appears on p. 14 of *Masses*, IX (April 1917).

34. Samuel Eliot Morison and Henry Steele Commager, *The Growth of the American Republic* (New York: Oxford University Press, 1942), II, 475–79.

35. David A. Shannon, *The Socialist Party of America* (New York: Macmillan Co., 1955), pp. 96–103, 109–17; Daniel Bell, "The Background and Development of Marxian Socialism in the United States," *Socialism and American Life*, eds. Donald Drew Egbert and Stow Persons (Princeton: Princeton University Press, 1952), I, chap. vi, 315–17; Hoffman, Allen, Ulrich, *The Little Magazine*, p. 30; *New York Times*, November 20, 1917, p. 4.

36. Letter from Dos Passos to M.L., February 1, 1957.

37. *Harvard College Class of 1916, Secretary's Third Report* (privately printed, June 1922), p. 109; *New York Times*, August 4, 1918, sec. 1, p. 19.

"Originally Henry James was chairman of the organization [the American Motor-Ambulance Corps]. The corps was connected with the British army, but soon the rule that no American could serve in any capacity within the British lines was discovered and the corps was divided, half continuing . . . under a British officer, half under Norton serving thenceforth with a French army corps. Norton's section was presently joined by one supported by [a banker] Mr. Harjes of Paris, under the Red Cross, and was later joined by other units, until by September, 1917, the entire body, known as the Norton-Harjes Ambulance Corps, was operating in many places. . . ." William Fenwick Harris, "Richard Norton, 1872–1918," *Harvard Graduates' Magazine*, XXVII (December 1918), 183.

38. Dos Passos, *The Best Times*, pp. 23–24, 51.

39. Letter from Dos Passos to McComb, June 28, 1917.

40. Ibid.

41. Ibid., July 20, 1917. The burden was that of "telling the truth about the world." Letter from Dos Passos to M.L., March 26, 1970.

42. Letter from Dos Passos to McComb, July 31, 1917.

43. Ibid., August 10, 1917.

44. Ibid., August 27, 1917.

45. Letter from Dos Passos to M.L., June 11, 1956; letter from Dos Passos to Clarence E. Walton, February 2, 1940 (Houghton Library, Harvard); Dos Passos, *The Best Times*, pp. 44–45.

46. Letter from Dos Passos to McComb, postmarked September 17 [1917].

47. Letters from Dos Passos to Walter Rumsey Marvin, October 2 and 26, 1917; November 12, 1917.

48. Letters from Dos Passos to McComb, December 10, 1917 (on Wright and for Dos Passos' being in Italy) and December 31, 1917 (on Cummings and on Dos Passos' negative attitude). See E. E. Cummings, *The Enormous Room* (New York: Boni and Liveright, 1922).

49. Letter from Dos Passos to McComb, May 7, 1918.

50. M.L. interview with Chandler Post.

51. Letter from Dos Passos to M.L., June 26, 1956. The quotation is complete; the ellipsis marks are Dos Passos' own.

52. Letters from Dos Passos to McComb, August 10 and August 19, 1918.

53. The fiction written aboard ship and in New York was supposed to be a part of the Jericho novel (nicknamed "Fibbie"), which Dos Passos was now

continuing alone. He ultimately detached this part and called it *One Man's Initiation—1917*. See Dos Passos, *The Best Times*, pp. 56, 70, and 71 on this new novel, Ewer, and the trip to England; Harry W. Schwartz, *This Book Collecting Racket* (rev. ed.; Chicago: Normandie House, 1937), pp. 75–77, on relative freedom of expression; letters from Dos Passos to McComb, April 9 and June 8, 1920, on bowdlerization. The publication date of the novel is in Potter's *Bibliography*, p. 15. An unexpurgated edition, based largely on old page proofs, has now appeared: Dos Passos, *One Man's Initiation: 1917* (Ithaca, New York: Cornell University Press, 1969). Dos Passos says in the introduction that he seems to have finished writing the novel in New York.

Fibbie exists in a manuscript titled "Seven Times Around the Walls of Jericho."

54. Dos Passos, *One Man's Initiation—1917* (London: George Allen and Unwin Ltd., 1920), p. 91. Unless otherwise identified, all references to the book are to this edition.

55. Ibid., p. 52.

56. Ibid., p. 104.

57. Ibid., p. 69.

58. Dos Passos, *First Encounter* (New York: Philosophical Library [1945]), p. 9.

59. Dos Passos, *One Man's Initiation*, pp. 114–15. The entire incident is on pp. 109–24.

60. Ibid., p. 128.

61. Ibid., pp. 41–46.

62. Henri Barbusse, *Under Fire*, trans. Fitzwater Wray (New York: E. P. Dutton and Co., 1917), p. 343. Dos Passos describes his reading of the novel in *The Best Times*, p. 44.

63. Letters from Dos Passos to M.L., February 1, 1957, and March 26, 1970 (the second quotation is in the latter); letter from Dos Passos to McComb, August 7, 1916. Dos Passos writes of his "youth against the world" zeal in *The Best Times*, pp. 24–25, 45. On Rolland's activities see William T. Starr, *Romain Rolland and a World at War* (Evanston, Illinois: Northwestern University Press, 1956), passim.

64. Dos Passos' letter to M.L. of February 1, 1957, specifically names Barbusse, Rolland, and Rimbaud as influences. "Never neglect Rimbaud," he says there. In *The Best Times*, p. 52, he speaks of carrying the verse about; he also speaks, on pp. 56–57, of enthusiastically reading some of Georg Brandes' *The World at War* in France in 1917.

Edmund Wilson sees Rimbaud as a prototype of the artist who flees modern industrial and bourgeois institutions. Wilson, *Axel's Castle* (New York: Charles Scribner's Sons, 1954), pp. 268–98.

65. Dos Passos, *First Encounter*, p. 9; Starr, *Romain Rolland*, p. 147; Randolph Bourne, *Untimely Papers*, ed. James Oppenheim (New York: B. W. Huebsch, 1919), pp. 104, 121–23; Shannon, *The Socialist Party in America*, pp. 119–20; Stephen Richards Graubard, *British Labour and the Russian Revolution, 1917–1924* (Cambridge: Harvard University Press, 1956), pp. 16–63.

66. Letter from Dos Passos to M.L., June 26, 1956; Dos Passos, *The Best Times*, p. 73.

67. Letter from Dos Passos to M.L., June 26, 1956; *Harvard College Class of 1916, Secretary's Third Report*, p. 109; letter from Dos Passos to McComb, October 5, 1918.

68. Letter from Dos Passos to McComb, October 21, 1918.

69. Ibid., n.d.

70. Ibid., October 5, 1918.

71. Letter from Dos Passos to M.L., June 26, 1956; Dos Passos, *The Best Times*, p. 75; *Harvard College Class of 1916, Secretary's Third Report*, p. 109.

72. Dos Passos, *The Theme Is Freedom*, p. 2.

73. Dos Passos, "Grosz Comes to America," *Esquire*, VI (September 1936), p. 128.

74. See *Nineteen Nineteen*, pp. 342–44, 400–402 (secs. 39 and 40 of "The Camera Eye").

75. Letter from Dos Passos to M.L., June 26, 1956 (on discharge, Spain, and work on *Three Soldiers*); letter from Dos Passos to McComb, April 9, 1920.

76. *Harvard College Class of 1916, Secretary's Third Report*, p. 109; Dos Passos, *The Best Times*, pp. 82, 85–86; George H. Doran, *Chronicles of Barabbas* (New York: Harcourt, Brace, and Co., 1935), pp. 285–86; Potter, *Bibliography*, p. 22. Dudley Poore helped me date Dos Passos' return.

77. Dos Passos, "Contemporary Chronicles," a draft (n.d.) that he used, he says, for a talk sometime between 1958 and 1964. It is on deposit at the University of Virginia Library. For a published account, differing in some details, see Dos Passos, "What Makes a Novelist," *National Review*, XX (January 16, 1968), pp. 29–32.

78. Dos Passos, *Three Soldiers* (New York: George H. Doran Co., 1921), p. 45.

79. Ibid., p. 44.

80. Ibid., p. 37 and, for quoted sentences, pp. 39–40.

81. Ibid., p. 92. Cohen's name became Cohan in the Modern Library edition.

82. Dos Passos, *Three Soldiers*, pp. 23, 27–28, 404–5.

83. Dos Passos, "In Defense of Kentucky," *New Republic*, LXIX (December 16, 1931), 137.

84. Dos Passos, *Three Soldiers*, p. 165.

85. Ibid., p. 168.

86. Ibid., pp. 265–67.

87. Ibid., p. 236.

88. Ibid., p. 27.

89. Ibid., p. 393.

90. Ibid., p. 421. Perhaps developments in Russia were responsible for the pessimistic remarks on politics which Dos Passos had Andrews voice. Dos Passos recollected that news of the Bolshevik capture of the soviets helped "put me off straight Marxism." Replies by Dos Passos to questionnaire in Thomas Chilton Wheeler, "The Political Philosophy of John Dos Passos" (unpublished undergraduate honors thesis, Division of History, Government, and Economics, Harvard College, 1951), Appendix.

91. Henry Seidel Canby, Review of *Three Soldiers* by John Dos Passos, *New York Evening Post*, October 8, 1921, sec. 3, p. 67.

92. W. C. Blum, Review of *Three Soldiers* by John Dos Passos, *Dial*, LXXI (November 1921), 606–8.

93. Coningsby Dawson, Review of *Three Soldiers* by John Dos Passos, *New York Times*, October 2, 1921, sec. 3, pp. 1, 16, 17.

94. *New York Times*, October 15, 1921, p. 12.

95. Ibid., October 16, 1921, sec. 3, pp. 1, 22.

96. Potter, *Bibliography*, p. 17; letter from Dos Passos to M.L., March 6, 1958.

97. *New York Times*, March 2, 1922, p. 20.

CHAPTER IV: A REVOLUTIONARY POSTWAR WORLD (PAGES 77–96)

1. Letters from Dos Passos to M.L., June 26, 1956, July 10 and November 22, 1965; Norman, *The Magic-Maker*, p. 215; Dos Passos, *The Best Times*, pp. 86–125. Dudley Poore helped me establish the time of return.

2. Theodore Draper, *The Roots of American Communism* (New York: Viking Press, 1957), pp. 101–13.

3. Ibid., pp. 315–18, 446; John S. Gambs, *The Decline of the I.W.W.* (New York: Columbia University Press, 1932), pp. 77–78, 89.

4. Bell, "The Background and Development of Marxian Socialism in the United States," *Socialism and American Life*, I, 319–27. Bell's account should be supplemented by Shannon, *The Socialist Party of America*, pp. 126–49, and by Theodore Draper's study. Draper complains that Bell appears to minimize the historical continuity between the Socialist left wing of 1912 and the American Communist movement. Draper, *Roots of American Communism*, pp. 105–6, 414.

5. The account which follows is based on Robert K. Murray's *Red Scare: A Study in National Hysteria, 1919–1920* (Minneapolis: University of Minnesota Press, 1955). Because a number of Murray's interpretations differ from my own, I have interpolated a few remarks about revolutionary leaders' aims in the steel strike, the effect of the January raids upon a generation of radicals, and the possible consequences of American Socialists' and anarchists' confused pro-Bolshevism in 1918 and 1919.

6. Murray, *Red Scare*, pp. 166–67.

7. Letter from Dos Passos to M.L., February 1, 1957.

8. Letter from Waldo Frank to M.L., September 15, 1956.

9. Dos Passos, "Young Spain," *Seven Arts*, II (August 1917), 473–88.

10. Dos Passos, "In Portugal," *Liberator*, III (April 1920), 25. The article, bearing the dateline December 14, 1919, probably contained much the same material that Dos Passos sent to the *Daily Herald* at the time. In a letter to M.L., October 22, 1966, he says, "I wrote a lot of stuff for the Daily Herald—as I remember they published very little of it." See Dos Passos, *The Best Times*, pp. 77–81.

The *Liberator*, which flaunted the subtitle "A Journal of Revolutionary Progress," was demanding revolution to achieve a socialist state. (*Liberator*, I [November 1918], 2; ibid., [December 1918], 8; Max Eastman, "The Clarté Movement," ibid., III [April 1920], 40–42.) But despite Max Eastman's dedication to Communism, the periodical allowed its contributors considerable freedom in their discussion of revolutions, a circumstance of which Dos Passos later took full advantage. He gave his article on Portugal to Crystal Eastman, Max's sister, whom he may have met in Europe. Max himself he did not meet until many years later. Letter from Max Eastman to M.L., June 19, 1956; letter from Dos Passos to M.L., July 10, 1965.

11. Letter from Dos Passos to M.L., December 1965, tells when most of the book was written. For a list of titles and dates of the articles, see Potter, *Bibliography*, p. 21.

12. Dos Passos, "America and the Pursuit of Happiness," *Nation*, CXI (December 29, 1920), 777–78.

13. M.L. interview with E. E. Cummings (source of information about the long journey); letters from Dos Passos to M.L., December 22, 1965, and August 1970. In the 1970 letter Dos Passos writes that they might have seen Pastora Imperio somewhat later.

14. Dos Passos, *Rosinante to the Road Again* (New York: George H. Doran Co., 1922), pp. 13–20.

15. Ibid., p. 38.

16. Ibid., p. 75.

17. Ibid., pp. 101–3.

18. Dos Passos, "Farmer Strikers in Spain," *Liberator*, III (October 1920), 28–30.

19. Dos Passos, *Rosinante to the Road Again*, pp. 107–9.

20. Ibid., pp. 202–20.

21. Dos Passos, "Two University Professors," *Broom*, II (April 1922), 59–71. The additional comment is on p. 71.

22. Dos Passos, *Rosinante to the Road Again*, pp. 120–32.

23. Dos Passos, "A Novelist of Disintegration," *Freeman*, II (October 20, 1920), p. 133. The passage on pp. 93–94 of *Rosinante to the Road Again* differs only slightly in wording. Alfred Kazin quotes from and discusses it in *On Native Grounds*.

24. Isaac Goldberg translated the trilogy into English under the titles *The Quest, Weeds,* and *Red Dawn*, but Dos Passos considered the translation "disastrously clumsy and insensitive." Dos Passos, "Baroja Muzzled," review of *The Quest* in *Dial*, LXXIV (February 1923), 199–200.

25. The date for his reaching Persia comes from a letter from Dos Passos to McComb, August 27, 1921.

26. Letters from Dos Passos to M.L., February 1, 1957, and July 10, 1965; M.L. interview with Mrs. Paxton Hibben, June 1957 (source of material about meeting at Dell's house); letter from Dos Passos to McComb, August 27, 1921 (speaks of the writer's spending a week at the mission); Dos Passos, *The Best Times*, pp. 90–94; Suzanne La Follette, "Paxton Pattison Hibben," *Dictionary of American Biography*, IX, 1–2.

27. George Vernadsky, *A History of Russia* (New Haven: Yale University Press, 1954), pp. 321–22; Isaac Deutscher, *Stalin: A Political Biography* (New York: Oxford University Press, 1949), pp. 217–27.

28. Dos Passos, "The Caucasus Under the Soviets," *Liberator*, V (August 1922). 7. The article is on pp. 5–8.

29. Dos Passos, *Orient Express* (New York: Harper and Brothers, 1927), pp. 42–43. After studying famine conditions in the Soviet Union in 1921, Hibben submitted a report on the effects of the famine and on the inefficiency of the relief organizations to a U.S. Senate investigating committee, but the report was for some reason destroyed. [Paxton Hibben], *An American Report on the Russian Famine: Findings of the Russian Commission of the Near East Relief* (New York: *Nation* [1921]), pp. 3–6; Suzanne La Follette, "Paxton Pattison Hibben," *Dictionary of American Biography*, IX, 1–2. Hibben subsequently became Executive Secretary of the American Committee for Relief of Russian Children, and Dos Passos became one of the scores of people on its national committee. Paxton

Hibben, *Report on the Russian Famine, 1922* (New York: American Committee for the Relief of Russian Children [1922]), p. 2.

30. Dos Passos, *Orient Express*, p. 45. These musings appear in the chapter "Red Caucasus," a substantial part of which was published as "In a New Republic," *Freeman*, IV (October 5, 1921), 81–83. For other articles by Dos Passos which included material later published in *Orient Express*, see Potter, *Bibliography*, p. 31.

31. Paxton Hibben, Review of *Orient Express* by John Dos Passos, *New Masses*, III (June 1927), 28; Dos Passos, *The Best Times*, p. 94.

32. Dos Passos, *Orient Express*, pp. 46–48.

33. William Henry Chamberlain, *The Russian Revolution, 1917–1921* (New York: Macmillan Co., 1935), II, 440–45.

34. Emma Goldman, *My Disillusionment in Russia* (Garden City, New York: Doubleday, Page and Co., 1923), pp. 3–5; idem, *My Further Disillusionment in Russia* (Garden City, New York: Doubleday, Page and Co., 1924), pp. 65–94. Dos Passos writes that Emma Goldman seemed in these early years "as she does now a sympathetic but a slightly comic figure." Letter to M.L., September 23, 1957.

35. Letter from Dos Passos to M.L., February 1, 1957; letter from Mrs. Charles R. Walker to M.L., February 12, 1958. See p. 169 below. A major problem in interpreting Dos Passos' reaction to Bolshevism in August 1921 is that we do not know what details about Kronstadt reached him before or during his stay in the Russian Caucasus.

36. Dos Passos, *The Best Times*, p. 94.

37. Dos Passos, *Orient Express*, pp. 77–78.

38. Unless otherwise attributed, the details that follow are from *Orient Express*.

39. Letter from Dos Passos to McComb, n.d.

40. Dos Passos, *Orient Express*, p. 178 (for quotation), 86 (on mass production), 80 (on retreat from struggle). The passage on p. 80 of *Orient Express* appeared with slight differences in "The Opinions of the 'Sayyid,'" *Asia*, XXII (June 1922), 465–66.

CHAPTER V: A STRAW HAT OUT OF SEASON (PAGES 97–123)

1. Letter from Dos Passos to McComb, May 28, 1922.

2. Letter from Dos Passos to M.L., August 12, 1964, speaks of inheritance; letter from Dos Passos to M.L., February 1, 1957, speaks of career.

3. Ibid., July 10, 1965 and October 22, 1966.

4. Letters from Dos Passos to McComb, 1922.

5. See, for example, part XIV of "Winter in Castile," in Dos Passos, *A Pushcart at the Curb* (New York: George H. Doran Co., 1922), pp. 40–42.

6. Replies by Dos Passos to questionnaire in Wheeler, "The Political Philosophy of John Dos Passos," Appendix.

7. Dos Passos, *Streets of Night* (New York: George H. Doran Co., 1923), pp. 49–51, 83–87. See pp. 138–39 below.

8. Letters from Dos Passos to McComb, December 5, 1922, and spring 1923. The quotations and the reference to a book on New York are in the letter of spring 1923. Dudley Poore provided further information.

9. Frederick Lewis Allen, *Only Yesterday* (New York: Harper and Brothers, 1931), p. 160.

10. James Warren Prothro, *The Dollar Decade* (Baton Rouge: Louisiana State University Press, 1954), passim. The quotation is on p. 210.

11. Letter from Dos Passos to M.L., February 1, 1957.

12. Malcolm Cowley, *Exile's Return* (New York: Viking Press, 1951), p. 292.

13. M.L. telephone conversation with Lewis Galantière, June 11, 1957.

14. Letter from Dos Passos to M.L., February 1, 1957.

15. Edmund Wilson, *The Cold War and the Income Tax: A Protest* (New York: Farrar, Straus and Co., 1963), p. 44.

16. Daniel Aaron, *Writers on the Left* (New York: Harcourt, Brace and World, 1961), 10–18. Letters from Dos Passos to M.L., February 1, 1957, and September 23, 1957, speak of his knowledge of I.W.W. men and his creation of Mac.

17. Dos Passos, *The Theme Is Freedom*, pp. 2–4.

18. Mabel Dodge Luhan, *Intimate Memories*, Vol. III, *Movers and Shakers* (New York: Harcourt, Brace and Co., 1936), p. 23.

19. Dos Passos, *The Best Times*, pp. 135–37, 140–41, 147. His contemporary fiction and drama seem to confirm his reminiscences about Greenwich Village. On the growth of the Village, see Frederick J. Hoffman, *The Twenties* (New York: Viking Press, 1955), pp. 16–18.

20. Dos Passos, *The Theme Is Freedom*, pp. 2–3.

21. Hoffman, *The Twenties*, p. 19; Cowley, *Exile's Return*, pp. 63–67.

22. Thorstein Veblen, *The Theory of the Leisure Class* (New York: Modern Library, 1934), passim.

23. Idem, *Absentee Ownership and Business Enterprise in Recent Times: The Case of America* (New York: Viking Press, 1923), p. 442 (quotation on "predatory dynastic State"); idem, *An Inquiry into the Nature of Peace and the Terms of Its Perpetuation* (New York: Macmillan Co., 1917), pp. 24–26, 62 (on benefit of businessmen); idem, *Absentee Ownership*, p. 438 (quotation on "underlying populations"); idem, *An Inquiry into the Nature of Peace*, p. 57 (quotation on "parasite"); ibid., p. 61 (quotation on "remedy for evils"); Veblen, *Absentee Ownership*, p. 28 (quotations on "unsanctified workday arrangement" and "neighborly fellowships"); idem, *The Vested Interests and the State of the Industrial Arts* (New York: B. W. Huebsch, 1919), p. 164 (on Veblen's favoring the I.W.W. and considering A.F.L. leaders a "kept class"); idem, *The Engineers and the Price System* (New York: Viking Press, 1947), 89–90 (on I.W.W.'s frightening authorities); ibid., pp. 1–3 (on "sabotaging" industry). The quotation about the purpose of the A.F.L. is in *The Engineers and the Price System*, p. 90.

24. Letter from Dos Passos to M.L., February 1, 1957.

25. Susan Jane Turner, "A Short History of *The Freeman*, a Magazine of the Early Twenties, with Particular Attention to the Literary Criticism" (unpublished Ph.D. dissertation, Faculty of Philosophy, Columbia University, 1956), p. iii (contains quotation), 9, 48.

26. [Albert Jay Nock], "In the Vein of Intimacy," *Freeman*, I (March 31, 1920), 52–53, quoted in Turner, "Short History of *The Freeman*," pp. 64–65.

27. Albert Jay Nock, *On Doing the Right Thing* (New York: Harper and Brothers, 1928), pp. 150–52. Although virtually all the essays in this volume were originally published after the demise of the *Freeman*, the ideas referred to are the same as those expressed in the periodical.

28. Ibid., pp. 171 (for quotation), 191–99; Turner, "Short History of *The*

Freeman,'' p. 9. Nock wrote a full-length study of Jefferson, which appeared in 1926.

29. It is not certain how much Jefferson he knew at Harvard. He writes: ''I certainly had my father's copy of Randall and Tucker's life—but I dont remember reading Parton at that time. That doesnt mean that I didnt.'' Replying to the questions: ''When did you first read Jefferson? When did you become strongly attracted to his ideas?'' he says: ''After returning from reporting Spanish Civil War. The process is described in The Ground We Stand On.'' Letters from Dos Passos to M.L., November 22, 1965, and November 1964 respectively. See Dos Passos, *The Ground We Stand On* (New York: Harcourt, Brace and Co., 1941), 3–20; idem, *The Theme Is Freedom*, pp. 151–52; idem, *The Head and Heart of Thomas Jefferson* (Garden City, New York: Doubleday and Co., 1954); idem, *The Men Who Made the Nation* (Garden City, New York: Doubleday and Co., 1957); idem, *The Shackles of Power* (Garden City, New York: Doubleday and Co., 1966).

30. Turner, ''Short History of *The Freeman*,'' pp. 106 (contains quotation), 111.

31. Ibid., pp. 121–35, 179–80, 197–99, 207. See also Hoffman, *The Little Magazine*, pp. 197–98. Some of Dos Passos' comments on the *Dial* appear in his letters to John Howard Lawson, September 12 and Columbus Day 1920. Library of Southern Illinois University, Carbondale.

32. Letter from Dos Passos to M.L., February 1, 1957, names Cummings as an influence. Dos Passos' review, which differs from one of *The Enormous Room* he had in the *Dial*, appeared in the *Philadelphia Ledger* May 27, 1922. A clipping of it is in the E. E. Cummings file of the Columbia University Journalism Library morgue; the page number is not included. Excerpts from the review are worth reprinting here as spirited social commentary:

''The writers who preceded in America this much-advertised younger group were only afraid of being innmoral [*sic*] now added to that is the fear of being unbalanced, of not being a perfect thirty-six . . . in other words, of being an individual, eternal and indissoluble. . . . At least the old fogies were willing to be themselves in the small realm of things unforbidden. . . .

''In these lilylivered days nerve of any sort seems a miracle. And it seems to me that if any man is going to master sufficiently this great clanging, dusty machine of American life to make of it something of his own, it is in this mood of adventure, of willingness to go the limit in emotion, in intensity, in imagination that he will have to work. The material about us is of such soggy, deadening weight that it is only at the whitest heat that it can be fused into anything alive. . . .

''The reviewer for the New Republic complained that he did not like the personality of the author of ''The Enormous Room.'' I wonder if that didn't mean that he would have been made uneasy by any exhibition whatsoever of personality. With all our fuss in advertisements and correspondence school methods for success in business about personality and all the little mimickings of speakers before women's clubs, I doubt if there has ever been an aggregation of people in the history of the world so puzzled and terrified by the smallest spontaneous gesture made by an individual man as these United States.''

33. Dos Passos, ''Looking Back on *U.S.A.*,'' in *New York Times*, October 25, 1959, sec. 2, p. 5.

34. Dos Passos, ''Benavente's Madrid,'' *Bookman*, LIII (May 1921), 226–30.

35. Dos Passos, ''The Misadventures of 'Deburau,' '' *Freeman*, II (February 2, 1921), 497–98. He excepted only the city's Yiddish theater, which he held to be, like the Madrid theater, a stable means of expression for a people. Idem,

foreword to John Howard Lawson, *Roger Bloomer* (New York: Thomas Seltzer, 1923), p. vi; idem, *Rosinante to the Road Again*, p. 186; idem, *Three Plays* (New York: Harcourt, Brace and Co., 1934), p. xiii.

36. Dos Passos says that although he was brought up to seek in visual matter a literary content, spectacle always attracted him. He loved the circus. While at Harvard, he attended whatever theater came to Boston; however, he remembers most the Diaghilev ballet and Urban's settings at the Boston Opera House. What contact he had with the literary theater was through friendship with Edward Massey (Harvard, 1917), who was taking one of George Pierce Baker's courses. In Italy, after Dos Passos' experiences with paintings in Spain and Paris, he found frescoes more important to him than anything else and spent much furlough time looking at them. After the war there were Cézannes, Picassos, and Juan Grises to see. Dos Passos followed with tremendous enthusiasm the productions of Diaghilev's Ballet Russe when it was dominated by Stravinsky's music. He and some friends were delighted to help Goncharova paint scenery for *Les Noces* in a loft near the Place des Combats. Dos Passos, "Grosz Comes to America," *Esquire*, VI (September 1936), 105; idem, "Looking Back on *U.S.A.*," in *New York Times*, October 25, 1959, sec. 2, p. 5.

37. Letter from Dos Passos to M.L., February 1, 1957, cites Seldes and *Dial* and tells of first meeting Lawson. Letter from Dos Passos to M.L., June 26, 1956, helps date the composition of *The Garbage Man*. Dos Passos and Lawson became good friends and would go out with the same girls. M.L. interview with Dawn Powell. The details about the two friends' discussing theater together are from the *New York Herald Tribune*, March 14, 1926, sec. 5, p. 4. The article reported an interview in which Lawson denied that *Processional* had influenced *The Garbage Man*.

38. Dos Passos, foreword to Lawson, *Roger Bloomer*, p.v; idem, "Is the 'Realistic' Theatre Obsolete?" *Vanity Fair*, XXIV (May 1925), pp. 64, 114.

39. John Chamberlain, Review of *Three Plays* by John Dos Passos, *New York Times*, May 23, 1934, p. 17; Dos Passos, *Three Plays*, p. 75. Dos Passos wrote McComb in the spring of 1922: "The M. is a G. is to be rewritten this summer. . . ." The next spring he wrote him from aboard ship: "Finished a play called the Garbage Man before I left." Dos Passos used the latter title for the original publication, *The Garbage Man* (New York: Harper and Brothers, 1926), and in *Three Plays*. He has referred to a New York production, in March 1926, as a "tryout" and "a garbled repetition" of the Harvard version. *Three Plays*, p. 75.

40. Dos Passos, *The Garbage Man*, p. 48.

41. Ibid., p. 68.

42. Ibid., p. 149.

43. Graham Wallas, "The Price of Intolerance," *Atlantic Monthly*, CXXV (January 1920), 116.

44. Dos Passos, *The Garbage Man*, p. 151.

45. Asked whether any literary works were particularly suggestive in determining the form of *Manhattan Transfer*, Dos Passos replied: "I dont know if Baroja's La Busca & Aurora Roja had anything to do with the form of Manhattan Transfer   Possibly some of Blaise Cendrars' early poetry and Verhaerens' Villes Tentaculaires had something to do with it. From Baroja I might have caught a certain attitude towards city life. The interest in form I might have caught from Zola. Flaubert's *Education Sentimentale* probably had a good deal of influence. I cant remember whether I read Stephen Crane's Maggie before or after M.T."

Letter from Dos Passos to M.L., September 23, 1957. In another letter to M.L., March 26, 1970, he wrote "influenced me" alongside the titles of Verhaeren's and Flaubert's works in Chapter V of this biography.

46. Dos Passos to M.L., March 26, 1970. The quotation about "rapportage" is from Dos Passos, "How the Contemporary Chronicles Began," draft (n.d.). A similar statement appears in Dos Passos, "What Makes a Novelist," *National Review*, XX (January 16, 1968), 31. On European experimental literature, see also Dos Passos' foreword to Blaise Cendrars, *Panama, or the Adventures of My Seven Uncles*, trans. John Dos Passos (New York: Harper and Brothers, 1931), p. vii.

47. Granville Hicks, "John Dos Passos," *Bookman*, LXXV (April 1932), 38–40.

48. Dos Passos, *Manhattan Transfer* (New York: Harper and Brothers, 1925), p. 119. For the eulogy of Dos Passos' father, see pp. 2–3 above.

49. Dos Passos, *Manhattan Transfer*, p. 220.

50. For the critical commentary on Dreiser, I am indebted to F. O. Matthiessen, *Theodore Dreiser* (New York: William Sloane Associates, 1951), pp. 75, 79.

51. Sinclair Lewis, Review of *Manhattan Transfer* by John Dos Passos, *Saturday Review of Literature*, II (December 5, 1925), 361. Coburn Gilman, advertising manager at Harper and Brothers in 1926, recalls that until Lewis' review appeared sales were quite moderate. M.L. interview, June 7, 1956.

52. Dos Passos, *Manhattan Transfer*, p. 398.

53. Letter from Dos Passos to M.L., November 22, 1965. The influence of James Joyce upon Dos Passos' narrative style demands a very careful study, one which seemed to me beyond the province of this book. Dos Passos, in his Introduction to the Modern Library edition of *Three Soldiers* (New York 1932), wrote: "You answer that Joyce is esoteric, only read by a few literary snobs, a luxury product like limited editions, without influence on the mass of ordinary newspaper readers. Well give him time. The power of writing is more likely to be exercised vertically through a century than horizontally over a year's sales. I don't mean either . . . that the influence of his powerful work hasn't already spread, diluted through other writers, into many a printed page of which the author never heard of *Ulysses*."

54. Dos Passos, *Manhattan Transfer*, pp. 212, 262.

55. Ibid., p. 261.

56. Ibid., p. 193.

57. Ibid., pp. 365–66.

58. Ibid., p. 401.

59. Ibid., p. 143.

60. Joseph Warren Beach, *American Fiction, 1920–1940* (New York: Macmillan Co., 1941), pp. 41–42.

61. Dos Passos, *Manhattan Transfer*, p. 264.

62. Ibid., p. 288.

63. Waldo Frank, *Our America* (New York: Boni and Liveright, 1919), pp. 171–201.

64. Barrett Wendell, *A Literary History of America* (New York: Charles Scribner's Sons, 1900), p. 472.

65. Blanche Housman Gelfant, *The American City Novel* (Norman: University of Oklahoma Press, 1954), pp. 138–66; Dos Passos, *Manhattan Transfer*, pp. 136, 194.

66. Walt Whitman, *The Inner Sanctum Edition of the Poetry and Prose of Walt Whitman*, ed. Louis Untermeyer (New York: Simon and Schuster, 1949), p. 815 n. See also below, pp. 225–26 and 256, n. 82.

CHAPTER VI: "CLASS WARFARE" (PAGES 124–60)

1. Dos Passos, *The Theme Is Freedom*, p. 10.

2. Leo Wolman, *Ebb and Flow in Trade Unionism* (New York: National Bureau of Economic Research, 1936), p. 23.

3. Ibid., p. 37. Unless otherwise credited, the above facts are based on the account of the labor history of the period in Harry J. Carman and Harold C. Syrett, *A History of the American People* (New York: Alfred A. Knopf, 1952), II, 424–25, 492–500.

4. Joseph Freeman, *An American Testament* (New York: Farrar and Rinehart, 1936), pp. 308–10; M.L. interview with Joseph Freeman, June 5, 1956; Robert Minor, "Growth," *Liberator*, VII (October 1924), 6.

5. Freeman, *An American Testament*, pp. 338–39; letter from Joseph Freeman to M.L., May 17, 1956.

6. Letter from Joseph Freeman to M.L., May 17, 1956. See Cowley, *Exile's Return*, p. 223.

7. *New Masses*, I (May 1926), 3.

8. Freeman, *An American Testament*, p. 379.

9. Dos Passos, *The Theme Is Freedom*, p. 7.

10. Dos Passos, "The New Masses I'd Like," *New Masses*, I (June 1926), 20. The debates at the editorial meetings are referred to in Freeman, *An American Testament*, p. 379.

11. Benjamin Gitlow, *I Confess* (New York: E.P. Dutton, 1940), pp. 363–66.

12. *New York Times*, April 18, 1926, sec. 1, p. 24.

13. Ibid., 1926: April 14, p. 25; April 15, p. 1; April 18, sec. 1, p. 24; April 30, p. 7; May 1, p. 19.

14. Dos Passos, "300 N.Y. Agitators Reach Passaic," *New Masses*, I (June 1926), 8; Freeman, *An American Testament*, p. 386.

15. Gitlow, *I Confess*, pp. 371–74.

16. Ibid., pp. 365–77.

17. *New York Times*, 1926: April 18, sec. 1, p. 24; July 28, p. 3; August 14, p. 18; September 3, p. 19.

18. Albert Weisbord, *The Conquest of Power* (New York: Covici, Friede, 1937), II, 115 n.

19. *New York Times*, November 12, 1926, p. 14; December 14, 1926, p. 1; February 15, 1927, p. 12; February 17, 1927, p. 12; March 1, 1927, p. 46.

20. Letters from Dos Passos to M.L., February 1 and September 23, 1957.

21. *New York Times*, April 18, 1926, sec. 1, p. 24; Gitlow, *I Confess*, pp. 366–70 (quotations, pp. 363, 369 respectively).

22. *New York Times*, December 17, 1929, p. 20, and April 8, 1930, p. 7; Daniel Bell in *Socialism and American Life*, I, 366.

23. Dos Passos, *The Big Money*, p. 539.

24. Edna St. Vincent Millay, *Wine from These Grapes* (New York: Harper and Brothers, 1934), p. 43.

25. For the history of the case, see G. Louis Joughin and Edmund M. Morgan,

The Legacy of Sacco and Vanzetti (New York: Harcourt, Brace and Co., 1948), passim.

26. Ibid., pp. 221–42.

27. Letter from Dos Passos to M.L., June 26, 1956.

28. Dos Passos, *The Best Times*, p. 166.

29. Letters from Dos Passos to M.L., June 26, 1956 (for Felicani), and September 23, 1957.

30. Ibid., February 1, 1957. See Joughin and Morgan, *The Legacy of Sacco and Vanzetti*, p. 245.

31. Nicola Sacco and Bartolomeo Vanzetti, *The Letters of Sacco and Vanzetti*, eds. Marion Denman Frankfurter and Gardner Jackson (New York: Viking Press, 1928), pp. 201–2.

32. Dos Passos, *The Theme Is Freedom*, p. 11.

33. Dos Passos, "The Pit and the Pendulum," *New Masses*, I (August 1926), 30; idem, "Two Interviews," *Official Bulletin of the Sacco-Vanzetti Defense Committee of Boston, Massachusetts*, I (December 1926), 3–4.

34. Dos Passos, *Facing the Chair* (Boston: Sacco-Vanzetti Defense Committee, 1927), pp. 19–20.

35. Ibid., p. 45.

36. Ibid., pp. 57–58.

37. Ibid., p. 116.

38. Ibid., p. 127.

39. See Joughin and Morgan, *The Legacy of Sacco and Vanzetti*, pp. 221–71, 299.

40. *New York Times*, August 7, 1927, sec. 1, p. 23. The quotation is from the report.

41. Dos Passos, "An Open Letter to President Lowell," *Nation*, CXXV (August 24, 1927), 176. The *New York Times*, August 8, 1927, quotes passages from the letter.

42. Dos Passos, *The Theme Is Freedom*, p. 39; idem, *The Best Times*, p. 172; *New York Times*, 1927: August 11, p. 1; August 12, p. 2; August 23, p. 4; August 24, p. 2.

43. Felix Frankfurter, *The Case of Sacco and Vanzetti* (Boston: Little, Brown and Co., 1927), p. 108.

44. M.L. interview with Gardner Jackson, October 16, 1957.

45. Dos Passos, "They Are Dead Now—" *New Masses*, III (October 1927), 7; letter from Dos Passos to M.L., September 23, 1957.

46. Dos Passos, *The Theme Is Freedom*, p. 42; letter from Dos Passos to M.L., July 12, 1966. Otto Kahn financed the New Playwrights Theatre for the first two years of its career. *New York Times*, April 26, 1929, p. 29.

47. Letter from Dos Passos to McComb, 1925; Dos Passos, "Abd el Krim," *New Masses*, I (July 1926), 21. The month of return is based on Dos Passos, *The Best Times*, p. 163.

48. *New York Times*, February 7, 1927, p. 17.

49. Letter from Dos Passos to M.L., July 12, 1966; Dos Passos, "They Want Ritzy Art," *New Masses*, IV (June 1928), 8.

50. Michael Gold, "A New Masses Theatre," *New Masses*, III (November 1927), 23.

51. Bernard Smith, "Machines and Mobs," *New Masses*, III (March 1928), 23. On Smith's observation about the playwrights' talk, Dos Passos comments: "It depended on who was doing the talking." Letter from Dos Passos to M.L., July 12, 1966.

52. Dos Passos, *The Theme Is Freedom*, pp. 41–42.

53. Dos Passos, "Towards a Revolutionary Theatre," *New Masses*, III (December 1927), 20.

54. Dos Passos, "Did the New Playwrights Theatre Fail?" *New Masses*, V (August 1929), 13.

55. Dos Passos, *Airways, Inc.* (New York: Macaulay Co., 1928); idem, *Three Plays*, p. 158.

56. Dos Passos, *Airways, Inc.*, p. 18.

57. Ibid., p. 48.

58. Weisbord was arrested in July 1926 for carrying a concealed weapon. He charged that the Passaic police were attempting a frame-up. *New York Times*, July 29, 1926, p. 3.

59. Dos Passos, *Airways, Inc.*, pp. 141–42.

60. Ibid., p. 147.

61. Dos Passos, *Three Plays*, p. 158.

62. *New York Times*, February 21, 1929, p. 30; *New York Herald Tribune*, February 21, 1929, p. 19.

63. *Daily Worker*, February 23, 1929, p. 4.

64. Ibid. (National Edition), February 28, 1929, p. 4.

65. Letter from Dos Passos to M.L., June 26, 1956; Dos Passos' replies to questionnaire in Wheeler, "The Political Philosophy of John Dos Passos," Appendix.

66. Dos Passos says that he did not read Marx with any of the enthusiasm he had felt for Veblen. Letter from Dos Passos to M.L., June 26, 1956. On Dos Passos and Veblen, see above, pp. 32–33 (including note), 103–4, and below, pp. 162–63, 221–24.

67. Thorstein Veblen, *Essays in Our Changing Order*, ed. Leon Ardzrooni (New York: Viking Press, 1945), pp. 219–31.

68. Gardner Jackson, "How About It, Lindbergh?" *Lantern*, I (January 1928), 3–4.

69. *New York Times*, March 5, 1926, pp. 1, 11.

70. Dos Passos, *Airways, Inc.*, pp. 100–101.

71. George A. Knox and Herbert M. Stahl, *Dos Passos and "The Revolting Playwrights*," Essays and Studies on American Language and Literature, ed. S. B. Liljegren, XV (Upsala: American Institute, Upsala University, 1964), 25, 58, 95. Dawn Powell spoke to me about the extent of Dos Passos' contribution.

72. Dos Passos, letters to the editor, *Daily Worker*, January 20, 1928, p. 4, and January 28, 1928, p. 6. For Garlin's review and reply, see *Daily Worker*, January 16, 1928, p. 4, and January 21, 1928, p. 6.

73. Dos Passos, "They Want Ritzy Art," *New Masses*, IV (June 1928), 8.

74. *New York Times*, April 26, 1929, p. 29; Dos Passos, *The Theme Is Freedom*, p. 42.

75. Dos Passos, "Porto Maurizio," *Dial*, LXXXI (November 1926), 425–26; idem, "A City That Died by Heartfailure," *Lantern*, I (February 1928), 11–12. Tresca is discussed in a letter from Dos Passos to M.L., June 26, 1956. Information

about the *Lantern* is from M.L. interview with Gardner Jackson, October 16, 1957.

76. Dos Passos, "Relief Map of Mexico," *New Masses*, II (April 1927), 24. The date is from Dos Passos, *The Best Times*, p. 170.

77. Dos Passos, "Zapata's Ghost Walks," *New Masses*, III (September 1927), 11–12; letter from Dos Passos to M.L., July 12, 1966.

78. Dos Passos, "Paint the Revolution!" *New Masses*, II (March 1927), 15.

79. Ibid.

80. His reasons for visiting, his route to Russia, and the period of his stay are from Dos Passos, *The Theme Is Freedom*, pp. 42, 43, 68; idem, *The Best Times*, p. 174; and letter from Dos Passos to M.L., November 1964.

81. Dos Passos, *The Theme Is Freedom*, p. 66.

82. Unless otherwise credited, the historical details above are from Vernadsky, *A History of Russia*, pp. 321–70, and Deutscher, *Stalin*, pp. 228, 294–344 (the quotation is from p. 294).

83. Dos Passos, *In All Countries* (New York: Harcourt, Brace and Co., 1934), pp. 9–36. The quotation is from pp. 35–36.

84. Letter from Dos Passos to M.L., November 1964.

85. Dos Passos, *In All Countries*, pp. 36–72, for material in the above paragraph not otherwise credited.

86. Dos Passos, *The Theme Is Freedom*, pp. 42, 59, 66.

87. Letter from Dos Passos to M.L., November 1964, speaks of the New Playwrights and Piscator, and letter from Dos Passos to M.L., July 12, 1966, explains his not meeting Meyerhold. *Roar China* is discussed in Dos Passos, *The Theme Is Freedom*, p. 59. On Meyerhold, see Marc Slonim, *Russian Theater from the Empire to the Soviets* (Cleveland, Ohio: World Publishing Co., 1961), p. 257.

88. Dos Passos, *In All Countries*, pp. 59, 60–62, for contrast between Russian and American theaters; idem, *The Theme Is Freedom*, p. 67, on Russian enthusiasm and powers of absorption; idem, "Looking Back on *U.S.A.*," *New York Times*, October 25, 1959, sec. 2, p. 5.

89. Dos Passos, *In All Countries*, pp. 20, 34.

90. Ibid., pp. 56–57. When he had trouble finding a room in Moscow in the fall of 1928, a Soviet writer and his wife (who was a high Gaypayoo official) put him up in their apartment, near a Red Army barracks. Dos Passos, *The Best Times*, pp. 193–94.

91. Dos Passos, *In All Countries*, pp. 25–26 (on students), 51–52. The comment "very little Russian" is in a letter to M.L. of November 1964.

92. Dos Passos, *In All Countries*, p. 23

93. Ibid., pp. 31–32.

94. Ibid., p. 66.

95. His prompt report was "Rainy Days in Leningrad," *New Masses*, IV (February 1929), 3–5.

96. Dos Passos, *The Theme Is Freedom*, p. 59.

97. Ibid., pp. 66–68.

98. Letter from Dos Passos to Lawson, n.d. Library of Southern Illinois University, Carbondale.

99. Letter from Dos Passos to M.L., February 1, 1957.

100. Dos Passos, "Looking Back on *U.S.A.*" *New York Times,* October 25, 1959, sec. 2, p. 5.

101. Letter from Dos Passos to M.L., March 26, 1970.

CHAPTER VII: DESPERATION, DILEMMA, HOPE (PAGES 161–86)

1. The personal history is from Dos Passos, *The Best Times,* pp. 200–220. Curiosity as well as debt, Dos Passos says here, took him to Hollywood briefly in 1934. His debt was due, at least in part, to rheumatic fever, the illness having put him in Johns Hopkins Hospital in 1933 and having made trips south necessary. In Hollywood, while bedridden from a relapse, he helped Josef von Sternberg with *The Devil Is a Woman.* A letter from Dos Passos to Theodore Dreiser, April 24, 1933, is from Johns Hopkins Hospital. Another to Malcolm Cowley, about October 4, 1934, describes the work as finished. Dos Passos says that he finds all the money going to pay off debts. For the trips abroad, see Dos Passos, *In All Countries,* pp. 106–68; idem, *Journeys Between Wars* (New York: Harcourt, Brace and Co., 1938), pp. 297–329.

2. Dos Passos, "Back to Red Hysteria!" *New Republic,* LXIII (July 2, 1930), 168–69. On the New York police, see *New York Times,* 1930: March 4, pp. 1, 16; March 22, p. 11; November 10, p. 3. On Easley, ibid., July 14, 1930, p. 1.

3. Dos Passos, "Whom Can We Appeal To?" in "A Discussion: Intellectuals in America," *New Masses,* VI (August 1930), 8.

4. David Sanders, typescript of an interview with John Dos Passos, 1962, in the University of Virginia Library (for conversations with Ivy Lee); Dos Passos, "Wanted: An Ivy Lee for Liberals," *New Republic,* LXIII (August 13, 1930), 371–72. The reminiscences referred to are Dos Passos' *The Theme Is Freedom,* p. 103.

5. So a letter from the secretary of the John Reed Club Press Committee asserted. *New Masses,* VI (August 1930), 23. Throughout this chapter the possibility that an organization used an individual's name without his approval can never be entirely discounted.

6. *Left,* I, No. 2 (1931), 100; Dos Passos, "Help the Scottsboro Boys," *New Republic,* LXXII (August 24, 1932), 49; idem, "The Two Youngest," *Nation,* CXXXV (August 24, 1932), 172; "An Appeal," *Student Review,* II (October 1932), 21. On the National Student League, see Irving Howe and Lewis Coser, *The American Communist Party: A Critical History (1919–1957)* (Boston: Beacon Press, 1957), pp. 200–201.

7. *New York Times,* 1931: September 28, pp. 1, 3; September 29, p. 3; October 11, sec. 5, pp. 9, 23.

8. National Committee for the Defense of Political Prisoners, *Harlan Miners Speak* (New York: Harcourt, Brace and Co., 1932), pp. 3–7.

9. *New York Times,* November 17, 1931, p. 14.

10. *Harlan Miners Speak,* pp. 101–293; Dos Passos, "Harlan: Working Under the Gun," *New Republic,* LXIX (December 2, 1931), 67.

11. Dos Passos, "Harlan . . ." in *New Republic,* December 2, 1931, p. 64; idem, *In All Countries,* p. 194.

12. *New York Times,* November 17, 1931, p. 14 (for quotation); ibid., March 2, 1933, p. 15; Dos Passos, *The Theme Is Freedom,* p. 86. On Frank, see *Harlan Miners Speak,* pp. 313–22.

13. *Harlan Miners Speak*, p. 91.

14. Dos Passos, "Harlan . . . " in *New Republic*, December 2, 1931, p. 63.

15. Ibid., pp. 62–67.

16. Dos Passos, "In Defense of Kentucky," *New Republic*, LXIX (December 16, 1931), 137. Dos Passos had asked the *New Republic* to send him to report on the Gastonia strike in 1929, but the editors thought him too far left for their purposes. Edmund Wilson, *The Shores of Light* (New York: Farrar, Straus and Young, 1952), pp. 497–98.

17. Dos Passos, *In All Countries*, p. 197, on his not being a lodgemember; letter from Dos Passos to M.L., September 23, 1957, on influence of I.W.W. men.

18. Letter from Dos Passos to M.L., February 1, 1957.

19. Mrs. Walker, in a letter to M.L., February 12, 1958, wrote:

"I remember very well the episode when, after the main hearings in the Kentucky coal fields, Mr. Dos Passos went to see the indicted miners of the UMWA and returned much shaken by what he had learned of the callous behavior of the ILD in their cases. I'm afraid all of us . . . paid much less attention than we should have to such clear warnings that the Communists' only interest was to promote themselves and their own policies. . . . In including Mr. Dos Passos in our gullibility I mean only to say that he did not at that time make an open scandal and he continued to support in a general way, the miners' revolt which the Communists largely dominated. He certainly made it very clear to his close friends that he found the whole situation very dubious and worrisome, and perhaps had we given him more support he would have made a more open issue of it. As I remember he did talk to some of the leaders of the Communist union and miners' defense about it and was met with the usual equivocal answers, which . . . I think convinced him much less than . . . [those answers convinced] some of us. . . .

". . . it is so difficult to get in all the elements that made us see things differently than they appear today. It is almost impossible to realize how uninterested the public, even the liberal public, was in what was going on in Kentucky in 1931. Later, when left wing activities became fashionable in intellectual circles; Hollywood, and Park Avenue, as well as bona fide liberals and labor people, made a tremendous outcry over situations much less extreme. But in 1931, literally only a few individuals and the Communists were concerned. That is why so many of us who never were Communists found ourselves associating with them. . . ."

20. Mimeographed letters to Theodore Dreiser and F. Scott Fitzgerald (n.d.) in the libraries of the University of Pennsylvania and Princeton University respectively.

21. Identification of references to Harlan County and the Red Caucasus are in a letter from Dos Passos to M.L., December 1965.

22. Dos Passos, *The Big Money*, p. 523. Dos Passos devoted a portion of *Adventures of a Young Man* (New York: Harcourt, Brace and Co., 1939) to industrial warfare in Harlan County. In that novel the Communists' policy toward the imprisoned miners is the chief reason that the leading character, Glenn Spotswood, breaks with the party.

23. Dos Passos, *The Theme Is Freedom*, pp. 75–87. The long quotation is from p. 87.

24. Dos Passos, "Red Day on Capitol Hill," *New Republic*, LXIX (December

23, 1931), 153–55; idem, "Washington and Chicago, I: The Veterans Come Home to Roost," *New Republic*, LXXI (June 29, 1932), 177–78.

25. Dos Passos, "Detroit: City of Leisure," *New Republic*, LXXI (July 27, 1932), 280–82.

26. Dos Passos, "Washington and Chicago, II: Spotlights and Microphones," *New Republic*, LXXI (June 29, 1932), 178–79.

27. Dos Passos, "Out of the Red with Roosevelt," *New Republic*, LXXI (July 13, 1932), 230–32.

28. "Whither the American Writer," *Modern Quarterly*, VI (Summer 1932), 11 (on near-beer); Dos Passos, "Four Nights in a Garden: A Campaign Yarn," *Common Sense*, I (December 5, 1932), 21–22 (on rallies).

29. Letter to the editor of *The Golden Book* (Frederica Pisek Field), November 29, 1932, in the Houghton Library (Harvard); League of Professional Groups for Foster and Ford, *Culture and the Crisis* (New York: Workers Library Publishers, 1932), p. 32.

30. "Whither the American Writer," *Modern Quarterly*, VI (Summer 1932), 11–12. Dos Passos' references to Marxism seem to invite offhand comment on *U.S.A.*, but the replies must be interpreted with much caution. See Chapter VIII below.

31. Dos Passos, "The Writer as Technician," *American Writers' Congress*, ed. Henry Hart (New York: International Publishers, 1935). The quotations are on pp. 79 and 81 respectively. See Aaron, *Writers on the Left*, pp. 280–85.

32. Dos Passos' comment is in his letter published in *Common Sense*, II (September 1933), 30. For the initial appearance, staff, and aims of the periodical, see *Common Sense*, I (December 5, 1932), 2, 3.

33. William E. Leuchtenburg, *Franklin D. Roosevelt and the New Deal, 1932–40* (New York: Harper and Row, 1963), p. 84.

34. Dos Passos, "The Radio Voice," *Common Sense*, III (February 1934), 17.

35. Dos Passos, "The Unemployed Report," *New Masses*, X (February 13, 1934), 11–12. A letter from Dos Passos to M.L., February 11, 1963, links *Fortune Heights* with the New Playwrights Theatre. Excerpts from the play appeared in *International Literature* (Moscow) in October 1933 (pp. 52–67) before the work was published in Dos Passos' *Three Plays* (1934). An article in *International Literature* in 1934 reported that the play was running simultaneously in two Moscow theaters, though in significantly altered versions, the Tairov one, in the Kamerny Theatre, and the Diki one. D. Mirsky, "Dos Passos in Two Soviet Productions," *International Literature*, July 1934, 152–54.

36. Letter from Dos Passos to M.L., November 1964.

37. Dos Passos, *Three Plays*, p. 189.

38. Ibid., p. 210.

39. Ibid., pp. 254–55. See pp. 223–24 below.

40. Ibid., p. 272.

41. Ibid., p. 275.

42. Ibid., pp. 244, 294, 249, respectively, for the first three quotations.

43. Dos Passos, "Thank You, Mr. Hitler!" *Common Sense*, I (April 27, 1933), 13. For his opinions about war, see idem, "The World's Iron, Our Blood, and Their Profits," *Student Outlook*, III (October 1934), 17–18 (reviews of *Merchants of Death* by Englebrecht and Hanighen, *Iron, Blood and Profits* by George Seldes,

and *Arms and the Man*, an article reprinted in a pamphlet by *Fortune*); Dos Passos, "Two Views of the Student Strike," *Student Outlook*, III (April 1935), 5.

44. M.L. telephone conversation with Herbert Solow, June 1957.

45. Deutscher, *Stalin*, pp. 403–19.

46. Aaron, *Writers on the Left*, pp. 149–60.

47. *New York Times*, February 16, 1934, p. 4.

48. Ibid., February 17, 1934, pp. 1, 3.

49. Letter from Dos Passos to M.L., September 23, 1957; M.L. telephone conversation with John McDonald, June 1957; M.L. interview with Elliot Cohen, December 1954.

50. "The Lesson of Madison Square Garden," an editorial in *New Masses*, X (February 27, 1934), 8–10.

51. Ibid., 9.

52. "To John Dos Passos," an editorial in *New Masses*, X (March 6, 1934), 8–9.

53. " 'Unintelligent Fanaticism,' " *New Masses*, X (March 27, 1934), 6, 8.

54. Letter from Dos Passos to Malcolm Cowley, n.d., in Lockwood Library, State University of New York at Buffalo. The episode can be reconstructed from the Dos Passos–Cowley correspondence there and Dos Passos' letters to Cowley in the Newberry Library. Correspondence on Quintanilla occurred between November 13 and December 1934. See also "Etcher and Revolutionist," *New Republic*, LXXXI (November 28, 1934), p. 73.

55. Letter from Dos Passos to Malcolm Cowley, n.d., in Lockwood Library, State University of New York at Buffalo.

56. Letters from Malcolm Cowley to Dos Passos, May 16, 1935, and from Dos Passos to Cowley, n.d., in Lockwood Library, State University of New York at Buffalo.

57. Hoffman, Allen, and Ulrich, *The Little Magazine*, p. 281. Joseph Freeman, in an interview with M.L., furnished some information on *New Masses*.

58. Dos Passos, "Grandfather and Grandson," *New Masses*, XXI (December 15, 1936), 19.

59. Dos Passos, "Grosz Comes to America," *Esquire*, VI (September 1936), 128.

60. Leuchtenburg, *Franklin D. Roosevelt and the New Deal*, p. 162.

61. Ibid., pp. 332 and 347 respectively for the quotations.

62. "How They Are Voting," *New Republic*, LXXXVIII (September 30–October 28, 1936), 223–24, 249–50, 277–78, 304–5, 347–48; LXXXIX (November 4, 1936), 14–15; Dos Passos, *The Theme Is Freedom*, pp. 161–62.

CHAPTER VIII: *U.S.A.* (PAGES 187–227)

1. Letter from Dos Passos to M.L., June 26, 1956.

2. Dos Passos, *The 42nd Parallel* (New York: Harper and Brothers, 1930), p. ix. This note does not appear in the Modern Library edition of the trilogy.

3. See Dos Passos, *Review of Georgian Poetry, 1913–1915* in *Harvard Monthly*, LXII (May 1916), 92–94 (on Chaucer); idem, *The 42nd Parallel*, p. 239 (sec. 19 of "The Camera Eye"); and pp. 21, 87–91, 173 above.

Replying to a number of questions about the literary origins of the trilogy, Dos Passos writes: "U.S.A. grew out of Manhattan Transfer." "Joyce's Ulysses was an example of a novel loaded to the gunnels with extraneous matter, so was Sterne's Tristram Shandy." "There might be some influence of Defoe and Fielding in the narrative style." (Letter to M.L., September 23, 1957.) Dos Passos also writes: "Rabelais was and still is my favorite Renaissance writer"; he names Erasmus and Villon as other favorites. He says that he "never could abide" *The Faerie Queene* but that he loved the *Morte d'Arthur*. (Letter to M.L., June 26, 1956.)

4. The quotation mentioning Italian futurists is from Dos Passos, "Contemporary Chronicles," a draft (n.d.) that was used, he says, for a talk between 1958 and 1964. It is on deposit at the University of Virginia Library. On montage, see Sanders, "Interview with John Dos Passos," *Claremont Quarterly*, XI (Spring 1964), 97. The quotation about everything going in is from Dos Passos, "How the Contemporary Chronicles Began," draft (n.d.). See also Dos Passos, "What Makes a Novelist," *National Review*, XX (January 16, 1968), 31.

5. The examples come, in order, from *The 42nd Parallel*, p. 110; *Nineteen Nineteen*, p. 229; and *The Big Money*, pp. 92, 255, 521.

6. *The Big Money*, pp. 28–29.

7. *The 42nd Parallel*, p. 54.

8. *The Big Money*, p. 28.

9. Ibid., p. 196.

10. Ibid., p. 437.

11. Whit Burnett (ed.), *105 Greatest Living Authors Present the World's Best* (New York: Dial Press, 1950), p. 124.

12. *The 42nd Parallel*, p. 368.

13. Ibid., p. 301.

14. Dos Passos, "Edison and Steinmetz: Medicine Men," *New Republic*, LXI (December 18, 1929), 103–4 (reviews of *Edison, His Life and Inventions* by Frank Lewis Dyer, Thomas Cummerford Martin, and William Henry Meadowcroft; *Loki: The Life of Charles Proteus Steinmetz* by Jonathan Norton Leonard; and *Forty Years with General Electric* by John T. Broderick).

15. Letter from Mark Saxton to Harvard University Press, 1963; letter from Dos Passos to M.L., July 23, 1965, in which Dos Passos added: ". . . looking back on it I realize now that the Morgan piece was a prejudiced piece of work. If I were to write the book over I would modify it. Actually old man Morgan, before his death, worked hard to avert the coming war."

16. *Nineteen Nineteen*, pp. 374–75.

17. Ibid., pp. 15, 104–6 for the quotations. See Randolph Bourne, *Untimely Papers*, pp. 140–230, and Dos Passos, *The Theme Is Freedom*, p. 162.

18. Letter from Dos Passos to M.L., June 26, 1956.

19. M.L. interview with Mrs. Paxton Hibben, for comparison of the two friends' enthusiasms; letter from Dos Passos to M.L., September 23, 1957, on their agreements. The quotation is from Suzanne La Follette, "Paxton Pattison Hibben," *Dictionary of American Biography*, IX, 1–2.

20. Gambs, *The Decline of the I.W.W.*, p. 233.

21. Dos Passos, "Grandfather and Grandson," *New Masses*, XXI (December 15, 1936), 19.

22. Freeman, *An American Testament*, pp. 61 (quotation), 94.

23. *The Big Money*, p. 433.

24. Ibid., p. 477.

25. Ibid., p. 525.

26. Dos Passos, Review of *Henry Ward Beecher: An American Portrait* by Paxton Hibben, *New Masses*, III (December 1927), 26.

27. Dos Passos, "A Case of Conscience," *Common Sense*, IV (May 1935), 17.

28. Sanders, "Interview with John Dos Passos," *Claremont Quarterly*, XI (Spring 1964), 97–98, for comment on fictional reportages; Dos Passos, draft (n.d.), in possession of or on deposit at the University of Virginia Library, for the two following sentences. Dos Passos thinks he wrote the draft in the 1950s.

29. Dos Passos, "Statement of Belief," *Bookman*, LXVIII (September 1928), 26.

30. Dos Passos, Review of *The Shadow Before* by William Rollins, Jr., *New Republic*, LXXVIII (April 4, 1934), 220.

31. *The Big Money*, pp. 491–92.

32. *The 42nd Parallel*, p. 115.

33. Ibid., pp. 408–9. Dos Passos probably based the scene on an incident at Rector's restaurant in New York. See *New York Times*, April 7, 1917, p. 3.

34. Shannon, *The Socialist Party of America*, pp. 4–5, 61, and, for a survey of the prewar party, 1–61. Shannon explains the great diversity among the Socialists by arguing that before World War I they constituted a "typically American party" rather than a sect.

35. Letter from Dos Passos to M.L., September 23, 1957.

36. Arthur Gelb and Barbara Gelb, *O'Neill* (New York: Harper and Brothers, 1962), pp. 350, 488.

37. Gambs, *The Decline of the I.W.W.*, pp. 13–14.

38. On the history of the organization between 1905 and 1912, see Brissenden, *The I.W.W.*, passim, and Shannon, *The Socialist Party of America*, passim.

39. Brissenden, *The I.W.W.*, pp. 191–201.

40. Gambs, *The Decline of the I.W.W.*, pp. 112, 182, 184–86; Brissenden, *The I.W.W.*, pp. 349–50.

41. Asked whether this narrative technique owes much to any particular influence, Dos Passos replied: "I dont know—everybody is influenced by everything he reads, sees, hears etc Zola may have tried something a little similar—Joyce certainly did in Ulysses." Letter from Dos Passos to M.L., July 23, 1965.

42. *The 42nd Parallel*, p. 197.

43. Ibid., p. 255.

44. Edward L. Bernays, *Public Relations* (Norman, Oklahoma: University of Oklahoma Press, 1952), pp. 64–66, 78. The last two quotations are on pp. 71 and 73 respectively.

45. Sanders, typescript of interview with John Dos Passos, in the University of Virginia Library; *New York Times*, November 10, 1934, p. 15. See p. 163 above.

46. *New York Herald Tribune*, November 10, 1934, p. 13.

47. Henry F. Pringle, *Big Frogs* (New York: Macy-Masius, 1928), p. 107.

48. Alvin F. Harlow, "Ivy Ledbetter Lee," *Dictionary of American Biography*, XXI (Supplement One), 489–90; *New York Times*, November 10, 1934, p. 15;

New York Herald Tribune, November 10, 1934, p. 13; Pringle, *Big Frogs*, pp. 93–114.

49. Pringle, *Big Frogs*, p. 132.

50. See C. Wright Mills, *White Collar* (New York: Oxford University Press, 1951), pp. 265–72.

51. *Nineteen Nineteen*, p. 171.

52. John Chamberlain, Review of *Nineteen Nineteen* by John Dos Passos, *New York Times*, March 13, 1932, sec. 4, p. 2.

53. *Nineteen Nineteen*, p. 211.

54. Ibid., p. 383.

55. Ibid., p. 427.

56. *Manhattan Transfer*, p. 384; *Nineteen Nineteen*, pp. 298–99.

57. *The 42nd Parallel*, p. 209.

58. She does indeed shed tears for embattled France while she and Moorehouse are out for an evening before April 1917, but the tears are facile and the cause is fashionable. The scene portrays the sentimental aspect of Eleanor's self-serving actions. Besides exhibiting the clichés in which she thinks, it illustrates another of Dos Passos' most successful satirical techniques, presenting a mechanical account of a character's acts and thoughts. Jean-Paul Sartre has written that it is through this technique, with its depiction of trite behavior, that Dos Passos links individual characters' experiences with men's collective experience under capitalism and makes his readers hate the social system. We quote from the scene with Eleanor:

"The sight of the French flag excited her always or when a band played *Tipperary*; and one evening when they were going to see *The Yellow Jacket* for the third time, she had on a new fur coat that she was wondering how she was going to pay for, and she thought of all the bills at her office and the house on Sutton Place she was remodeling on a speculation and wanted to ask J.W. about a thousand he'd said he'd invested for her and wondered if there'd been any turnover yet. They'd been talking about the air raids and poison gas and the effect of the war news downtown and the Bowmen of Mons and the Maid of Orleans and she said she believed in the supernatural, and J.W. was hinting something about reverses on the Street and his face looked drawn and worried; but they were crossing Times Square through the eighto'clock crowds and the skysigns flashing on and off. The fine little triangular men were doing exercises on the Wrigley sign and suddenly a grindorgan began to play *The Marseillaise* and it was too beautiful; she burst into tears and they talked about Sacrifice and Dedication and J.W. held her arm tight through the fur coat and gave the organgrinder man a dollar. When they got to the theater Eleanor hurried down to the ladies' room to see if her eyes had got red." (*The 42nd Parallel*, p. 353.)

Beach cites and comments on this passage in his *American Fiction, 1920–1940*, p. 65. Sartre analyzes Dos Passos' technique of reporting "all his characters' utterances to us in the style of a statement to the Press" in his *Literary and Philosophical Essays*, trans. Annette Michelson (New York: Collier Books, 1962), pp. 94–103.

59. Letter from Dos Passos to M.L., July 23, 1965; *Nineteen Nineteen*, p. 431.

60. Georges Sorel, *Reflections on Violence*, trans. T. E. Hulme (New York: Peter Smith, 1941), p. 137.

61. For views of the A.F.L. see pp. 103–4 above and Brissenden, *The I.W.W.*, pp. 83–110.

62. *The Big Money*, p. 146.

63. Ibid., p. 458.

64. Ibid., p. 540.

65. Letter from Dos Passos to M.L., June 26, 1956.

66. Granville Hicks, Review of *The Radical Novel in the United States, 1900-1954* by Walter B. Rideout, *New Leader*, XXXIX (November 12, 1956), 23.

67. See pp. 140–42 and 173 above.

68. Dorfman, *Thorstein Veblen and His America*, pp. 484–85.

69. *The Big Money*, pp. 217, 301, 309–10.

70. Thorstein Veblen, *The Place of Science in Modern Civilisation* (New York: Viking Press, 1932), pp. 444–45.

71. Ibid., pp. 441–42.

72. See pp. 103–4 above.

73. For Stead see p. 177 above.

74. Veblen, *An Inquiry into the Nature of Peace*, pp. 153–57. The quotation is on p. 154.

75. Veblen, *The Engineers and the Price System*, passim. The "contrivance" phrase is on p. 73.

76. *The Big Money*, p. 66.

77. Letter to William Henry Bond, March 26, 1938. Houghton Library (Harvard).

78. *U.S.A.*, pp. v–vi.

79. *The Big Money*, p. 150. See also pp. 45, 122–23, 191 above.

80. The quotation is from Whitman, *The Inner Sanctum Edition of the Poetry and Prose* . . . p. 860.

81. Ibid., pp. 817–18.

82. Ibid., pp. 812–13. On pp. 813–14 Whitman continues: "Never was there, perhaps, more hollowness at heart than at present, and here in the United States. Genuine belief seems to have left us. The underlying principles of the States are not honestly believ'd in, (for all this hectic glow, and these melodramatic screamings,) nor is humanity itself believ'd in. . . . We live in an atmosphere of hypocrisy throughout. The men believe not in the women, nor the women in the men. . . . A lot of churches, sects, &c., the most dismal phantasms I know, usurp the name of religion. Conversation is a mass of badinage. From deceit in the spirit, the mother of all false deeds, the offspring is already incalculable. An acute and candid person, in the revenue department in Washington, who is led by the course of his employment to regularly visit the cities, north, south and west, to investigate frauds, has talk'd much with me about his discoveries. The depravity of the business classes of our country is not less than has been supposed, but infinitely greater. The official services of America, national, state, and municipal, in all their branches and departments, except the judiciary, are saturated in corruption, bribery, falsehood, mal-administration; and the judiciary is tainted. The great cities reek with respectable as much as non-respectable robbery and scoundrelism. In fashionable life, flippancy, tepid amours, weak infidelism, small aims, or no aims at all, only to kill time. In business, (this all-devouring modern word, business,) the one sole object is, by any means, pecuniary gain. . . . The best class we show, is but a mob of fashionably dress'd speculators and vulgarians. True, indeed, behind this fantastic farce, enacted on the visible stage of society, solid things and stupendous labors are to be discover'd, existing

crudely and going on in the background, to advance and tell themselves in time. Yet the truths are none the less terrible. I say that our New World democracy, however great a success in uplifting the masses out of their sloughs, in materialistic development, products, and in a certain highly-deceptive superficial popular intellectuality, is, so far, an almost complete failure in its social aspects, and in really grand religious, moral, literary, and esthetic results.''

SELECTED BIBLIOGRAPHY

The following is neither a complete bibliography of works by and about Dos Passos nor a full list of the materials I read or consulted. Rather, it is a list of sources which I drew upon or found especially useful in preparing this book. The writings of John Dos Passos and those of and about John Randolph Dos Passos are listed in order of the date of publication; in other sections the arrangement is alphabetical.

WRITINGS BY JOHN RANDOLPH DOS PASSOS

BOOKS AND PAMPHLETS

Argument of John R. Dos Passos, Esq. of New York in Favor of Recognition of Cuba by the United States. N.p.: n.n., n.d.

A Treatise on the Law of Stock-Brokers and Stock-Exchanges. New York: Harper and Brothers, 1882.

A Defence of the McKinley Administration from Attacks of Mr. Carl Schurz and Other Anti-Imperialists. N.p.: n.n., 1900.

Commercial Trusts. New York: G. P. Putnam's Sons, 1901.

The Anglo-Saxon Century. New York: G. P. Putnam's Sons, 1903.

The Trend of the Republican Party. New York: n.n., 1904.

The American Lawyer: As He Was — as He Is — as He Can Be. New York: Banks Law Publishing Co., 1907. Also New York: Consolidated Law Book Co., 1919.

The Results and Responsibilities of Our Representative Democracy. N.p.: n.n., n.d.

Observations of John R. Dos Passos upon the Question of Direct Primary. N.p.: n.n., 1909.

Some Observations on the Proposition to Elect United States Senators by the People. N.p.: n.n., 1911.

Equality of Suffrage Means the Debasement Not Only of Women But of Men. New York: National Association Opposed to Woman Suffrage, n.d. According to John Dos Passos, the pamphlet appeared after 1910, perhaps in 1912.

Commercial Mortmain. New York: Bench and Bar Co., 1916.

MATERIAL IN PERIODICALS

Letter to the editor. *New York Times*, January 4, 1914, sec. 2, p. 14.

Special article on desirable reforms in administration of New York State criminal law. *New York Times*, March 1, 1914, sec. 5, p. 4.

Letter to the editor. *New York Times*, February 7, 1915, sec. 8, p. 1.

MANUSCRIPT MATERIALS

Letter to Eliot Norton, November 12, 1916. In the Houghton Library, Harvard University.

BIOGRAPHICAL ARTICLES ABOUT JOHN RANDOLPH DOS PASSOS

New York Times, January 28, 1917, sec. 7, p. 3 (obituary).

Wollman, Henry. "John R. Dos Passos," *Case and Comment*, XXIV (July 1917), 163–65.

Knott, H. W. Howard. "John Randolph Dos Passos," *Dictionary of American Biography*, V. Edited by Allen Johnson and Dumas Malone. New York: Charles Scribner's Sons, 1930. Pp. 388–89.

Landsberg, Melvin. "John R. Dos Passos: His Influence on the Novelist's Early Political Development," *American Quarterly*, XVI (Fall 1964), 473–85.

WRITINGS BY JOHN DOS PASSOS

BOOKS AND PAMPHLETS

One Man's Initiation — 1917. London: George Allen and Unwin Ltd., 1920. Also Ithaca, New York: Cornell University Press, 1969.

Three Soldiers. New York: George H. Doran Co., 1921. Also New York: Modern Library, 1932 (the introduction by Dos Passos is new).

Rosinante to the Road Again. New York: George H. Doran Co., 1922.

A Pushcart at the Curb. New York: George H. Doran Co., 1922.

Streets of Night. New York: George H. Doran Co., 1923.

Manhattan Transfer. New York: Harper and Brothers, 1925.

The Garbage Man: A Parade with Shouting. New York: Harper and Brothers, 1926.

Orient Express. New York: Harper and Brothers, 1927.

Facing the Chair. Boston: Sacco-Vanzetti Defense Committee, 1927.

Airways, Inc. New York: Macaulay Co., 1928.

The 42nd Parallel. New York: Harper and Brothers, 1930.

1919. New York: Harcourt, Brace and Co., 1932.

In All Countries. New York: Harcourt, Brace and Co., 1934.

Three Plays. New York: Harcourt, Brace and Co., 1934.

The Big Money. New York: Harcourt, Brace and Co., 1936.

U.S.A. 1. The 42nd Parallel; 2. Nineteen Nineteen; 3. The Big Money. New York: Harcourt, Brace and Co. The volume lists 1937 as the final copyright date but was published on January 27, 1938.
Also New York: Modern Library [1939]. This edition of *U.S.A.*, like the first edition, lists 1937 as the final copyright date but was actually published later. References to *The 42nd Parallel, Nineteen Nineteen*, or *The Big Money* are, unless otherwise identified, to this volume.

Journeys Between Wars. New York: Harcourt, Brace and Co., 1938.

Adventures of a Young Man. New York: Harcourt, Brace and Co., 1939.

The Ground We Stand On. New York: Harcourt, Brace and Co., 1941.

First Encounter. New York: Philosophical Library [1945].

Chosen Country. Boston: Houghton Mifflin Co., 1951.

The Theme Is Freedom. New York: Dodd, Mead and Co., 1956.

The Best Times. New York: New American Library, 1966. I have made a number of additions from these memoirs, which appeared after I had completed most of my manuscript.

CONTRIBUTIONS TO BOOKS AND PAMPHLETS

Lawson, John Howard. *Roger Bloomer*. New York: Thomas Seltzer, Inc., 1923. Pp. v–viii contain a foreword by Dos Passos.

Cendrars, Blaise. *Panama, or the Adventures of My Seven Uncles*. Translated by John Dos Passos. New York: Harper and Brothers, 1931. P. vii contains a foreword by Dos Passos.

League of Professional Groups for Foster and Ford. *Culture and the Crisis*. New York: Workers Library Publishers, 1932. P. 32 of this pamphlet contains a political declaration signed by fifty-two men and women, including Dos Passos.

National Committee for the Defense of Political Prisoners. *Harlan Miners Speak*. New York: Harcourt, Brace and Co., 1932. Pp. 91–228 and 277–97 contain material written by Dos Passos.

American Writers' Congress. Edited by Henry Hart. New York: International Publishers, 1935. Pp. 78–82 contain Dos Passos' paper "The Writer as Technician."

Portraits and Self-Portraits. Collected and illustrated by Georges Schreiber. Boston: Houghton Mifflin Co., 1936. P. 23 contains an autobiographical note by Dos Passos.

105 Greatest Living Authors Present the World's Best. Edited by Whit Burnett. New York: Dial Press, 1950. P. 124 contains a comment by Dos Passos on *U.S.A.*

Potter, Jack. *A Bibliography of John Dos Passos*. Chicago: Normandie House, 1950. P. 13 contains an introduction by Dos Passos.

MATERIAL IN PERIODICALS

"The Almeh," *Harvard Monthly*, LVI (July 1913), 172–79.

"The Honor of the Klepht," *Harvard Monthly*, LVII (February 1914), 158–63.

Review of *Insurgent Mexico* by John Reed, *Harvard Monthly*, LIX (November 1914), 67–68.

"The Poet of Cordale," *Harvard Monthly*, LIX (December 1914), 77–82.

Review of *Small Souls* by Louis Couperus, *Harvard Monthly*, LIX (February 1915), 169.

"Malbrouck," *Harvard Monthly*, LIX (March 1915), 192–94.

Review of *Brittany with Bergère* by William M. E. Whitelock, *Harvard Monthly*, LIX (March 1915), 200.

"An Aesthete's Nightmare," *Harvard Monthly*, LX (May 1915), 77–80.

"An Interrupted Romance," *Harvard Monthly*, LX (June 1915), 119–22.

"Conrad's 'Lord Jim,'" *Harvard Monthly*, LX (July 1915), 151–54.

"Summer Military Camps: Two Views. I," *Harvard Monthly*, LX (July 1915), 156. Unsigned.

"Romantic Education," *Harvard Monthly*, LXI (October 1915), 1–4.

"The Evangelist and the Volcano," *Harvard Monthly*, LXI (November 1915), 59–61.

"The Shepherd," *Harvard Monthly*, LXI (January 1916), 115–21.

"The World Decision," *Harvard Monthly*, LXII (March 1916), 23–24. A letter from Dudley Poore led me to attribute this editorial, signed "D.P.," to Dos Passos. Poore wrote me that he published only a story and some poems in the *Harvard Monthly*. Letter to M.L., October 30, 1956.

"Les Lauriers Sont Coupés," *Harvard Monthly*, LXII (April 1916), 48–51. Published anonymously.

"Incarnation," *Harvard Monthly*, LXII (May 1916), 89.

Reviews of the *Catholic Anthology* and *Georgian Poetry, 1913–1915, Harvard Monthly*, LXII (May 1916), 92–94.

"A Conference on Foreign Relations," *Harvard Monthly*, LXII (June 1916), 126–27.

"A Humble Protest," *Harvard Monthly*, LXII (June 1916), 115–20.

Review of *The War in Eastern Europe* by John Reed, *Harvard Monthly*, LXII (July 1916), 148–49.

"Against American Literature," *New Republic*, VIII (October 14, 1916), 269–71.

"Young Spain," *Seven Arts*, II (August 1917), 473–88.

"In Portugal," *Liberator*, III (April 1920), 25.

"Farmer Strikers in Spain," *Liberator*, III (October 1920), 28–30.

"A Novelist of Disintegration," *Freeman*, II (October 20, 1920), 132–34.

"America and the Pursuit of Happiness," *Nation*, CXI (December 29, 1920), 777–78.

"The Misadventures of 'Deburau,'" *Freeman*, II (February 2, 1921), 497–98.

"Benavente's Madrid," *Bookman*, LIII (May 1921), 226–30.

"Out of Turkish Coffee Cups," *New York Tribune*, October 2, 1921, sec. 5, p. 2.

"In a New Republic," *Freeman*, IV (October 5, 1921), 81–83.

"One Hundred Views of Ararat," *Asia*, XXII (April 1922), 272–76, 326.

"Two University Professors," *Broom*, II (April 1922), 59–71.

Review of *The Enormous Room* by E. E. Cummings. *Philadelphia Ledger*, May 27, 1922. A clipping of the review is in the E. E. Cummings file of the Columbia University Journalism Library morgue. The page number is not available.

"The Opinions of the 'Sayyid,'" *Asia*, XXII (June 1922), 461–66.

"The Caucasus Under the Soviets," *Liberator*, V (August 1922), 5–8.

"Baroja Muzzled," Review of *The Quest* by Pío Baroja, *Dial*, LXXIV (February 1923), 199–200.

"July," *transatlantic review*, II (August 1924), 154–79.

"Is the 'Realistic' Theatre Obsolete?" *Vanity Fair*, XXIV (May 1925), 64, 114.

"The New Masses I'd Like," *New Masses*, I (June 1926), 20.

"300 N.Y. Agitators Reach Passaic," *New Masses*, I (June 1926), 8.

"Abd el Krim," *New Masses*, I (July 1926), 21.

"The Pit and the Pendulum," *New Masses*, I (August 1926), 10–11, 30.

"Homer of the Transsiberian," *Saturday Review of Literature*, III (October 16, 1926), 202, 222.

"Porto Maurizio," *Dial*, LXXXI (November 1926), 425–26.

"Two Interviews," *Official Bulletin of the Sacco-Vanzetti Defense Committee of Boston, Massachusetts*, I (December 1926), 3–4.

"Paint the Revolution!" *New Masses*, II (March 1927), 15.

"Relief Map of Mexico," *New Masses*, II (April 1927), 24.

"Lese Majeste," *New Masses*, III (July 1927), 3.

"An Open Letter to President Lowell," *Nation*, CXXV (August 24, 1927), 176.

"Zapata's Ghost Walks," *New Masses*, III (September 1927), 11–12.

"They Are Dead Now — " *New Masses*, III (October 1927), 7.

Review of *Henry Ward Beecher: An American Portrait* by Paxton Hibben, *New Masses*, III (December 1927), 26.

"Towards a Revolutionary Theatre," *New Masses*, III (December 1927), 20.

Letter to the editor. *Daily Worker*, January 20, 1928, p. 4.

Letter to the editor. *Daily Worker*, January 28, 1928, p. 6.

"A City That Died by Heartfailure," *Lantern*, I (Feburary 1928), 11–12.

Letter on E. E. Cummings' play *Him*. *New York Times*, April 22, 1928, sec. 9, p. 2.

"They Want Ritzy Art," *New Masses*, IV (June 1928), 8.

"Statement of Belief," *Bookman*, LXVIII (September 1928), 26.

"Rainy Days in Leningrad," *New Masses*, IV (February 1929), 3–5.

"Did the New Playwrights Theatre Fail?" *New Masses*, V (August 1929), 13.

"Edison and Steinmetz: Medicine Men," *New Republic*, LXI (December 18, 1929), 103–5 (reviews of *Edison, His Life and Inventions* by Frank Lewis Dyer, Thomas Cummerford Martin, and William Henry Meadowcroft; *Loki: The Life of Charles Proteus Steinmetz* by Jonathan Norton Leonard; and *Forty Years with General Electric* by John T. Broderick).

Report of encounter with John Reed, *Monde* (Paris), January 18, 1930, p. 3.

"Back to Red Hysteria!" *New Republic*, LXIII (July 2, 1930), 168–69.

"Whom Can We Appeal To?" in "A Discussion: Intellectuals in America," *New Masses*, VI (August 1930), 8.

"Wanted: an Ivy Lee for Liberals," *New Republic*, LXIII (August 13, 1930), 371–72.

Advertisement signed by Dos Passos, *Left*, I, No. 2 (1931), 100.

"Harlan: Working Under the Gun," *New Republic*, LXIX (December 2, 1931), 62–67.

"In Defense of Kentucky," *New Republic*, LXIX (December 16, 1931), 137.

"Red Day on Capitol Hill," *New Republic*, LXIX (December 23, 1931), 153–55.

"Whither the American Writer," *Modern Quarterly*, VI (Summer 1932), 11–12.

"Washington and Chicago. I: The Veterans Come Home to Roost. II: Spotlights and Microphones." *New Republic*, LXXI (June 29, 1932), 177–79.

"Out of the Red with Roosevelt," *New Republic*, LXXI (July 13, 1932), 230–32.

"Detroit: City of Leisure," *New Republic*, LXXI (July 27, 1932), 280–82.

"Help the Scottsboro Boys," *New Republic*, LXXII (August 24, 1932), 49. A letter.

"The Two Youngest," *Nation*, CXXXV (August 24, 1932), 172. A letter.

"An Appeal," *Student Review*, II (October 1932), 21. A letter signed by Dos Passos and thirteen others.

"Four Nights in a Garden: A Campaign Yarn," *Common Sense*, I (December 5, 1932), 20–22.

"Thank You, Mr. Hitler!" *Common Sense*, I (April 27, 1933), 13.

A letter. *Common Sense*, II (September 1933), 30.

"Fortune Heights," *International Literature* (October 1933), 52–67. Excerpts from the play.

"The Radio Voice," *Common Sense*, III (February 1934), 17.

"The Unemployed Report," *New Masses*, X (February 13, 1934), 11–12.

A letter, quoted in the editorial "Unintelligent Fanaticism," *New Masses*, X (March 27, 1934), 6, 8.

Review of *The Shadow Before* by William Rollins, Jr., *New Republic*, LXXVIII (April 4, 1934), 220.

"The World's Iron, Our Blood, and Their Profits," *Student Outlook*, III (October 1934), 17–18 (reviews of *Merchants of Death* by Englebrecht and Hanighen; *Iron, Blood and Profits* by George Seldes; and *Arms and the Man*, an article reprinted in a pamphlet by *Fortune*).

"Etcher and Revolutionist," *New Republic*, LXXXI (November 28, 1934), 73. Composed in part by Malcolm Cowley.

"Two Views of the Student Strike," *Student Outlook*, III (April 1935), 5.

"A Case of Conscience," *Common Sense*, IV (May 1935), 16–19.

"Grosz Comes to America," *Esquire*, VI (September 1936), 105, 128, 131.

"Grandfather and Grandson," *New Masses*, XXI (December 15, 1936), 19.

"The Communist Party and the War Spirit," *Common Sense*, VI (December 1937), 11–14.

"Adlai Stevenson: Patrician with a Mission," *National Review*, II (Octboer 27, 1956), 11–15.

"Looking Back on *U.S.A.*" *New York Times*, October 25, 1959, sec. 2, p. 5.

"What Makes a Novelist," *National Review*, XX (January 16, 1968), 29–32.

MANUSCRIPT MATERIALS

Various drafts, n.d. In the University of Virginia Library.

Letters to Arthur K. McComb. 1916–1936 (?). In the Library of the American Academy of Arts and Letters, New York.

Letters to John Howard Lawson. 1920 and n.d. In the library of Southern Illinois University, Carbondale.

Letters to Theodore Dreiser. 1920s and 1930s, or n.d. In the University of Pennsylvania Library.

Letters to F. Scott Fitzgerald. 1920s and 1930s, or n.d. In the Princeton University Library.

Letters to Malcolm Cowley. 1930s. In the Lockwood Library, State University of New York at Buffalo, and in the Newberry Library, Chicago.

Letter to editor of *The Golden Book* (Frederica Pisek Field). November 29, 1932. In the Houghton Library, Harvard University.

Letter to William Henry Bond. March 26, 1938. In the Houghton Library, Harvard University.

Letter to Clarence E. Walton. February 2, 1940. In the Houghton Library, Harvard University.

Replies to questionnaire in Thomas Chilton Wheeler, "The Political Philosophy of John Dos Passos" (unpublished thesis, Division of History, Government, and Economics, Harvard College, 1951), Appendix.

Letters to Melvin Landsberg. June 11, 1956; June 26, 1956; July 20, 1956; February 1, 1957; September 23, 1957; March 6, 1958; February 11, 1963; August 12, 1964; November 1964; December 12, 1964; July 10, 1965; July 23, 1965; October 4, 1965; November 22, 1965; December 1965; December 22, 1965; January 3, 1966; July 12, 1966; October 22, 1966; March 26, 1970; August 1970. The dates February 1, 1957, July 23, October 4, and November 22, 1965, and January 3, 1966, are those of the postmarks.

OTHER BOOKS, THESES, AND PAMPHLETS

Aaron, Daniel. *Writers on the Left.* New York: Harcourt, Brace and World, 1961.

Allen, Frederick Lewis. *Only Yesterday.* New York: Harper and Brothers, 1931.

Aron, Raymond. *The Century of Total War.* Garden City, New York: Doubleday and Co., 1954.

Astre, Georges-Albert. *Thèmes et structures dans l'oeuvre de John Dos Passos.* Vol. I. Paris: Lettres Modernes, 1956.

Barbusse, Henri. *Under Fire.* Translated by Fitzwater Wray. New York: E. P. Dutton and Co., 1917.

Bates, Ernest Sutherland. "John Reed," *Dictionary of American Biography*, XV. Edited by Dumas Malone. New York: Charles Scribner's Sons, 1935. Pp. 450–51.

Beach, Joseph Warren. *American Fiction, 1920–1940.* New York: Macmillan Co., 1941.

Bell, Daniel. "The Background and Development of Marxian Socialism in the United States," Vol. I, chapter vi, of *Socialism and American Life.* Edited by Donald Drew Egbert and Stow Persons. Princeton: Princeton University Press, 1952. Pp. 213–405.

Bernays, Edward L. *Public Relations.* Norman, Oklahoma: University of Oklahoma Press, 1952.

Bourne, Randolph. *History of a Literary Radical.* Edited by Van Wyck Brooks. New York: B. W. Huebsch, 1920.

_____. *Untimely Papers.* Edited by James Oppenheim. New York: B. W. Huebsch, 1919.

Brissenden, Paul Frederick. *The I.W.W.: A Study of American Syndicalism.* Studies in History, Economics and Public Law, edited by the Faculty of Political Science of Columbia University, Vol. LXXXIII, Whole No. 193. New York: Columbia University, 1920.

Brooks, Van Wyck. *Scenes and Portraits: Memories of Childhood and Youth.* New York: E. P. Dutton and Co., 1954.

Carman, Harry J., and Harold C. Syrett. *A History of the American People.* Vol. II. New York: Alfred A. Knopf, 1952.

Chamberlain, William Henry. *The Russian Revolution, 1917–1921*. Vol. II. New York: Macmillan Co., 1935.

Cowley, Malcolm. *Exile's Return*. New York: Viking Press, 1951.

Cummings, E. E. *The Enormous Room*. New York: Boni and Liveright, 1922.

Deutscher, Isaac. *Stalin: A Political Biography*. New York: Oxford University Press, 1949.

Doran, George H. *Chronicles of Barabbas*. New York: Harcourt, Brace and Co., 1935.

Dorfman, Joseph. *Thorstein Veblen and His America*. New York: Viking Press, 1934.

Draper, Theodore. *The Roots of American Communism*. New York: Viking Press, 1957.

Filler, Louis. *Randolph Bourne*. Washington, D. C.: American Council on Public Affairs, 1943.

Forcey, Charles. *The Crossroads of Liberalism*. New York: Oxford University Press, 1961.

Frank, Waldo. *Our America*. New York: Boni and Liveright, 1919.

Frankfurter, Felix. *The Case of Sacco and Vanzetti*. Boston: Little, Brown, and Co., 1927.

Freeman, Joseph. *An American Testament*. New York: Farrar and Rinehart, 1936.

Gambs, John S. *The Decline of the I.W.W.* New York: Columbia University Press, 1932.

Gelb, Arthur and Barbara Gelb. *O'Neill*. New York: Harper and Brothers, 1962.

Gelfant, Blanche Housman. *The American City Novel*. Norman: University of Oklahoma Press, 1954.

Gitlow, Benjamin. *I Confess*. New York: E. P. Dutton and Co., 1940.

Goldman, Emma. *My Disillusionment in Russia*. Garden City, New York: Doubleday, Page and Co., 1923.

––––––. *My Further Disillusionment in Russia*. Garden City, New York: Doubleday, Page and Co., 1924.

Graubard, Stephen Richards. *British Labour and the Russian Revolution, 1917–1924*. Cambridge: Harvard University Press, 1956.

Harlow, Alvin F. "Ivy Ledbetter Lee," *Dictionary of American Biography*, XXI (Supplement One). Edited by Harris E. Starr. New York: Charles Scribner's Sons, 1944. Pp. 489–90.

Harvard College Class of 1916, Secretary's Third Report. Privately printed, June 1922.

Harvard University Catalogue, 1912–1913. Also 1913–1914, 1914–1915, 1915–1916.

Herrick, Robert. *The World Decision*. Boston: Houghton Mifflin Co., 1916.

[Hibben, Paxton]. *An American Report on the Russian Famine: Findings of the Russian Commission of the Near East Relief*. New York: *Nation* [1921]. A pamphlet.

Hibben, Paxton. *Report on the Russian Famine, 1922*. New York: American Committee for the Relief of Russian Children [1922].

Hicks, Granville. *John Reed: The Making of a Revolutionary*. New York: Macmillan Co., 1936.

Hoffman, Frederick J. *The Twenties*. New York: Viking Press, 1955.

————, Charles Allen, and Carolyn F. Ulrich. *The Little Magazine*. Princeton: Princeton University Press, 1946.

Howe, Irving, and Lewis Coser. *The American Communist Party: A Critical History (1919–1957)*. Boston: Beacon Press, 1957.

Jones, P. Mansell. *Emile Verhaeren: A Study in the Development of His Art and Ideas*. Cardiff: University of Wales Press Board, 1926.

Joughin, G. Louis, and Edmund M. Morgan. *The Legacy of Sacco and Vanzetti*. New York: Harcourt, Brace and Co., 1948.

Kazin, Alfred. *On Native Grounds*. New York: Harcourt, Brace and Co., 1942.

Knox, George A., and Herbert M. Stahl. *Dos Passos and "The Revolting Playwrights."* Essays and Studies on American Language and Literature, edited by S. B. Liljegren, Vol. XV. Upsala: American Institute, Upsala University, 1964.

La Follette, Suzanne. "Paxton Pattison Hibben," *Dictionary of American Biography*, IX. Edited by Dumas Malone. New York: Charles Scribner's Sons, 1932. Pp. 1–2.

Leuchtenburg, William E. *Franklin D. Roosevelt and the New Deal, 1932–1940*. New York: Harper and Row, 1963.

Link, Arthur S. *Woodrow Wilson and the Progressive Era, 1910–1917*. New York: Harper and Brothers, 1954.

Luhan, Mabel Dodge. *Intimate Memories*, Vol. III: *Movers and Shakers*. New York: Harcourt, Brace and Co., 1936.

Matthiessen, F. O. *Theodore Dreiser*. New York: William Sloane Associates, 1951.

Millay, Edna St. Vincent. *Wine from These Grapes*. New York: Harper and Brothers, 1934.

Mills, C. Wright. *White Collar*. New York: Oxford University Press, 1951.

Morison, Samuel Eliot. *Three Centuries of Harvard, 1636–1936*. Cambridge: Harvard University Press, 1936.

————, and Henry Steele Commager. *The Growth of the American Republic*. Vol. II. New York: Oxford University Press, 1942.

Munson, Gorham B. *Waldo Frank*. New York: Boni and Liveright, 1923.

Murray, Robert K. *Red Scare: A Study in National Hysteria, 1919–1920*. Minneapolis: University of Minnesota Press, 1955.

Nock, Albert Jay. *On Doing the Right Thing*. New York: Harper and Brothers, 1928.

Norman, Charles. *The Magic-Maker: E. E. Cummings*. New York: Macmillan Co., 1958.

Pringle, Henry F. *Big Frogs*. New York: Macy-Masius, 1928.

Prothro, James Warren. *The Dollar Decade*. Baton Rouge: Louisiana State University Press, 1954.

Sacco, Nicola, and Bartolomeo Vanzetti. *The Letters of Sacco and Vanzetti*. Edited by Marion Denman Frankfurter and Gardner Jackson. New York: Viking Press, 1928.

Sartre, Jean-Paul. *Literary and Philosophical Essays*. Translated by Annette Michelson. New York: Collier Books, 1962.

Schwartz, Harry W. *This Book Collecting Racket*. Rev. ed. Chicago: Normandie House, 1937.

Shannon, David A. *The Socialist Party of America.* New York: Macmillan Co., 1955.

Slonim, Marc. *Russian Theater from the Empire to the Soviets.* Cleveland, Ohio: World Publishing Co., 1961.

Sorel, Georges. *Reflections on Violence.* Translated by T. E. Hulme. New York: Peter Smith, 1941.

Starr, William T. *Romain Rolland and a World at War.* Evanston, Illinois: Northwestern University Press, 1956.

Turner, Susan Jane. "A Short History of *The Freeman*, a Magazine of the Early Twenties, with Particular Attention to the Literary Criticism." Unpublished Ph.D. dissertation, Faculty of Philosophy, Columbia University, 1956.

Veblen, Thorstein. *Absentee Ownership and Business Enterprise in Recent Times: The Case of America.* New York: Viking Press, 1923.

_____. *The Engineers and the Price System.* New York: Viking Press, 1947.

_____. *Essays in Our Changing Order.* Edited by Leon Ardzrooni. New York: Viking Press, 1945.

_____. *An Inquiry into the Nature of Peace and the Terms of Its Perpetuation.* New York: Macmillan Co., 1917.

_____. *The Place of Science in Modern Civilisation.* New York: Viking Press, 1932.

_____. *The Theory of Business Enterprise.* New York: Charles Scribner's Sons, 1904.

_____. *The Theory of the Leisure Class.* New York: Modern Library, 1934.

_____. *The Vested Interests and the State of the Industrial Arts.* New York: B. W. Huebsch, 1919.

Verhaeren, Emile. *Les Villes tentaculaires.* 7th ed. Paris: Mercure de France, 1911.

Vernadsky, George. *A History of Russia.* New Haven: Yale University Press, 1954.

Weisbord, Albert. *The Conquest of Power.* Vol. II. New York: Covici, Friede, 1937.

Wendell, Barrett. *A Literary History of America.* New York: Charles Scribner's Sons, 1900.

Wheeler, Thomas Chilton. "The Political Philosophy of John Dos Passos." Unpublished undergraduate honors thesis, Division of History, Government, and Economics, Harvard College, 1951.

Whitman, Walt. *The Inner Sanctum Edition of the Poetry and Prose of Walt Whitman.* Edited by Louis Untermeyer. New York: Simon and Schuster, 1949.

Wilson, Edmund. *Axel's Castle.* New York: Charles Scribner's Sons, 1954.

_____. *The Cold War and the Income Tax: A Protest.* New York: Farrar, Straus and Co., 1963.

_____. *The Shores of Light.* New York: Farrar, Straus and Young, 1952.

Wolman, Leo. *Ebb and Flow in Trade Unionism.* New York: National Bureau of Economic Research, 1936.

Wrenn, John H. *John Dos Passos.* New York: Twayne Publishers, 1961.

Zweig, Stefan. *Emile Verhaeren.* London: Constable and Co., 1914.

OTHER MATERIAL IN PERIODICALS

Bernardin, Charles W. "John Dos Passos' Harvard Years," *New England Quarterly*, XXVII (March 1954), 3–26.

Blum, W. C. Review of *Three Soldiers* by John Dos Passos, *Dial*, LXXI (November 1921) 606–8.

Canby, Henry Seidel. Review of *Three Soldiers* by John Dos Passos, *New York Evening Post*, October 8, 1921, sec. 3, p. 67.

Common Sense. Vols. I (December 5, 1932) to III (February 1934).

Garlin, Sender. Review of production of *The International* written by John Howard Lawson, *Daily Worker*, January 16, 1928, p. 4.

_____. Reply to Dos Passos on Lawson's *The International*. *Daily Worker*, January 21, 1928, p. 6.

Gold, Michael. Article on *Airways, Inc.* written by John Dos Passos, *Daily Worker* (National Edition), February 28, 1929, p. 4.

Harris, William Fenwick. "Richard Norton, 1872–1918," *Harvard Graduates' Magazine*, XXVII (December 1918), 181–86.

Harvard Crimson. November 8, 1912–June 16, 1916.

Harvard Monthly. Vols. LV (October 1912) to LXII (July 1916).

Hicks, Granville. "John Dos Passos," *Bookman*, LXXV (April 1932), 32–42.

_____. Review of *The Radical Novel in the United States, 1900–1954* by Walter B. Rideout, *New Leader*, XXXIX (November 12, 1956), 23.

Jackson, Gardner. "How About It, Lindbergh?" *Lantern*, I (January 1928), 3–4.

Kallich, Martin. "A Textual Note on John Dos Passos' 'Journeys Between Wars,'" *Papers of the Bibliographical Society of America*, XLIII (Third Quarter 1949), 346–48.

Lewis, Sinclair. Review of *Manhattan Transfer* by John Dos Passos, *Saturday Review of Literature*, II (December 5, 1925), 361.

Liberator. Vols. I (August 1918) to VII (October 1924).

McComb, Arthur K. "Art and Industry," *Harvard Monthly*, LXII (June 1916), 121–23.

Magil, A. B. Review of production of *Airways, Inc.* written by John Dos Passos, *Daily Worker*, February 23, 1929, p. 4.

Masses. Vols. V (May 1914) to IX (August 1917).

Mirsky, D. "Dos Passos in Two Soviet Productions," *International Literature* (July 1934), 152–54.

New Masses. Vols. I (June 1926) to XXI (December 15, 1936).

New Republic. Vols. I (November 7, 1914) to X (April 14, 1917); Vols. LXXXVIII (September 30, 1936) to LXXXIX (November 4, 1936).

New York Herald Tribune, March 14, 1926, sec. 5, p. 4. Report of an interview with John Howard Lawson.

New York Herald Tribune, November 10, 1934, p. 13. Obituary of Ivy Lee.

New York Times. 1912–1934.

New York Tribune. 1912.

Pierhal, Armand. "Le Grand Romancier Dos Passos est à Paris," *Les Nouvelles littéraires*, June 5, 1937, p. 9.

Sanders, David. "Interview with John Dos Passos," *Claremont Quarterly*, XI (Spring 1964), 89–100.

Seven Arts. Vols. I (November 1916) to II (July 1917).

Stearns, Harold. Review of *Character and Opinion in the United States* by George Santayana, *Freeman*, II (December 29, 1920), 378–81.

Wallas, Graham. ''The Price of Intolerance,'' *Atlantic Monthly*, CXXV (January 1920), 116–18.

Watts, Richard, Jr. Review of production of *Airways, Inc.* written by John Dos Passos, *New York Herald Tribune*, February 21, 1929, p. 19.

OTHER MANUSCRIPT MATERIALS

Cowley, Malcolm. Letters to John Dos Passos. 1930's. In the Lockwood Library, State University of New York at Buffalo.

Sanders, David. Typescript of interview with John Dos Passos. 1962. In the University of Virginia Library. The *Claremont Quarterly* interview-article contains excerpts.

Saxton, Mark. Letter to Harvard University Press. 1963.

Letters to Melvin Landsberg from : Cyril F. dos Passos, June 16, 1957; Max Eastman, June 19, 1956; Waldo Frank, September 15, 1956; Joseph Freeman, May 17, 1956; Dudley Poore, October 30, 1956; Mrs. Charles R. Walker, February 12, 1958.

INTERVIEWS AND CONVERSATIONS

Landsberg, Melvin, personal interviews with: Elliot Cohen, December 1954; E.E. Cummings, October 22, 1956; Mrs. Margaret DeSilver, May 1956; Joseph Freeman, June 5, 1956; Coburn Gilman, June 7, 1956; Mrs. Paxton Hibben, June 1957; Gardner Jackson, October 16, 1957; Kenneth Murdock, May 3, 1956; Chandler Post, spring 1956; Mrs. Dawn Powell, June 7, 1956; Morris R. Werner, 1957.

————, telephone conversations with: Lewis Galantière, June 11, 1957; John McDonald, June 1957; Herbert Solow, June 1957.

INDEX

Abortion, 118, 219
Academic freedom, 89
Action, Dos Passos on, 57–58. *See also* In-
tellectuals and thinkers, Dos Passos
on; Writer, Dos Passos on
Actors, 107, 111, 162
in *Manhattan Transfer*, 114, 117
in *U.S.A.*, 196, 199, 202
Addams, Jane, 47
Adventures of a Young Man, 250 n.22
Advertising, 112, 189–90, 205
Aestheticism, 21–24 passim, 28, 31, 73,
198, 213–14. *See also* Art and art-
ists
A.F.L. (American Federation of Labor)
Dos Passos and, 170, 218–19
in *U.S.A.*, 131, 205, 218–19, 220
history of, 78, 80, 81, 125, 130, 136, 164,
180, 208, 219
Veblen and, 104, 218–19
Agail people, 96
"Against American Literature," 44–45, 49,
68, 77
Agitation, 48, 57–58, 77, 97, 176
Agitprop, 97, 176
Agrarianism, 20
"Ah, Sunflower" (Blake), 94
Aims of life, Dos Passos on, 33
Airplane, 39, 148, 151–52, 197, 198, 224
Airways, Inc., 145, 147–52, 169, 217
Goldberg, Walter (fictional), in, 131, 147–
48, 150, 151
and Marxism, 150
and Passaic strike, 147, 151–52
production of, 147, 149, 152
public figures, use of, 131, 151
realism in, 147, 149
reviews of, 149–50
and Sacco-Vanzetti affair, 145, 147, 148–
49
U.S.A., similarities with, 151–52
Veblenite ideas in, 150–51
mentioned, 175

Alexander the Great, 200
Alexandra (of Sanitary Propaganda The-
atre), 158
Aliveness and "living," 31, 52, 98. *See
also* "Deadalive"; "Feather dust-
er"; *Garbage Man, The*; Joy and
vitality; Spiritual death
Allen, Frederick Lewis, 100
Allentown, Pennsylvania, 64
"Almeh, The," 26, 95
Alonso, Don (fictional), 88, 94, 101
Alsace, 65
Amalgamated Clothing Workers of Ameri-
ca, 180
"Ambulance, always in . . ." (comment),
183
Ambulance service of Dos Passos, 44, 51–
58 passim, 64, 108, 213, 235 n.37
and class war, 183
America. *See* United States
American Civil Liberties Union, 129, 161
American Committee for Relief of Rus-
sian Children, 239 n.29
American Defense Society, 80
American Federation of Labor. *See* A.F.L.
American Fiction, 1920–1940 (Beach), 255
n.58
American Fund for Public Service, 125
American Lawyer, The (Dos Passos, Sr.),
14
American Legion, 80, 81, 121, 147, 148
American literature. *See* "Against Ameri-
can Literature"
American plan, 124
American Revolution, 12, 19, 168
American Sugar Refining Company, 3
American Thread Company, 3
American Writers' Congress, 174, 183
Anacostia Flats, 171
Anarchists and anarchism. *See also* I.W.W.;
Syndicalists and syndicalism
Dos Passos and, 50, 61, 103, 126, 179
in fiction, 61–62, 88, 119, 121, 217;
mentioned, 204, 216